The Psychology of
Apartheid

Peter Lambley

The Psychology of Apartheid

The University of Georgia Press
Athens

The University of Georgia Press
Athens, Georgia 30602

Introduction copyright © Anthony Storr 1980
Text copyright © Peter Lambley 1980

Library of Congress Catalog Card Number 80–53595
International Standard Book Number 0–8203–0548–0

Printed and bound in Great Britain by
REDWOOD BURN LIMITED
Trowbridge & Esher

For my children,
Catherine, Rupert and Simone

Contents

Acknowledgements

This book most certainly would not have been written without the help of Jack and Irene Lambley, Dorrian McLaren, Miranda Caldis and Sadie Forman. My parents, Miranda and Sadie, helped me to survive the turmoil of my flight in 1978, while Dorrian did research and interviews for me in South Africa before I fled. She also bravely organised the smuggling out of precious data I was unable to take with me and risked certain arrest or detention by returning to Cape Town to fetch her young son in order to stay with me to help complete the work.

I am grateful, too, for the assistance that Sergia Hyams, Merle Baum, Michelle Sank, Stephen Bloom and Shelley Power gave over the last two years, and also to my patients and students, people like Shirley Jenner, who over the years did work for me or gave me information. I am only sorry that I cannot name them all personally but, since many occupy vulnerable positions in South Africa, they must remain anonymous.

Peter Lambley
Zurich, September 1979.

Introduction
by Anthony Storr

Peter Lambley was born in Britain but finished his schooling in Kitwe. In 1965 he went as a student to the University of Cape Town. After obtaining his degree, he was given an appointment to teach sociology in the same university, and then went on to gain higher degrees in psychology. As a psychologist he worked both in hospitals and in private practice, and so had the opportunity to study a wide variety of persons from all the different racial groups which comprise South African society. His intention in going to Cape Town was not to study *apartheid*, but to obtain a degree; but, after a while, he became so puzzled and disturbed by the extraordinary society in which he found himself that he decided to study its history and the methods by which it maintains itself in spite of world-wide criticism and opposition. Anyone pursuing research of this kind runs obvious risks; and it is not surprising that Mr Lambley had to flee the country in 1978 to avoid arrest by the authorities.

South Africa, since 1948, has been governed by the Afrikaners. I believe Mr Lambley when he affirms that we shall never understand *apartheid* unless we realize how very different the Afrikaners are from the British, or indeed from any other nation. The fact that South Africa was once under the control of the British, and that the governmental institutions appear to be modelled on those of Britain, has misled people into thinking that the government of South Africa today is behaving like a British government might under similar circumstances. Moreover, South Africa wears a smiling face. Students come to England to pursue courses at universities. South African scholars attend conferences and freely exchange information. The English inhabitants of South Africa are, all too often, content with their lot. Surely, it is often argued, although some of the features of *apartheid* are deplorable, this is a passing phase in South African history, and one may expect that, within a decade or so, a more democratic regime will take control. Mr Lambley thinks otherwise. He argues, convincingly to my mind, that the South African government is composed of men who are very different indeed from those who govern any of the free countries of the world, and he sees the peculiarities of their personalities as springing directly from their history.

Voluntary emigrés, as opposed to political refugees, are seldom persons of the highest quality, and the early Dutch settlers were no exception. Many of them seem to have been failures in their own country; and Mr Lambley paints a picture of them, derived from his historical research, as being unsophisticated, isolated, and poorly informed. Moreover, the boers who engaged in the Great Trek to avoid being swamped by the British succeeded in perpetuating the isolation of their society from outside influences. Boer society remained Calvinistic, authoritarian, narrow, and prejudiced. In addition, the 'inferiority' of Africans became a necessary prop for that society, just as the supposed inferiority of blacks became a prop for the self-esteem of the poorest whites in the Southern States of the USA. Whenever men feel isolated and despised by their fellows they tend to search desperately for some group of human beings to whom they can feel superior; and so the inferiority of the Africans and the superiority of the whites became an article of faith for the Afrikaners. When the Union of South Africa was formed, the British supposed that the leaders would be men like Smuts and Botha. What has happened is that the leadership has reverted to rigid, fundamentalist, narrowly prejudiced boers of the old-fashioned variety, many of whom showed considerable sympathy with the Nazis. Mr Lambley points out that *apartheid* was not only designed to separate white from black, but also designed to protect the Nationalist Afrikaner community from infiltration by English and non-boer whites. He therefore made it his object to study the Afrikaner's attitude to the other white inhabitants of South Africa, rather than his attitude to the blacks. His findings, blocked as they were by the authorities, suggest that the more authoritarian the

Afrikaner, the more is he prejudiced against the English. As a trained psychologist, Mr Lambley was well qualified to administer tests of various kinds designed to reveal the attitudes and prejudices of different groups in South African society. Psychological tests, more especially the so-called 'projection' tests, like the Rorschach and the Thematic Apperception Test, are susceptible of different interpretations; and no doubt South African critics of *The Psychology of Apartheid* will dismiss the author's findings as being tainted with his own prejudices. However, he has opened up a field of research which cries out for repetition of his tests and their confirmation; something which will never be allowed under the present government. *Apartheid*, and the apparatus of harassment and terror which is needed to sustain it, has evil effects upon the whole society, even upon those who do not appear to be directly involved. For example, a study of parental attitudes in families who were mostly liberal and progressive revealed that the parents went in such terror of the police that they constantly urged their children to avoid politics or anything which might engage police attention.

The author practised for some time as a psychotherapist. He found that the symptoms of anxiety presented by his patients were often the result of the regime under which they lived rather than springing from any internal conflicts of their own. One black nursing sister, who suffered from migraine, had to break off treatment with him, rather than modify the structure of her defences against her true feelings of resentment at the way in which white doctors and others ordered her around. It was better to continue to have migraine than to face the consequences of standing up for herself. He also reports that the police constantly telephoned him to ask him for information about certain of his patients, and were both surprised and offensive when he refused to divulge confidential information.

The brutality of the South African police is now so well known as hardly to need further documentation; but Mr Lambley's account of the methods employed to harass suspects who are still at large reveals much which is both horrifying and unfamiliar to most people. Imagine returning to your house every day to find the front door open, the larder ransacked, books and papers disturbed. The police even descend to such childish nastiness as putting nails in sanitary towels, or irritants on toothbrushes. Even those who are not naturally suspicious become paranoid when ceaselessly harassed by unknown persecutors; and not a few commit suicide. Mr Lambley worked in one South African mental hospital which is worse than any American 'snake-pit'. Indeed, the only comparable institutions are those mental hospitals in Soviet Russia which are used to confine criminal lunatics together with political dissidents. Drugs and electro-convulsive therapy are used as methods of control and punishment rather than as treatment; and psychological tests which have only been standardized on white populations are given without modification to blacks, with the consequence that the abilities and characteristics of the black population are grossly distorted. Corruption is widespread, not only amongst members of the government, as the 'Muldergate' scandal has revealed, but also throughout the whole Afrikaner society. Lambley discovered, for example, that the chief psychologist in the hospital in which he worked claimed a degree from the University of London which he did not possess. When this was brought to the notice of the authorities, he was duly sacked; but, within a short time, had been found another post at a higher salary.

There have been many books about *apartheid* and the evils of South African society, but Mr Lambley's experience as a clinical psychologist and a psychotherapist entitles him to a special hearing. His position enabled him to hear much which is usually concealed for fear of reprisals; and his attempts to compare the attitudes of the different sections of the South African populations by means of psychological testing is unique in my experience. I hope that his book will be widely read, and that it may bring home to some of those who have not fully understood what is going on in South Africa how corrupt and evil the Afrikaner government really is.

Anthony Storr

Preface

Let me say at the outset that I did not intend writing this book. When, in 1965, at the age of nineteen, I went to study sociology and psychology at the University of Cape Town, it was with the simple intention of getting a university degree. I was not politically motivated or charged with a desire to expose the workings of a racist or corrupt society, neither was I a believer in racial separatism. My choice of university was dictated by the fact that I had matriculated in Kitwe, Zambia, in 1963 and this qualification did not permit me entry into either a British university or the University of Rhodesia in Salisbury, at the time a college of London University. In the early sixties most young people in 'white' central Africa, the Rhodesias, the Congo, Malawi, Botswana, aimed to go to university in Europe; if you could not afford it, you went to South Africa, which is what I did. I had to work for a year after leaving school in order to earn money and get bursaries to attend university; my parents were not well off and there was no spare cash, so I considered myself lucky to at least go to a university.

I was British, from a working-class family in Yorkshire, and, like most working-class families, mine was primarily concerned with making ends meet and getting on with our own lives; politics was something that seldom touched us in any material way. My parents, born and bred in the United Kingdom, had the usual British belief that things were generally all right and roughly fair and so tended to trust the institutions of the countries they lived in. Politics was something best left to the politicians. I was no different. I was born in Yorkshire and left for Central Africa with my parents at the age of six. We lived first in Southern Rhodesia then in Zambia until I was eleven, when we went back to England. The family's movements were determined by economic and educational considerations, not by politics; I went to grammar school in Hampshire and finished my education in Kitwe. My parents returned to Africa in 1962 for the same reason: there was more chance there of their being able to send me to a university. In England I had had potential but not enough to get a grant.

We did discuss politics but in a pragmatic way: what was likely to happen in the future? Would there be a repeat of the Congo in Zambia? Would we have to leave? I read the newspapers and followed current events just as my friends did. I knew about Verwoerd and about *apartheid*; I had once in fact won a debate at an African school in Kitwe by attacking separate development and yet none of this did I ever consider in any way to be political. This is reflected in the fact that while I was far more deeply involved in local affairs in Kitwe than ever I was in Cape Town, neither I nor my parents considered this to be 'political'. I chaired a multiracial junior council in Kitwe as Junior Mayor for a year; I worked for Northern Rhodesian television where, amongst other things, I interviewed Kenneth Kaunda, and later I worked for the Anglo-American Corporation as an industrial relations officer. Part of my duties there involved being loaned to the Zambian army to help with Kitwe's Independence Day festivities.

I therefore went to South Africa as a most unlikely candidate to write a book exposing the country and its function. Not only was I English, a foreigner and thus an outsider, prone to be blinded by the similarities between South Africa and Britain – the same parliamentary system, same institutions, same language – but I was an ordinary citizen. And in this day and age, ordinary citizens do not, as a rule, gain access to the corridors of power.

Contemporary societies, whatever the benefits they have brought to the average person, have distanced him or her inordinately from the processes of power and political decision-making. It is in fact only through exposés or memoirs and the like that the ordinary citizen gets an occasional glimpse inside high places. Even then, the exposé is inevitably used more to replace the guilty party by someone else rather than to fully examine the system itself.

Ask yourself, who really knows what's going on in any modern state? Admittedly, South Africa is a special case – getting inside the skin (as it were) of the Afrikaner body politic is virtually impossible, repressive legislation aside – but is it any different in so-called free states like Britain or America? The formal structure of the open democracies is simply a bare framework which the average citizen is invited to participate in once every four or five years or so. The real day-to-day substance of the possession and manipulation of power is in the hands – as it always has been – of two or three hundred elite families or associations of interest. Their affairs are even more closely guarded than those of prominent politicians, a state of affairs helped along by the general unwillingness of people to examine cherished institutions too closely: Richard Nixon's resignation and the Watergate affair, for example, gave many Americans a disturbing insight into the intimate and personal power games engaged in by some of their leading politicians, but failed to produce a critical re-examination of the structure and personal scope of presidential power.

You could argue that since I trained as a social scientist, as a sociologist and a psychologist, surely I had an advantage over ordinary people? One expects such people to know about their fellow-beings and about society and as a *scientist* – one of the *epistemological gods* – if they do not know, then for God's sake, who does? Well, natural scientists, perhaps. Physicists, chemists, are among the most well-informed of people about the aspects of reality they study. But sociologists, psychologists? They know *something* about people, quite a lot about rats, but it is far more likely that journalists, ex-members of the elite, secretaries, wives, mistresses and lovers would provide more information and more insight about how top people function than any professional could. The deprived, the underdeveloped, the mentally ill are really the only people psychologists and sociologists are allowed to practise on. The corridors of power are very much out of bounds.

I say all this because this is not an ordinary straight-forward book about South Africa and *apartheid*. It is not an analytic academic treatise explaining how the system arose or how it is maintained, neither is the book a moral polemic showing how bad or evil South Africa is. It is very much a book of raw material produced by an ordinary person wanting to know about how a society and its people operate. In the process of discovering what went on in my ten years, between 1967 and 1977, of active research in South Africa, I became aware of many problems and limitations that characterize contemporary societies everywhere; in order to understand South Africa, I had to understand myself better and the context in which I was reared. I had to question my faith in the values and traditions of the British way of life and in Western political philosophy because South African society is ostensibly modelled on them. Any visitor to South Africa is in fact struck by the modernity and 'European-ness' of the country. Its parliamentary system is derived from West-minster; many of its institutions are derived from those found in Western countries, and, of course, it was a British colony and fought for Britain in two world wars. Its cities are busy, modern, bustling; its services are comparable with those in Europe and America and its institutions look and sound the same. Each city has active programmes in the arts: opera houses, theatres, parks mingle with huge office and leisure complexes; giant freeways get clogged up with rush-hour traffic just like they do in New York, London or Rome. It is possible in fact to travel the length and breadth of the country without encountering very much evidence of the effects of the reputedly harsh and callous regime in power.

I believe South Africa has survived because of the similarity it shares with the Western world. People who visit it or who criticize it give it and its institutions a credibility and a status – just as I did – because it is all so familiar. And this is why I say the book is not solely an academic or moral treatise. Academic books about South Africa try to explain it in terms derived from and developed in social traditions more fitting to America or Europe than Southern Africa. They explain South Africa by using such concepts as reli-gion – the Afrikaner believes *apartheid* is a God-ordained system; they use such concepts as the struggle of the Afrikaners for survival, referring to the Boer War and to the Boer Republics' fierce resi-stance to encroachments by Imperialists and Capitalists. Moralistic treatises alternately approve or condemn South Africa depending on the polemic of their authors; South Africa is either a brave Chris-tian attempt to maintain civilization and standards in a sea of Black turmoil or it is a fascist, Nazi-like state, repressing millions of Afri-cans and depriving them of their rights.

What worries me about the existing polemical, moralistic and academic works about South Africa is that they explain *apartheid* and all it involves by using slogans and expressions – such as fascism, or the maintenance of civilization – which while familiar, are labels used to describe other, European, phenomena that in themselves we do not fully understand. The term fascism, for example, we associate with Mussolini's Italy and Nazi Germany – power structures that even now, forty years later, we still do not really know how or why they arose and what they mean. The truth of the matter is that to examine something as complex as South Africa properly, you have also to examine Western society properly. One of the reasons we do not understand fascism is because to analyse it properly means to analyse ourselves and our own institutions properly: it is far safer and far simpler to seek an obvious scapegoat – a Hitler, a Mussolini – than to say that modern states and their organization are at fault, anachronistic or inefficient. This is too threatening, too close to home. Hitler and Mussolini are safely and conveniently dead and gone, but the social problems and the technological and political systems that gave rise to them remain firmly entrenched in our modern way of life.

In writing *The Psychology of Apartheid*, I have tried to get behind the façades and the appearances of the South African society, to dispense with academic concepts and theoretical explanations that obscure ignorance and lack of information. It was as an ordinary person that I went into South Africa; it was as an ordinary person that I researched what actually goes on, and this account is written so that ordinary people can understand it and relate it to themselves and their own lives.

Like a social scientist in Britain or America, I started off doing quite ordinary and routine academic and historical research. When I probed too deeply, I was stopped; if I had been in Britain or America, it is more than likely that I would quite happily have stopped where I was told. As I said earlier, no one is permitted into the *real* seat of power, anywhere. But the South African authorities stopped me in odd and bizarre ways. And they stopped me at crucial points of my studies while pretending to want to help me with my work.

My approach to do studies at Afrikaans and at government-created ethnic universities for Coloureds and Africans got bogged down in red tape and eventually in blank refusals. My attempts to get grants from government councils such as the Human Science Research Council to study South Africa were refused while less well-qualified researchers got substantial sums for non-political work. And I was warned off – sometimes by friends, sometimes by officials, always subtly, 'for my own good' but always effectively. No one seemed interested in South Africa. Few of the psychologists, psychiatrists or sociologists I came into contact with actually wanted to research South Africa; they were involved politically but they thought I was crazy to want to study it – and they could not say why. It was like finding yourself in a fog with all around you pretending they can see clearly.

Part of my research involved looking into the history of South Africa and I found that trying to establish the history of the country from 1948 was like living in an Orwellian world. I had expected to find good post-graduate research in the history departments of Afrikaans universities where Master's and Doctoral students would have had direct access to archives I couldn't easily get to. Yet this was not the case; Afrikaners do not produce critical self-analyses. Most theses I saw were on safe subjects or adopted pro-government viewpoints using the political present to explain past history. Wherever I came across good critical studies done by radicals, they were inevitably mutilated by black pencil marks where librarians had had to eliminate the writings of 'banned' persons. In some books, whole sections were missing or torn out; in one case, pages left blank because one of the contributors had been banned after the book had been published overseas but not in South Africa.

I discovered that the history of South Africa since 1948 is largely journalistic. Most of the books inside and outside South Africa are full of references to newspaper reports: actions, statements, key developments are not validated by referring to academic authors, to the private papers of participants or to historical journals, which is the custom; they simply refer to items that first appeared in the newspapers of the time. There is no *personal* feel of South Africa in the books I read; the Afrikaners' actions have been recorded at a distance, almost as if some controlling officer has carefully shaped press releases to be handed out. There is no inside information, no thrust and parry that marks the best in historical research elsewhere.

So I was left after three years of superficial, conventional work with the sort of choice we all face at one time or another in our lives – to give in and accept the *status quo* or to push on, to take risks and hopefully discover the truth. In the South African context, to choose the latter was suicidal; you risked imprisonment, intimidation, ruin, deportation, even death. Worse, you faced all this and the sure knowledge that whatever you did would have little effect and little impact in the long run. Certainly there may have been personal gain in choosing the latter – you could become a martyr or famous – you could get deported or exiled and get jobs and status on the strength of it – but by and large it was not an option favoured by many people. I wanted to discover the truth all right but I was not interested in the risks. There was a way, though, that I had discovered that seemed to offer accurate insight with few risks and it was to this I was drawn.

There is one kind of professional who does have a special access to those in power – the psychiatrist, the analyst, the clinical psychologist. Of all social scientists, it is probably true to say that the work of any one of these people takes them closest to the human data source that we need to know about. Questionnaires, experiments, systematic observation tell us about human behaviour in general, but treating people, especially in private practice, provides specific, full and accurate information about personalities, about what really goes on in the lives of people. If you treat people who fall into the top echelons of society there is a very good chance that you will get a good idea of the ins and outs of power.

Now despite the elaborate security employed by the South African government and the rigid and closed nature of the Afrikaans community, the Afrikaner has an Achilles heel; treat prominent people, and more especially their wives, children, lovers, mistresses and servants, and slowly but surely it is possible to develop the insights needed with relatively little risk. Broaden this to include South Africans in general and a gold mine of data opens up.

Once I had stumbled upon this Achilles heel, it became clear that in fact with a little bit of ingenuity and deception, a great deal could be achieved because of the very enormity and nature of the pervading pressures the South Africans applied to contain inquiry. Put simply, the authorities, expecting and geared for frontal inquiry, were quite unprepared for someone employing the methods of deception they themselves used.

Much of what I did after 1972 was in secret and involved deception and, in some cases, intricate, long-range data collection. As a lecturer in psychology, for example, I made use of the opportunities that came my way to get subjects or data; some of my students or researchers conducted studies in such a way as to allay the suspicions of the authorities while providing the required information. Some of them did small, seemingly unrelated studies on things like depression or self-disclosure or attitude to divorce, which are permitted, but which in reality contained hidden questionnaires to tap the dimensions I was interested in. Constructing these questionnaires and putting the data together was a straightforward matter – I simply used my training in scale construction and data collection. Some of my students gave false names or said their work was being supervised by psychologists acceptable to the authorities but gave me their data or did studies I wanted done. I also used bursaries and grants from the Human Science Research Council, a government agency, to finance some of my projects, applying for money to carry out non-political studies that never materialized.

These studies alone though were not enough. At best, they confirmed my existing ideas; I could write them up as proof for academic journals, some of which I did. But from 1972 onwards, I gained access to that special world I mentioned earlier: I went into private practice.

South Africa has a small white population and its elites in the worlds of art, science, politics, the professions, business and so on are small in number and closely inter-related. In few countries is it possible for a single clinician to get an insight into such a broad cross-section of important people and their private lives, but because of the structure of South African society, this was possible in Cape Town. In the six years I was in practice, I saw over five hundred people drawn from all walks of life in South Africa and Rhodesia; through them I learned some of the secrets of the Afrikaner state and Afrikaner psychology. A number of my patients were prominent in the arts, in business, the professions, politics; some were ordinary people like doctors, nurses, policemen; many were the sons and daughters of influential people; some were black, some were Afrikaans; all of them had information about South Africa. In some cases I used them to help me collect data, in others, people offered to help and turned out to be indispensable and reliable sources of information. How I justified my use of this privileged information and position will be found in the course of the book.

More importantly, the people I saw were part of South Africa and its history: in my waiting-room at any one time, it was possible for descendants of some of South Africa's prime ministers and some of South Africa's great parliamentarians to sit across from radicals and revolutionaries; for army officers to wait for appointments alongside conscripts whom I was getting out of the army, and for criminals, priests, policemen, businessmen and professionals to chat together, quite unaware of one another's role and status in the process of either maintaining or trying to undermine *apartheid*.

What I did in Cape Town was to create a channel for people to express their discontent and distress at the system in a way that could be useful to them while at the same time not expose them to any danger. I was surprised at how many ordinary South Africans wanted to see things change and at the risks they were prepared to take to help me. Some of my patients stole documents, copied others, took secret tape-recordings and so on to prove what they knew; others had to talk to unburden themselves because what they had seen or heard was too much for them to cope with.

I think if I had deliberately set out to achieve the results I got or to write about *apartheid*, I would have got nowhere. None of the major moves I made were planned; I did not go to South Africa deliberately, I studied *apartheid* almost by accident; I did not train as a clinician or go into private practice because I thought I would get the data I present here. I went into it for other reasons, more personal. I did not know I would get these insights until *after* I had got into practice – but what I did do was to make use of the opportunities that came my way and, later, to systematize them, trying to integrate the empirical studies I had done with the interpersonal data I was given.

The result is highly personalized. I do not claim to be able to explain everything, but I think I have caught the main developments. I worked in South Africa in a decade in which the Afrikaner state was both at its height of power – between 1967 and 1974 – and when it was under its greatest pressure – between 1974 and 1978 – following the collapse of the Portuguese buffer states, Mozambique and Angola, and the escalation of civil war in Rhodesia. In the first period, the Afrikaners seemed supreme, complacent and unassailable. In the second period the reality behind the cracks in the propaganda began to be visible as the state moved to re-assess and adjust to the changes. Soweto and other uprisings of 1976 came as a complete and unsettling surprise to white South Africa, and it was through these and other cracks that I recorded and observed.

This account is personal because I saw South Africa through *my* eyes and heard its secrets through *my* ears. In fact I think the book is analogous to a film I have seen several times and which always has the same awesome effect on me. In 1964, a crewman on board a ship in Noam Harbour, Alaska, was shooting film in his camera of the docks when a massive earthquake struck the region. He survived the catastrophe and we see through the lens of his camera the ocean floor opening up and sea water flooding into a black trench across the harbour mouth. Nothing I have seen or read captures the force and effect of earthquakes more vividly than this shakily held black-and-white film. As if in slow motion, the camera shows masts and sky as the crewman's ship topples over into the empty harbour. It is these frozen images that I find similar to my research in South Africa. In many respects, South Africa is a frozen society, frozen in the myths of an anachronistic past transformed into a model for its current functioning by the Afrikaans power elite. In South Africa one can find some of the key processes at work in most modern states without the camouflage and mists that usually accompany them.

Although personal, the work was done in accordance with the academic traditions in which I was trained. What I present is the evidence that I personally could objectively establish, either through experimental and statistical analysis or clinical testing, or through careful cross-questioning of my subjects and patients and cross-validating of their information. I have left out anything I could not check or reliably establish, no matter how much I believe it to be true. I have written it as it happened so that the reader can experience the same shock and awe as I did as time went by and I uncovered more and more about the real processes at work in South Africa.

Lastly, I worked independently. I severed all my ties with the University of Cape Town and with Groote Schuur Hospital by the end of 1973. I had no affiliation with any group, political, social or academic before or since then because I wanted to produce an *objective* account of South Africa. I wanted to stand outside of the system and be freely critical in my attempts to avoid moral judgements. After 1973, funds for the work, where necessary, came from my private practice but these were seldom needed – most people who helped gave of their time, energy and resources voluntarily.

I bear the responsibility for the resulting research programmes as

I do for the findings presented in this book, but in doing this work I was not alone. Throughout the later period of my research – from 1970 to 1978 – I was helped by a wide range of people, some black, some white but nearly all of them South Africans. They acted as sources of information – often at risk to themselves – as research assistants, as interviewers, as fronts for me so that I was able to obtain the data I needed to write *The Psychology of Apartheid*. It was quite an experience.

Peter Lambley

Chapter One

Preliminary Explorations in Authoritarianism and Some Historical Investigations

South Africa presents an awkward problem for Westerners. It is too much like home and we are too much a part of its history. Holland sent the colonists there – the people who became the boers and then the Afrikaners – Britain occupied the country and added to the population, French and German Huguenots and later immigrants helped to broaden the base of the white population, while nearly every major Western power has in one way or another benefited from what South Africa has to offer. Gold, diamonds, uranium, fruit, wine, cheap labour, all still have a valuable role and significance in European and American economies.

Perhaps this is why when people criticize South Africa or condemn its race policies, many, if not most of them, stop short of outright rejection or outright intervention. It would be easier to condemn *apartheid* and the Afrikaners if South Africa were a strange and alien land or if its rulers were yellow or black-skinned people. Then, no doubt, they would be both unacceptable *and* barbaric.

But South Africa is *too* familiar. And accordingly, no matter how much we dislike barbarism, we always tend to hold back if the perpetrators of injustice and brutality are familiar; we give it a second chance. We give the Afrikaner the benefit of the doubt.

We *understand* the Afrikaner. Not only have we Europeans practised at one time or another the same kind of separatism and denial of rights in our colonies, but worse: the British actually repressed the boers themselves. How, it is argued, can *we* condemn them for acting now with a feeling of historical and self-righteous justification? What would we have done in the same circumstances?[1]

Then, of course, there are the people themselves – the Afrikaners. How many visitors to South Africa, critics, investigators, have not returned grudgingly impressed by the sincerity and generosity of the Afrikaners? How many of us credit the Afrikaner with honesty and frankness on account of his leaders' open admittance of their problems and their earnest expression of concern for all South Africa's citizens?[2] It is this mixture of historical sympathy and familiarity that first impresses the visitor to South Africa and helps him to slip into what has become a routine procedure – *de rigeur* criticism and quiet acceptance. Nobody likes the idea of *apartheid* – it runs counter to most trends in contemporary social thinking – and nobody, unless they are really disturbed mentally, likes the idea of cruelty and oppression. But once these obvious points are out of the way, it is a rare person who pushes beneath them and wants to know more.

Nothing in my first few years in South Africa as an undergraduate really altered this run of events for me. I was critical, certainly, but it did not for one moment stop me from fitting quite easily into the progressive-liberal white community of Cape Town. I studied and taught at an English-language university known for its liberalism and high academic standing, all of which helped to further mask any personal sense of involvement I might have felt in helping to maintain *apartheid*. It was not I who was doing all those bad things to the Africans; if anything, by going on protest marches and so on, *I* was doing something to change the system – attitudes that well reflected the *zeitgeist* of the academic circle I was part of.

I even went further. I began to study South Africa, to do research on *apartheid*, and even then could not really get underneath the bland familiarity that South Africa had for us all – at least not at first. The research reports I read, the academic theories, all calmly and carefully explained the phenomenon of *apartheid* in terms of familiar constructs. Familiar, again, because they had been used in the past to explain events in other parts of the world: in India, in the American South, in the Caribbean – anywhere in fact that power has been retained by an ethnic minority for long periods of time.[3]

For the authorities, I read, South Africa is merely an example of the kind of social structure that emerges in societies with complex ethnic groupings as they evolve. The theories developed to explain *apartheid* reduce the South African experience to one of many; the Afrikaners' behaviour being interpreted in the same way as the whites in the Southern American states, the Upper castes in India and so on.[4]

What troubled me was that South Africa was not India nor the American South. What differentiated it from them was that they had changed, were progressing, whilst South Africa, if anything, was being attacked for standing still, even going backwards in time. What, I wanted to know, was *specific* to South Africa or the Afrikaner that had resulted in this? Everything about South Africa was familiar – except in one important respect: South Africa was as Britain and its colonies or the American South *had* been. They were no longer like South Africa.

The academic literature explained this quite simply: the Afrikaners, unlike other minorities, had been themselves oppressed so, once in power – remember, only as recently as 1948 – they were not yet ready either to relinquish it or to share it, hence the oppression and the determination. Desperate acts of a desperate people, 'cruelly treated by history'.[5]

It was all too simple and straightforward. According to the literature, South Africa is the same as any other industrialized Western nation; it differs solely in the fact that its process of government excludes non-whites. *Apartheid* arose for historical reasons just as it had in a less formal form elsewhere in the British Empire. Outside the phenomenon of segregation, white South Africa is just like any other modern state – the same institutions, the same 'democracy'. Reading Marxist formulations about South Africa added to this picture because Marxist writers make the same complaint about South Africa and use the same model as they do for Western non-communist states.[6]

All this created a dilemma. Not only did my own background and personal experiences in the country predispose me to seeing South Africa as a familiar Western society, but so did my sociological and psychological training and my preliminary reading and research. If a prominent academic or respected historian said such and such, who was I to disbelieve or dispute him? Think about what you know about your own country's history, think of who you read or listen to, to explain things. Nine times out of ten, it will be an authority you would not dream of disputing. If you are more sophisticated and you read more than one book, listen to more than one authority, and if they still agree on a common theory about things, then you give up and accept it. I did not know too much about the history of South Africa nor too much either about how Western institutions functioned in general or how they functioned in South Africa. Since people who did know presumed the two were the same and history accounted for any differences, I gave in and accepted it. One occurrence, though, and two coincidences saved me from complacency.

In December 1967, I was employed by the Department of Sociology to prepare background material on the history of education in South Africa. I had three months in which to do it, and in that time I began to delve into modern South African history to broaden my understanding of South Africa. Two things I read surprised me and made me realize how inadequate was my grasp of South African history and that of many of the South Africans I knew.

The first thing consisted of the statistics presented in government year books that showed in every respect that separate development definitely did not mean separate and equal. This was especially true in education but it applied in all other respects; government spending was overwhelmingly weighted in favour of the whites. I think I had expected the government to be roughly fair at least but the figures showed gross unfairness and neglect.

My second discovery came when, in order to better understand the motivation behind the Native Education Act of 1953, I decided to look at the parliamentary debates about the Act. This act, incidentally, was amongst the first that Verwoerd had used to create Bantu Affairs and his own personal empire. For the first time, reading Verwoerd's actual words and those of his fellow Nationalists, I could put a mentality, an actual way of thinking to the images I had formed of him and his party from the South African press. I was able to see the spirit in which the system of *apartheid* was applied.

Quite unconsciously and because of the way we are all brought up to accept public figures unthinkingly, Verwoerd, in my mind, was given a status equal to that of people like Macmillan, de Gaulle or even Kennedy. He was head of state and, in a small-boy way, I expected him to show intelligence and maturity, even if I did not agree with his politics. To my surprise and dismay, I discovered that in parliament, this man was a crass boor, a crude megalomaniac who knew only the language of the racist gutter. That was not all.

The level of debate in parliament, with the exception of the native representatives, seemed to me to be embarrassingly insular, prejudiced and uninformed – especially Dr Verwoerd's. I researched further and discovered that this 'paragon of virtue', as he was so often described, had been Professor of Applied Psychology and held the chair of Sociology at Stellenbosch University and that he, along with many of his colleagues, had not only been impressed with Nazi Germany but had actively flirted with Hitler and his ideology during the war years. Several cabinet ministers, including the late state president, Nico Diederichs, had spent time in Germany working and studying with the Nazis.

Discovering the Nazi link I think had more effect on me than anything else. Ever since I can remember, I had heard about Fascism and the Nazis. Born in 1946, I remember post-war rationing and the struggle at the time to make ends meet; both my grandfathers were war heroes and the enemy against whom they had fought had been soundly defeated and, we believed, removed once and for all. It came as a complete surprise to find that some Afrikaners had not only been against the war but had been imprisoned for aiding and abetting the Germans. These same men were today driving around in chauffeur-driven limousines and held powerful positions in South Africa. I knew because I saw them drive past me every day as I walked to university.

Discrimination was not unfamiliar to me. I had encountered hurtful class discrimination in Britain where what you wore or how you spoke determined how well people treated you; I had seen British colonial discrimination against Africans at close range in the colonial Rhodesias; moreover I had seen, also, blacks in power discriminate against whites and against less fortunate blacks. I did not like it but everybody seemed to tolerate it as a fact of life. South Africa's discrimination did not seem to me to be all that different from that I had met elsewhere. What concerned me was the Nazi links that Afrikanerdom had. Did the Afrikaners' discrimination against the blacks serve the same function that anti-Semitism had done in Germany? Had the Afrikaner Nationalists learnt their methods from the Nazis and then implemented them in South Africa after 1948?

These questions bothered me for other reasons. By coincidence, at the same time that I was doing this reading into South African history I was preparing a final year project in Psychology. During

1967, I had done personality theory in my psychology course and spent a lot of time on the authoritarian personality and I had decided to do some research on it for my project.

In America after the war, a group of psychologists and psychiatrists investigating the psychological roots of Fascism and Nazism, published the *Authoritarian Personality* (Adorno *et al.*, 1950). This attempted to explain the extremes of the events of the thirties and forties by taking Freudian theory and integrating it with advances made in the measurement of personality. The authors described and defined a cluster of variables that they felt were related to the kind of personality that had responded to Nazism and Fascism and they constructed a scale, the F. Scale, to measure this (F. for Fascism). They argued that in every society there were people who, through possessing attributes of this personality cluster, were liable to act and think in the same way as had the Nazis.

The authoritarian personality idea thus satisfied several needs I had in 1968. It linked my reading about Verwoerd and the Nationalist Afrikaners to the Nazis and Fascism and it gave me a course three project. Further, it involved one of the only academic theories that did not explain South Africa in conventional, closed-circle ways. Quite simply, it posited that people with authoritarian personalities had caused Nazi and Fascist outrages and thus, by inference, the same type of people may have created the situation in South Africa.

Personally I felt that the authoritarian personality concept seemed to explain pretty well what was going on in South Africa. It explained, I thought, the Afrikaners very well because it predicted most of their attitudes and ideas not just their racial prejudice. The essential features of the authoritarian personality clusters are rigidity, conformity, conventionality, a belief in power and toughness, in the ends justifying the means – especially in dealing with outgroups – in the use of force and aggression, and in myth and superstitious ritual in so far as these referred to their own group's concepts of leadership and power. The cluster also contains the tendency to use stereotypes, rigid in-group out-group discrimination and projection of human failings onto others while remaining uncritical of one's own actions.

Here in South Africa was a culturally isolated group who, through its isolation, had been able to raise unhindered generation after generation of its offspring on authoritarian values. This pattern would create a society in which, like Nazi and Fascist societies, the unpleasant and self-perpetuating acts of the Afrikaner were glossed over in favour of the kind of ends-justify-the-means morality already described as being part of the authoritarian personality's style. The authoritarian personality seemed made for South Africa and as such, it seemed to me at the time, an ideal point at which to start my work.

By using Adorno *et al.*'s F. Scale (to measure authoritarianism) I thought it would be quite easy to prove that South Africans were more fascist-prone than others and that this accounted for their unusual behaviour. More specifically, I hypothesized, since South Africans differed from others only apparently in terms of their *apartheid* policy, it followed that they would be authoritarian and fascist-like only in relation to non-white races who threatened them the most.

At the time I did not think that this was a radical departure from the accepted academic explanation of *apartheid*. I had not read a great deal of South African history by 1968 and I presumed that proving the authoritarian link would simply be explaining in rather more detail the psychology behind the historical events that had shaped the Afrikaner and thus South Africa. Verwoerd's racialism, unpleasant though I found it, and the Nazi links did not put them in the same class as the Nazis – it just showed, I thought, how desperate people could become under pressure of annihilation and after years of being oppressed.

The difficulty was that the authoritarian personality theory had already been used and tested in South Africa and been discarded. There was ample research to show that white South Africans were highly prejudiced towards non-white race groups, that they were discriminatory and in general more prejudiced than other people in other parts of the world with similar ethnic or pluralistic problems.[7] There was also evidence to show that South African whites, especially the Afrikaners, showed more authoritarianism (as measured by the F. Scale) than people in comparable cultures; that is, they showed a higher tendency for Fascism. The difficulty was that these two findings were not significantly related to each other; that is, the correlations between measures of authoritarianism and prejudice were no different to those in places such as the American South. In some cases they were even lower. This was a body blow to the authoritarian-fascism theory. If fascist tendencies had created the context in which *apartheid* arose, it followed that there should have been a consistently high relationship between the F. Scale and anti-black prejudice. Several careful studies were done in the fifties and early sixties in various parts of South Africa, some by eminent American psychologists. All reported consistently low correlations between the F. Scale and prejudice measures. Studies done in Cape Town, for example, showed that while Afrikaans-speaking white students showed more prejudice towards blacks and held more authoritarian attitudes than English-speaking students, the relationship between the Fascist and prejudice measures was the same for the two groups.[8]

In rejecting the authoritarian-fascist theory, psychologists and sociologists pointed to several factors that they felt showed that South Africa was not analogous to Nazi Germany or Fascist Italy. For one thing, South Africa had had discrimination since the arrival of the Dutch in 1652, it was not something the Afrikaans Nationalists had created in 1948. Secondly, South Africa was a democracy – at least for the whites; the Nationalists had been democratically and legitimately elected and theoretically they could be deposed by the same process. Thirdly, Africans to the Afrikaners, unlike the Jews to the Nazis, were *not* dreaded outsiders. Since 1652, the Afrikaners had included Africans in their communities as servants and helpers and assumed responsibility for them. The *apartheid* policy formalized what had been an ongoing system and allowed, in its home-land policy, for the eventual progression of the 'inferior' African to full adult, equal and national status. A far cry from the sub-human dogma of Hitlerian philosophy and, given the problems of other plural societies, one from which South Africa emerged with some credit for attempting a potential solution to a pressing and urgent problem.

The prejudice attitudes to be found in South Africa were not part of a fascist personality syndrome but were simply culturally tolerated attitudes that had developed over the three centuries of South African history. Afrikaners were more prejudiced and more rigid because they had had to fight hardest for their survival. As a young student, it was hard for me to go against the overwhelming weight of this academic opinion. 'Afrikaners are paternalistic towards Africans, which is irritatingly anachronistic but it is not Nazism,' I was told firmly by a Professor of Sociology. 'They look after the African better than the English ever did. There are no concentration camps in South Africa.' The fascist-authoritarian theory had, in the face of poor empirical results, been swamped by the weight of historical evidence.

The Afrikaner had adopted his race policy to protect himself from being swamped by the African tribes. His suspicion and hostility towards the British arose over the way he had been mistreated and exploited. The writings of Afrikaans academics stress repeatedly the heroism and determination of their community now and in the past; parallels are often drawn between the dangers faced by the *trekboers*, the Afrikaans-speaking colonists who left the British-occupied colony in the 1830s, and those faced by contemporary Afrikaners in order to illustrate how Afrikaner psychology had enabled its community to survive.[9] Many liberal Afrikaans academics with whom I discussed these issues were very skilful in constructing explanatory systems. Instead of using National Party dogma or sounding like devotees to the cause – which is academically suspect – they made use of sophisticated psychological arguments citing reputable studies reported in scientific journals to back up their arguments. They talked, for example, of the type of environmental exigencies that give rise to adaptive forms of behaviour. They saw the Afrikaner as having developed more power and survival-orientated behaviour than other race groups, carefully avoiding sounding like racists or believers in the inherent superiority of the white man.[10]

To a certain extent, I knew that arguments emerging from Afrikaans universities were suspect. From the experiences of my friends and my own contact with Afrikaans sociologists and psychologists, I knew that Afrikaner academics were generally committed to a narrow scientific deductivism; research being used not to uncover the secrets of reality but to prove Afrikaner ideology, namely that the Afrikaner is a superior being culturally and intellectually and that his position of power in the country is due to this superiority. I knew too that some researchers made good propaganda use of research reports by international researchers who had expressed themselves in favour of superior-versus-inferior attributes based on skin colour. The debate over Eysenck's views on race, for example, was gleefully seized upon and closely followed in South Africa, and I know of at least two professors at Afrikaans universities who employed full-time research assistants to comb international publications for any research report in the least bit supportive of Afrikaner philosophy. Still others varied their views according to the audience they were speaking to, saying one thing to doctrinaire audiences and another to professionals from overseas. Some departments at Afrikaans universities even insisted on probing a lecturer's theoretical orientation before allowing him or her to teach students. Two colleagues of mine, one from overseas and one an Afrikaner, transferred to departments of Psychology and Sociology at Afrikaans universities; both were required to be completely familiar with the main ideas behind Christian National Psychology and Sociology before they were permitted to start teaching.[11] They protested, but they were told that it was their job as a matter of principle to teach Afrikaans students Afrikaans psychology; if they did not like it, they could leave.[12]

I could treat Afrikaner academic dogma with suspicion but not the feelings of my English colleagues, empirical failure and the facts of history taken together. When my own studies in 1968 and later in 1969 failed to produce anything startling or unexpected, I had only one alternative left – to examine the history of South Africa closely.[13]

I had tried in my studies to improve the measuring instruments used, hoping that more accurate scales would show up a clearer link between prejudice and authoritarianism-fascism, but this proved not to be the case. I was left, though, with several puzzles from the studies; putting aside anti-African prejudice, for instance, why did the whites of South Africa hold such authoritarian attitudes? According to Adorno *et al.*, authoritarianism is usually accompanied by an outward threat that forces a community to behave in a closed and restrictive manner. What outside group had psychologically threatened the whites, especially the Afrikaners, to the extent of causing them to hold narrow and austere values and to behave in the way they did? Something was disturbing the white students that had been tested to make their personality structures more closed and regimented than need be the case; students in other countries are usually free from excessive authoritarianism. The question was to find out what was causing it. If it was in fact the Africans – which everyone said it was – then why was there no significant relationship between authoritarianism and anti-African prejudice?

There were other anomalies. Threats can be real or imaginary. In terms of what I knew of the history of South Africa, the Afrikaners had fought their last war with the Africans in the nineteenth century and had in fact dominated in their contacts with Africans ever since. English-speaking South Africans had even less cause to fear Africans. What was it that was making these young people, most of them born after 1948 and with no direct exposure to the African threat, hold threat-orientated attitudes?

The more I thought about it, the more I came to realize that the conventional explanations for *apartheid* rested on historical assumptions that few people had queried. While I had not been able to prove the authoritarian-fascist theory empirically, no one had yet provided empirical evidence to prove the alternative, namely that the Afrikaners had been an oppressed minority acting to protect themselves. Its support came from widely held beliefs about the history of South Africa that I had to accept through ignorance. I expected South Africans to know more about their history than I did. But what if their beliefs were wrong? Perhaps I could find support for the authoritarian theory by making out a case based on historical facts and, in the process, check the cherished assumptions that most whites held about South African history.

My historical research took some time to complete, mainly because many of the sources I wanted to study were not available in South Africa through being censored or banned and had to be consulted on my overseas trips. But there was enough evidence in the University of Cape Town's libraries to help me initially get a far better overview of South Africa's history than I had previously had.[14]

What I wanted to do with my historical research was to examine the basic axioms on which the historical justification that continually entered into the explanations I read were based. I wanted to know if the Afrikaners had really suffered at the hands of the Africans and the British, and if their historical role justified in any way their current behaviour. The history that follows therefore is very much geared to these questions; I wanted to try and understand the psychology behind the Afrikaner.

To begin with, I listed my own ideas – what I knew about South Africa. The Dutch had ruled the Cape from 1652 to 1795 and developed part of the interior; the British had taken over the Colony finally in 1806 and had run things until the Act of Union in 1910 when the country had become self-ruling. I knew that the Dutch colonists had resented British rule and trekked inland to form the

Orange Free State and the Afrikaans Republic between 1830 and 1860, that they had resisted attempts by the British to invade them once, and that in the 1870s or so gold and diamonds had been discovered. These, the British coveted and this eventually led to the Boer War breaking out in 1899. The British had won and South Africa had been peaceful and quiet until 1948 when the Afrikaans Nationalists won a general election, pushed out General Smuts and created the *apartheid* state.

The Afrikaners I knew claimed to be Africans; they claimed to have brought civilization to South Africa and to have as much right as anyone to remain. Further, since they had done the most for the country, they said, they had a right to rule. The British had proved themselves unreliable, over-eager to give the country to the blacks and, moreover, only interested in what they could get out of the country. The Afrikaners, on the other hand, were steadfast, loyal and had the blood of past generations on their hands to prove that they were sincere and had fought overwhelming odds to maintain their beliefs. Weighty stuff indeed.

The history of South Africa is fundamentally the history of man's use of the land and resources of the country and the conflict that arose between the various ethnic groups over how this was to be achieved. One of the basic assumptions of modern Afrikaner thought is that it was their ancestors who brought civilization in the form of science, art and Christianity to South Africa. Historical fact, however, tells a rather more complicated story. True, over time, the advent of the whites did bring with it the advances that were being made in Europe. But the Dutch settlers who came to the Cape between 1652 and 1795 came to a country which was already rich in its own form of civilization and tradition. Far from imposing radical change on these traditions, the settler community tended to take over the very patterns that had been developed over the years by the indigenous population. This can be seen in many ways.

Of the many African tribes that inhabited South Africa, some, like the Sotho, worked in iron and copper, others mined gold. Many followed essentially pastoral activities and others a semi-nomadic hunting existence. Some traded, others laboured and still others formed mutually beneficial economic relationships with each other. Some hunters, for example, attached themselves from time to time to groups of herders and served them in the form of clientship whereby in return for food and shelter, they hunted and tracked for themselves and the herders while the herders moved with their animals from pasture to pasture (Wilson, 1969).

The Dutch were used to having slaves to do lowly tasks and this was matched in some of the native tribes who, through their clientship systems, were familiar with the idea embodied in slavery. It was a straightforward matter, therefore, for these two people to form interdependent relationships. Other tribes not familiar with this system or not essentially nomadic fought the Dutch and, through the superior fire-power of the latter, were driven back north into the Cape and east into the Eastern Cape.

Until the discovery of gold and diamonds in the second half of the nineteenth century, South Africa was used by black and white alike to pasture herds, to grow crops and very little else. Until the British took over, Cape Town was essentially a replenishment station for Dutch East India Company ships, and the company operated the colony for much of the time on a shoe-string budget; the settlers who came were there to provide for the company, but owing to the general corruption obtaining amongst company officials and the inability of the company to assert its will, settlers began to trade with the Africans and later, as time went on, they began to farm and rear animals in much the same way as the African had done before them.

In a very real sense, then, the advent of the Dutch in South Africa imposed a white presence and organization on an existing black pattern which in turn had been dictated by the geography of South Africa. What was new was the considerable intermingling that occurred mainly in the towns between the Dutch, the slaves they had brought with them and the Africans who became integrated with the new society. Miscegenation saw the emergence of a coloured people and a local version of Dutch, *die taal*, became widely spoken by whites as well as non-whites. Within this matrix, some aspects of a multiracial society began to emerge. The colonists, caught between the demands of the Company's government and the pressure of guerrilla wars with the Africans, established a culturally distinct society which created a bond of compromise and a form of isolation and independence between white, Coloured and African. Cultural barriers dissolved and a sense of uniqueness began to evolve in the colony. Africans and whites alike were willing to give up some of their overt cultural habits in order to maintain the relatively stable life-style they had established. The use of *die taal* further helped to establish the distinctions between the non-settler company, non-colonial Africans and the new society. So what was specifically new or European-like was to be found in the relatively stable multiracial communities that sprung up and which in time created a form of liberalism and egalitarianism.

For some Dutch settlers, especially those on the frontiers, life was very different. The *trekboers*, nomadic farmers engaged in animal-rearing, trekked annually, like some African tribes did, for new pastures. Each such farmer, because of his superior fire-power and his favoured status with the Dutch East India Company, took over the role previously held by the stronger of the native tribes; he collected Africans in a kind of hierarchy in which clientship and slavery existed side-by-side. As the African tribes were pushed back and their land taken or their capital, their herds, taken or sold, the dispossessed Africans could choose to serve either the *trekboers* or the more settled boers who farmed in one place, or they could set up on their own. For the nomadic boer and his slaves and clients, life was a simple matter of rule by the strongest, a straightforward matter of continuing the systems that both had for years been used to.

Whatever the type, the settler communities gave very little to the country as such. The people who came from the Netherlands to form the bulk of the colony's white population were essentially people who had either failed for one reason or another in their own country or who had had so little in the first place that a move could only be for the better. Either way, life in the Cape was an improvement on that at home. As Katzen (1969) has pointed out, the Cape in the eighteenth century remained an intellectual backwater: few, if any, were the advances in art, science, technology, music, or literature. Because of their isolation from Europe, partly circumstantial and, especially amongst the people on the frontiers, partly deliberate, the cultural and social life of the Dutch colonists remained throughout their time, restricted and insular.[15]

In the colony, a sense of specialness and 'God-given' ingroupness arose, but not in a racial sense. *Die volk* was not 'pure' white. They had no need to conceptualize themselves as such because the colonists were not threatened by blacks alone. The nomadic boer especially regarded his 'own' blacks and Coloureds as an integral part of his community, the basic unit of these wandering communities being the single family comprised of whites *and* their black retainers. Hostility was directed towards whites who were not of it: Company officials, new immigrants – especially those from France and Germany who were rapidly and deliberately assimilated and prevented from forming their own communities – and to unfriendly blacks. The fact that the colonists were not well-educated, were isolated from the influence of Europe, had no newspapers or journals and the like, all helped to cement their simple survivalist values. Their lives were defined by cycles of warfare, farming, hunting and cheating on the Company, and their entertainment by sessions of eating, drinking, card-playing, music, dancing and gossiping. In such circumstances, the value system that arose had by definition to reflect on the glorification of mundane, commonplace human traits. Intellect, constructive thinking, insight had no place in such a community. As these people learnt that not only could they survive but advance materially by applying these standards, they tended to reify them.

Few people realize that until the late 1800s, South Africa was regarded not only as a backwater but as an unhealthy place to live in – life was hard, the climate harsh and relentless and the rewards few. Hence the lack of interest shown by the Dutch and British governments. Because of this and because of the vastness of the country, the new colonists survived successfully in isolation. The country was forbidding enough to discourage outside intervention and large enough to prevent a determined resistance from the African tribes for a considerable period of time. Faced with choosing life dominated by the colonists or moving into the deserted hinterland, many Africans chose the latter. Only when these factors changed, as they did after the British took over in 1806, were the flaws inherent in the Dutch colonists' existence exposed.

Understanding the nature of these boer communities is very important. It was clear from my research that the events of the nineteenth century shaped the future of South Africa but not for the reasons usually given, namely that the Afrikaner, through trekking into the interior, helped to stabilize the country and create a firm base for its leadership into the twentieth century. As I understand it, the history of South Africa since 1800 is essentially the history of how, through a series of unfortunate circumstances, the worst features of Dutch colonial existence were preserved intact well into the twentieth century.

I have already pointed out that the Dutch brought precious little to South Africa and that, at best, the beginnings of a healthy multi-racial society – such as occurred in Brazil at about the same time – were laid down while, at worst, the colonists simply mimicked the African tribes. Under the British occupation, some of the benefits and advances of European civilization were at last introduced into South Africa, and it was how some of the Dutch colonists reacted to these reforms that next interested me.

When the British took over finally in 1806, and began to make changes in the structure of government in the Cape, the colonists, especially the boers, encountered problems with authority. Gone were the days of the easily corrupted and evaded Company; the British meant business and they had some of the power and, above all, the will to see that their policies were carried out. Settling the colony meant, to the British, encouraging permanent farming, making the best use of the land and, of prime importance, bringing peace and prosperity – in particular this meant peace with the African tribes. All this meant change for the Dutch, and those who coped with it best were the settled farmers and the people who lived in the towns. Their policy of multiracialism and egalitarianism accorded well with the aims of the British administration of the Cape.

The advent of the British brought mixed fortunes to the colony. In some respects it prospered, and certainly life for its inhabitants was never the same again because the most fundamental effect of the British occupation was to bring change and reform into their lives. Legislative, judicial and land reform were introduced along with new English settlers, emancipation of the slaves and the beginnings of an equal rights political framework.

Many of the colonists made the adjustment well, especially those who had already begun to adjust to the new ideas of the nineteenth century which the British were introducing. For the *trekboers*, though, adjustment was difficult because it meant giving up patterns of behaviour that had been established over nearly a century and a half; the changes frightened and threatened the boers who, like all poorly informed, isolated and unsophisticated people, built them into major obstacles out of proportion to the actual reality. The changes imposed on the colonists were less stringent in fact than both those imposed by the colonists on the indigenous Africans, the French and German refugees who came to the country in the eighteenth century and those imposed on the colonists by the Dutch East India Company. In some instances, the British were a good deal more liberal than the company or the colonists themselves had been.

The African tribes who had earlier trekked away from the colonists did so for substantial reasons, the least of which was that the Dutch refused to use their languages in the official life of the colony – which is one of the reasons given in justification for the Great Trek (Van Jaarsveld, 1961). The Africans trekked because their lands were being taken by people who shot and killed them if they resisted and who made some of them into little more than serfs if they gave in. None of this happened to the boers.

The boers had had complex problems, with officialdom, with the Africans and with each other, long before the British came to South Africa (Walker, 1957, p.100). Some had earlier even trekked away from the frontier society set up by the boers, no doubt to avoid those problems. In addition, the frontier boers were essentially nomadic and, like the African tribes before them, they trekked seasonally.

The British, I believe, were a convenient target; a means of explaining the myriad problems the boers had and of justifying resistance to change. What the British proposed doing in the colony, the status the boers were to obtain, in reality cannot in any way be compared with the hardships and tribulations experienced by the African tribes at the hands of the Dutch colonists themselves. The boers were reacting to a civilizing and organizing force – whatever its logistic and interim shortfalls were – in a way that was entirely predictable, given the social and psychological frameworks that had become well-established parts of their personalities. It takes a certain psychology to act in the way the trekboers did. The crucial question, then, was why did some of these colonists decide, again, to mimic the African tribes and trek away from the 'oppression'?

We can, I think, get closer to understanding the real psychological reasons behind the Afrikaners' desire to trek by looking at what the new changes introduced by the British meant to the individual boer. The basic trekker unit was the farming family. Each man had on his farm his own family as well as the families of those non-whites who served him, and he was basically overlord of this small community, the family head being responsible for maintaining law and order and discipline. These small family communities were often on trek and so were isolated from each other and from whatever broad communal influences existed. The status of the boer head of family was therefore considerable, and it remained so for years.

This, then, was the base of the boer personality and society: success and adjustment to life was essentially a physical and individualistic one. Given the high degree of insularity of their life-style there was little desire to improve it. For the boer family head, life was very comfortable psychologically, better than the drudgery and toil in Holland where his status was lowly and inferior. South Africa was a psychological paradise – here he was top dog and led the life he chose; someone else, the non-white, now performed the drudgery.

This, I believe, is one of the central psychological reasons why the boers fought the British administration. Simple people, in fact all of us from time to time, tend to equate improvements in their lives with certain symbols or occurrences – like a lucky charm, good weather. When things go 'wrong', they cling to these symbols with a stubbornness that can become, if accompanied by a feeling of helplessness, a totally absorbing obsession. Having blacks underneath them was to the boers one such symbol; without it they felt threatened. Somewhere inside was an idea, transmitted from generation to generation and elaborated on through the one hundred and forty years of their 'new lives', of what life back in Holland had been like. Faced with this, they became convinced that giving Africans equal status meant a return for them to the lowly status they had had in Holland – something they feared more than anything else. Like a gambler who rubs his lucky charm harder and harder the more he loses, the boers became obsessed with keeping the African in servitude on the grounds that this was the only way they could maintain their own status.

This rationale, I think, became eventually – because the boer actually succeeded in isolating himself in trekking – an unquestioned axiom of his culture, an emotional rallying point. It became, like all axioms that emerge when simple uneducated people are frightened, a guiding myth – so much so that, in time, it became a *suicidal* obsession of hard-core Afrikaners. Rather than do their own work, boers committed atrocities like deliberately taking African women and children as slaves on their raids, and would rather die than do an African's work (Bird, 1888). Later, in the Depression of the 1920s, unemployed Afrikaners preferred facing starvation for themselves and their families rather than take the labouring jobs they thought were beneath them (De Kiewiet, 1975, Chapter ix; Welsh, 1969, pp. 202–221).

The British threatened to undermine a simple, almost primitive psychological structure. Once the boer head of family's special position was altered, he would lose his *personal* power and status and become a normal human being like everyone else. He would have to learn a different, static, kind of farming, stop seasonal trekking, socialize more, lose many of his servants who, under the British, were being encouraged to farm for themselves and, above all, he would have to learn to accept authority. The *trekboers* left because these changes were, to them, more dangerous – because they were personal, individual and essentially psychological – than any *physical* threat posed by the land, hardship and the Africans. Trekking with all its dangers allowed them to continue to function in the way they always had. In short, the male family heads – the power base of the trekker community and the people who made all the decisions – wanted to maintain the power that they had become used to.

Reading the history of this time, I was struck by the simple psychology at work. I had expected to read about great men, about a great people fighting and struggling for their beliefs and for their survival. What I found was a story about how an essentially insular and backward folk, through circumstance, actually defied the advance of civilization. One can understand and sympathize with the boers' problems, but could one admire their way of solving them? I could not; history is too full of the consequences of foolhardy actions, ignorant understanding and wasted effort. To reify the behaviour of this colonial minority, born out of an all too human but dangerous phobia, as the boers and their descendants did, is to defy logic and common sense. It amounted to institutionalized madness in which the phobia I have described became elevated to the status, virtually, of a state religion.[16]

Some of the central axioms of Afrikaner morality arose in this time. When I read about them it was, again, with surprise that anyone could have taken this nonsense seriously for so long. One of them concerns the Afrikaners' religious conviction – the belief that his system was ordained by the Almighty. People under pressure tend to use anything to justify remaining as they are; the more insular and uneducated they are, the more they rely on primitive arguments founded in myth. After over a century of having things their own way, the *trekboers*, unable to adjust to the new demands that reality and the British were making on them, had to reify their vaunted sense of their own capabilities and their past deeds in order to justify their resistance. This defensiveness easily mingled with the fundamentalist Calvinistic religion that, until 1780, had had a monopoly in the colony. Calvinism preaches a separatism between the godly and the ungodly and this was easily taken, in *trekboer* communities, as further justification for the *status quo* that had emerged between themselves and their African followers.

The real test of religious conviction, however, lies in assessing the role it plays *before* things get tough. Like the unbeliever who asks God to help him when he is frightened, did the *trekboers* use religion when it suited them? The answer from the history I read was that this was exactly what they did. The Dutch colonists, to some extent, 'bent' Calvinism to their own needs where and when it suited them; orthodox Calvinism became less than orthodox, for example, when it came to entertainment. If the *trekboers* had strictly applied the embargoes advocated by Calvinism on immorality – gambling, drinking, gossiping and dancing – their social lives would have quickly come to an end for there was little else to do but gambling, drinking, gossiping and dancing. Like everything else, the religion, the morality and the values of the *trekboer* were blended with and adjusted to the circumstances in which they found themselves. They incorporated into their culture that which they found acceptable and rejected or gave lip-service only to that which they did not. How the colonists actually regarded their religion, though, as opposed to what their modern descendants want us to believe, can be seen in the fact that before 1792 there were only five congregations in the colony – all of them near Cape Town and none in the areas occupied by *trekboers* (Katzen, 1969). Further, as Walker (1957, p. 136) notes, like all forms of authority in the Cape, the Dutch Reformed clergy were respected but were known to be apathetic. It suited the colonial society to have religion so long as it did not interfere with their lives.

The migration of this relatively small group of *trekboers* in the 1830s shaped the future of South Africa.[17] When the boers left, they took with them their African and Coloured servants; behind them, they left a multiracial community of English, Dutch, Africans and Coloureds. This act created an irrevocable split in the development of South African society in the following way: the Dutch who remained began gradually to integrate with the English and received in the process the benefits of the colony as it developed; that is, the new developments in European culture and education and an increased prosperity. More important for our understanding of the psychological development of South Africa's white groups, those who remained made the adjustment demanded by the situation and developed a psychological structure similar to that of the British settlers, itself being one that was in accordance with the demands of nineteenth-century reality.

The gulf that separated the two communities was a very broad and deep one. The hostility of the trekkers towards the British was expressed by their keeping contact to a minimum and rejecting anything that was the least bit British. At the same time, the Cape Colony community, including the Dutch, continued on its way, relatively disinterested in the *trekboers*. Because of this split, the boers and those with them were able to systematically avoid having to adjust to the normal changes to which people in nineteenth-century and early-twentieth-century societies were exposed. In America, Europe, and even in parts of the colonial empires of European nations, people were, in this time, being exposed to education, industrialization, cultural changes, changes in notions of human rights and so on. The foundations of our twentieth-century understanding of social responsibility involving ideas of degrees of balance between individual needs and social needs were being established at a time when the boers were standing still. Frontier people in the American west acted in a similar way to the boers and at the same time and for similar psychological reasons, yet they remained a part of American society and, in time, the areas they appropriated were settled by other Americans who created a continuity between frontier and civilized life.

In place of these civilizing processes, the boers chose to contend with hardship and to fight the Africans for the land and available cattle. While the Cape colonists were settling into a relatively safe communal existence, gradually leaving the police and the army – professional career militarists – to deal with the Africans, each boer family had to fight. This became a family tradition and the personality of these families was shaped in the early years by having to be continually on guard for danger – something that was becoming increasingly more alien to the whites left behind. This helped the Boer Republics to resist the British army so well in both wars of independence, but it did little else.

Where I think the tragedy lay was in the fact that this toughening process obscured, possibly forever, the kind of phobic psychopathology that I described earlier. Any chance the boers and the societies they created had for critical or reflective self-analysis was lost when the psychological division of South Africa occurred. Commitment to boer morality meant then, as it does now, a denial of reality as we in the Western world know it.

Split led to inability to analyse self

This is an important point. Denying the reality of the Western world as we know it does not mean that those who do so are incapable of dealing with reality; far from it – very often they excel in certain respects that we do not. Primitive tribes are usually, for example, better at hunting than computer programmers. What matters is that no matter how similar in appearance and behaviour they may be to us of the West, they retain a fundamentally different idea about how life should be lived, societies formed, the rights of the individual and, above all, the meaning of cruelty and human suffering.

Instead of survival being based on intellect, technical skill and education, as it was for those who remained in the Cape, it was for the boers a matter of physical animal cunning – familiarity with the terrain, with animals, Africans and the rifle. All of these demands served to accentuate and referent in reality the very values and way of life that the boer was familiar with (and the British wanted to take away). The boer family head's status and power became even more firmly entrenched by the hardships he and his family faced. While Western families were changing their structure from a semi-feudal male-dominated one in which the family depended on the male to protect them, to a peaceful, more broadly based, egalitarian emphasis in which physical survival was taken for granted, the boer family structure was becoming reified, fixed in an anachronistic and false image. I was surprised that the relevance of these points had escaped historians and social scientists because, for me, they went a long way towards explaining the incomprehensibility of the Afrikaners' behaviour in general and the acts of the Nationalists since 1948.

The Afrikaners' phobia towards the British was of course further entrenched both by their lack of contact with the Cape Colony and their hardships. Their belief in their God-giveness and their belief in the rightness of their approach to and their superiority over the African was confirmed, in their view, because they succeeded. Hardships and failings were blamed on the British; what the boers conveniently forgot was that their success was due in part to the disinterest of the British and to the fact that the British supplied the boers with arms and not the Africans.

These simple explanatory systems were easily accepted by the boers who, until the turn of the century had few, if any, leaders who were sufficiently well-educated and had sufficient insight to provide a proper assessment of the situation. Paul Kruger, for example, perhaps the most able political leader in the Boer Republics and the most well-known, was a fundamentalist who believed the sun went round the earth.

There were, then, by the mid-nineteenth century, three major social systems in South Africa. The boers formed one, essentially the one that the Afrikaner has imposed on South Africa today. African and coloured people in this community were servants and slaves, materially looked after but because of their subhuman status between man and animal, never permitted to improve or advance on this status.[18] The Cape Dutch, the English and their non-white fellows formed a second system, and the African tribes at war with either the British or the boers formed the third grouping, eventually settling for compromise and protection from the British in preference to subjugation by the boers. As the Native wars ended, the Africans of these tribes settled into a relatively peaceful co-existence with the whites and blacks from the Cape colony and Natal until the turn of the century. This tripartite split amongst the Africans and whites helps in part to explain the recent history of white-black interaction in South Africa because it is a split that has been maintained and formalized by the Afrikaner nationalists. The Afrikaners' Africans and Coloureds became an integral part of that society and were, as such, equally isolated from events elsewhere. Thus, they have had a long unchanging history of an Afrikaner-dominated *status quo*.

The Africans who were part of the Cape Colony developed white-orientated class structures, partially integrated socially, partially not, alongside the British and Dutch whites. They formed, however, an integral part of an economic and cultural system that was radically different from that in which their counterparts in the

Afrikaans Republics lived. Their values, aspirations and life-styles were similar to whites', and in some respects they were regarded as equal.

The tribal Africans were caught in between: their experiences of the boers were not pleasant and there was, they knew, no possibility of an honourable compromise with a group of people who regarded them, their kings and their institutions as inferior. When they compromised with the British, their individuality and their rights were to some extent respected – so much so that the Swazi and Sotho were able to avoid becoming part of the Union in 1910 (Forman, 1961). Thus, the orientation of these tribal Africans was towards English South Africa, and it was to the English-Dutch cities in the Cape colony or Natal that they moved in search of employment. As the nineteenth century progressed, potential disruption from Africans as a whole was not only curtailed by warfare but neutralized either by English or Afrikaans institutions.

When gold and diamonds were discovered after mid-century, these three social groups had to adjust to the new wealth. South Africa shifted from a country being exploited for its land to one in which the people mobilized to control its resources and to exploit them. Gold mines needed capital investment, technical know-how, labour and a marketing system. All three groups re-shaped their structure to cope with these new demands: the Afrikaners owned the land in which lay the gold; the English had the capital, the know-how and the markets, the Africans had the labour. The rush to exploit the new wealth created the conditions for contact between all three groups and soon exposed the structural faults that the previous state of isolation had obscured.

The wealth earned from labour created an easy opportunity for thousands of Africans to earn money in mines run by companies formed by the familiar English whites. South African Africans became richer and that more quickly than those from surrounding countries, and the gold mines became a mecca for foreign Africans as far away as the Congo and Nyasaland. However, this process, while materially improving the lot of South Africa's African tribes, created a growing urban society which learned to tolerate some hardship and few rights in order to continue making money quickly. Instead of augmenting and extending the middle class of Africans and Coloureds that had grown up over the past two centuries, the new wealth created a massive, cheap-labour class out of which grew a secondary class providing services that helped to maintain the undesirable *status quo*: traders working in and for a purely black, sometimes transitory society, on the fringes of white cities. Because these developments improved the lot of many Africans, they were not closely and clearly examined for what they were – in the long run, vulnerable to the machinations of an unscrupulous authority that eventually used them for its own ends.

The English and Dutch colonists profited. Many Dutch colonists, with the advent of wealth in the Republics, moved there, bringing with them their years of exposure to English ideology and education. English and other foreign companies poured personnel and capital into the Republics and created the infrastructure for the mining industries and, of course, took massive profits in the process. They also behaved unscrupulously in many respects, seeking to undermine the Afrikaner governments and, in order to maximize profits or appease the boers, reduced and undercut the status of Africans and their rights (Simons and Simons, 1969, Chapters 2 and 3).

Of all three systems, the Afrikaner Republics were the least able to cope with the new demands that wealth imposed. The Republics were direct outgrowths of the trekker communities, and the fact that war occurred between them and the British can be seen as a direct result of the inability of these communities to deal with the kind of reality that the rest of South Africa, in common with the outside world, had faced for some time. Under the weight of managing the new wealth, the Boer Republics collapsed and adopted the same tactics to fight off the *interlopers* as they had against the African tribes.

The Republics had not developed adequate institutions for controlling their wealth and foreign exploitation and were easily vulnerable to the sometimes unscrupulous power-seeking people who came in search of fortunes. A common presumption about the causes of the Boer War is that the English wanted the new wealth of the country and the boers had to fight to retain it. While some of the English undoubtedly wanted it, the pressure of the last two decades of the nineteenth century exposed the Afrikaans Republics for what they were: a backward and insular collection of fragmented communities operating on principles that had been current a century before.

The original trekkers had separated into four groups who differed and quarrelled with one another and who never really became reconciled or united. Once settled in the 1840s and 1850s, they discovered that the ability to organize and order themselves was lacking. They had never been called upon to live in such close proximity to one another, nor had they to deal with one another honestly and fairly. They had been used to manipulating a corrupt company; now they had to manage their own affairs and none of it came easily.

The essential unifying factor in the trekkers' communities was the dominant personality in each small community. Just as each boer family was dominated and took its lead from the male head of the family, so each community took its lead from its most dominant, articulate personality. This was inevitably the person who appeared to manifest the particular qualities of the local community.

In a simple, unsophisticated society, these leaders became God-like figures and their word was law. They had to act and operate for the good of the community and in the way the community expected or they would be replaced by someone who would. This straightforward leader-follower system has been the model for Afrikaans society ever since – the populace, including the clergy and the local police, giving their complete loyalty and trust to the leader who, in turn, kept close contact with his community. This system was essentially *personal*. Contact with the leader was through direct means and *vice versa*. If you had a problem, you went to see the leader. If he needed something, it was done informally; little was committed to paper, little was formalized.

In the Boer Republics, the informal style of unification and leadership, which was quite adequate at the level of village communities, began to disintegrate, and this gave rise to one of the major problems that is still a disrupting factor in Afrikaans society. The personal model works only when the number of people in the community is small enough to allow each person in it to know and have access to the leader. It cannot survive when this access does not exist because a formal structure is then required to ensure access to all on an order-of-priorities level. In the Boer Republics, just such a problem arose and the leadership structure, then as now, could not cope with the demands placed upon it. Factions of leadership cliques were unable to be unified, and public life became a matter of belonging to one or the other of the personal leadership systems in operation. (Thompson, 1969).

Within these systems, corruption and inefficiency became as familiar as they had been in dealing with the Dutch East India Company; personal contact became the key to organization and with it, favour and intrigue. For the trekkers, long familiar with this system and by tradition, with its off-shoots of corruption and favouritism, these practices became an established and accepted part of their daily lives.

What little organization existed in the Republics was provided by foreigners (Houghton, 1969; Thompson, 1969). The boers' approach to economic necessity was rashly anachronistic. They had become so used to other people doing the type of work they deemed beneath themselves that the Republics were completely dependent on cheap labour for their existence, notably from Africans and Coloureds. So obsessed were the *trekboers* with their social structure of Africans at the bottom of the ladder that they sometimes went on raids with the express purpose of abducting African women and children to serve them as slaves and servants. Bird (1888) contains an account of this which shows clearly the attitudes of the boers to raids against the Africans. Depriving Africans of their property, their wives, children and stock was regarded as little more than a hunting expedition; some boers went on them to make their fortunes. This unrealistic dependence on others applied at all levels of development in the Republics; trade, for example, was in the hands of non-boers, mainly British and Jewish entrepreneurs; mining and other services in the Republics were also performed by non-boers. Even the existing newspapers were run by English people. In fact, once again, the boers did little for the lands they occupied save use it for their herds without improving it.

As I said earlier, the boers and their societies managed through a combination of luck and circumstance to survive long after they should have either perished or been made to face ordinary reality. The vastness of South Africa saved the *trekboers* from having to adapt to British rule in the 1820s. Gold and diamonds saved the Boer Republics from manifesting failure after 1870, and losing the Boer War fought with the British in 1899–1902 further ensured that the boers never faced up to inadequacies in their social, cultural and psychological systems. They were then able to explain their 'failure' by once again blaming the British. World sympathy of course furthered the process. We only learn properly when our acts can

clearly be shown to be foolish or inhumane or lead to disaster; if we succeed every time, we behave ignorantly or indulge in fantasy; we never learn to criticize our ideas or acts. If values and actions such as these persist for over a hundred years in relative isolation, they become the basis for a *sociopathic* society and culture – one that is out of step with the rest of mankind. This is what I meant when I wrote earlier that the worst features of Dutch colonial existence were preserved through a series of lucky circumstances.

The two cultures that clashed in the Boer War were psychologically of different centuries. The British sent troops, the boers mobilized families and small communities – it was, for the boer, total war. The boer head of family was fighting once again for his psychological survival in terrain that he knew well and with methods he had long mastered. In losing the war, the boers gained a psychological respect from the British, a respect which is always engendered in those more used to negotiation and compromise by those stubborn and physical people who are prepared to fight. The Act of Union in 1910 which created modern South Africa was one result. In it, the Afrikaners gained everything they had fought for: political power, the English and non-boer Dutch to provide the institutions so lacking in the Boer Republics; the capital, the contact and marketing with the outside world; and the Africans firmly removed from their position in the triangle of power.

This Act had several crucial effects: under British rule, the African tribes in South Africa had developed an institutional way of living that had brought them a measure of prosperity and stability. They had got used to dealing with a white authority who in most part seemed capable of providing protection and who had gradually attempted to improve their status and well-being. The terms of the Act of Union effectively cut off the Africans from the power processes and, although there were protests and uprisings, by and large the African population, under assurances from the British and I think to some extent blinded by their wealth and status obtained from the mines, accepted the change-over peaceably. Part of the reason was that the past century had given them little cause to mistrust the judgement of the British.

The British had had very little contact with the growing Afrikaner nation in the Republics. South Africa was handed over, they clearly thought, to educated and responsible Afrikaners. One of them, Smuts, had even been educated at Oxford. Under the circumstances, the Act of Union relieved the British of a sizeable headache and placed the responsibility for African protection in the hands of the new Union government. My reading of the situation is that the British, the non-boer whites and the African chiefs were relying on the new government continuing in the role developed by the British; the new constitution was modelled on Westminster and incorporated many English institutions. Yet this expectancy could only be fulfilled if those administering the system held the same psychology, the same cultural values, beliefs and morality as the British who had laid it down. While this was partially true of the new leaders, Smuts and Botha and their followers, it was far from true of the hard-core Afrikaner.

The Act of Union was in a profound sense a betrayal of the trust placed in the British by the rural chiefs who had turned to them in the closing years of the nineteenth century for protection against the boers. Weakened and rendered powerless by the onslaughts of boer domination and the British administration's desire for peace, these African tribes had to stand by helplessly while the Afrikaners, once in power and working in concert with other white profiteers, dismembered the last remnants of formal African rights. Under Smuts and Botha, the Union government quickly passed a series of acts to contain the movement of Africans, to remove the power of the chiefs and to restrict the development of the African and Coloured middle class which functioned as part and parcel of white society. They left untouched the middle class that served the mining and other industrial interests, and which had arisen to support the cheap labour system that had 'tranquillised' the change-over for both English and African opposition. Successive governments added to this process until, by the time Malan's Afrikaner Nationalist Party took over in 1948, they had little to do but to reinforce and toughen up the application of already existing measures to control and contain the African population.

Even the moderate Afrikaner felt obliged – purely as an Afrikaner – to uphold the values and morality that had dominated the Afrikaner Republics. This morality, as we have seen, was grounded on the myths of the *trekboers* and the psychology I described earlier – a physical matter of survival and personal power. In South Africa, the British and non-boer South Africans had built institutions based on a set of standards that reflected the educational and historical background of the advanced societies in Western Europe. The Afrikaner had no such institutions, no history of responding to academic argument, no history of communality and, above all, no sense of rule of law and the rights of individuals or groups of individuals. Since 1910, South Africa has been ruled by Afrikaners: Botha, Smuts, Hertzog, Malan, Strydom, Verwoerd, Vorster and Botha, using British institutions and African labour.

It was clear to me from my studies that the boers' most feared enemy had always been the English and, to a lesser extent, the Anglicized Dutch. The Africans had been an irritant, easily controlled through ruthlessness, determination and superior weaponry. Moreover, they were a valuable commodity to the boer nation, both as a source of property and stock and then as labourers. The British were powerful, organized and skilful – a far more serious proposition. Afrikaner affairs from 1830 onwards have been dominated by an obsessive hatred and antagonism towards the British.

It also occurred to me that my thinking about *apartheid* had been shaped by a Western world concerned with its own racial problems rather than by actual events in South Africa. Slowly, I came to realize that South Africa is more than just a prejudiced society – its racism is a by-product of a much deeper process. European countries with immigrant minorities and the United States with its ethnic minorities are essentially states in which race problems arose because of an historical attitude held by *majority* whites about its Negro or non-white *minorities*. Where these states erected formal and even legal barriers to impede the progress of its minorities to full citizenship, it was as a means of protecting the interests of the *majority* of its citizens. Change occurred, albeit slowly, through education and increased communication between people. But it was achieved because the minorities discriminated against were not the majority in any given population. Removing overt prejudice in America or Britain did not mean for Americans and Britons giving up power or disrupting their political systems. Often it meant little more than having neighbours with different coloured faces, bus conductors, ticket collectors, black, white and brown.

South Africa is not a highly prejudiced society. It is a society in which prejudice is *used* as a highly effective means of camouflaging the efforts of just under 11% of the population to maintain itself in power. It is clear that *apartheid* had no base in religion or in colour prejudice. The modern Afrikaners have used the fact that it is the blacks who are apparently suppressed to draw a red herring across the noses of critics inside and outside the country. I could see that when people attacked South Africa for its prejudicial behaviour, they played into the Afrikaners' hands because they know that many people in Britain and America as well as in South Africa sympathise with an 'honest and open' attempt to deal with 'the problem'. As I was aware from my own experience, foreigners, conscious of their own prejudice, give South Africa a certain sympathy.

I also saw how the Afrikaners used anti-African prejudice as a means of distracting attention away from the way it had extended its own power; the government could afford to give way slowly on race matters because these matters were essentially unrelated to the power structure and gained it a certain favour and a reputation for pragmatism and reasonableness which it did not deserve. While liberal South Africans were watching the South African government for any signs that it was easing its race policy, I realized from these historical studies that the Afrikaners continued unabated with entrenching themselves firmly in control of the country. While the authorities busied themselves with strategic supplies, building up armed forces infiltrating its neighbouring countries, fermenting unrest in Angola, Zambia, Rhodesia, Mozambique and Zaire, we in Cape Town watched to see if black cricket teams would be allowed to play in white leagues.

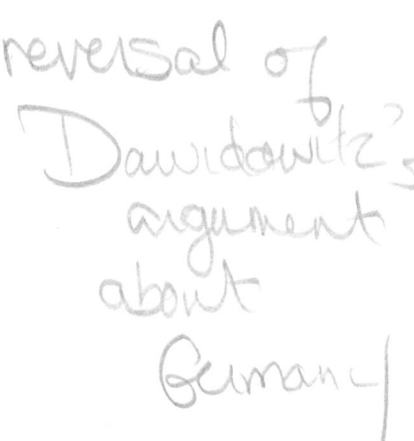

reversal of
Davidowitz's
argument
about
Germany

Chapter Two

Afrikanerism, Fascism and Their Contemporary Traces

These preliminary historical explorations revealed three crucial things to me. Firstly, the boers had actually won the Boer War – by 1910, the country was theirs, the Africans were conveniently subjugated, the English departing, turning their attentions elsewhere. Secondly, Afrikaner society was insular and sociopathic – they had a phobia about the British, completely unrealistic ideas about their own capabilities and a hopelessly irrelevant view of their past. Thirdly, all of this had been achieved by an incredible series of co-incidences, all of them operating to help cement the Afrikaner's beliefs in his myths and in his sociopathic way of life.

All right. These insights fascinated me, but how to build a research programme around them? How to relate them to contemporary South Africa and, above all, how to link this sociopathic culture with the authoritarian-fascist framework I was working on? Perhaps the South African experience was a completely new one that required a new concept and a new framework? What was clear was that relating authoritarianism-fascism to anti-African prejudice was a mistake. The historical evidence indicated that the Afrikaners' feared out-group was not the black but rather the white English-speaking South Africans who had been the phobic enemy for most of the nineteenth century.

The more I thought about it, the more I realised how irrelevant to the Afrikaners' equation the Africans really were. From the late nineteenth century until the guerrilla incursions of the 1960s and

70s, the Africans as a possible physical threat – the only kind of threat the boers understood or recognised – ceased to exist. The real task was to find out how the Afrikaners' anti-British phobia and sociopathic culture had developed and how they had coped with the demands of running South Africa from 1910 onwards.

Once in power, the Afrikaners could no longer trek away from their problems; they had to stand and fight, which meant a radical departure from their historical tradition. Strangely enough, their previous experience stood them in good stead – not in forming and leading a democratic South Africa – but in preserving and protecting their own power base as leaders of the new Union: they were the only group in South Africa psychologically equipped and motivated for ruthless self-preservation.

The newly acquired institutions of state had to be filled with trusted, educated and trained Afrikaners. To cope with this, the Afrikaans leadership embarked on a campaign to educate their community and to help them manage the demands of the new situation; the new wealth and new power could easily have been usurped by the powerful English business and professional communities eager to exploit South Africa's potential. Two ways of protecting the poorly educated and insular Afrikaans community were set up. One was to make use of the Afrikaans *Broederbond*, and the other to create Afrikaans institutions in all areas to parallel those of the English.

The Afrikaans *Bond*, formed in 1879 by a church minister to protect the rights and interests of Afrikaners in the Cape Colony, was reconstituted in 1918 as the *Broederbond* and operated openly until 1924 when it became a secret society. The *Broederbond*'s job was to serve as a watchdog on Afrikaans-English interaction and to further the ends of Afrikanerdom where possible. It was organised to prevent exploitation of the Afrikaner by the English and to maintain and unify the development of the Afrikaans community. One way it did this was through a system of placing cells of its members in as many settings as possible where English-Afrikaans joint ventures were operating. It also infiltrated existing English institutions and ensured that its members held power in all Afrikaner institutions. This body became in time *the* central organising factor in the Afrikaans community. It established charities and institutions to look after the Afrikaner and directed the actions of people in a wide range of institutions and associations in the fields of religion, the professions, politics, business, the academic community, and so on.

The degree to which the Afrikaans community constructed a state within a state since 1910 was quite staggering. Every possible English institution was copied, from professions down to service and business organisations, from the Voortrekkers (modelled on the Boy Scouts and Girl Guides) down to Afrikaner language preservation societies.

The Afrikaner applied a kind of reverse trek. No longer able to escape territorially, the community effectively psychologically isolated itself from the rest of South Africa, pushing the English and the non-whites even further away from themselves and the centre of power. This slow and systematic imposition of Afrikaner values and control over South African society was achieved largely because it moved at such a pace and made such use of the appearance of co-operation and stability that it successfully camouflaged its real intent. English whites were encouraged to concentrate on business and finance and they found this as rewarding as the African working class did in providing labour for South African industries.

When the time came in 1948 for a hardening of the processes, the hard Afrikaner Nationalist core of the community was more than ready. It set about completing the final links in the chain which kept white from white and black from white that had helped it to maintain power since 1910. By using techniques gained from first-hand experience of Nazi methods of control and propaganda, it used the constitution to gain power. Then it entrenched itself firmly by a series of actions that ensured it could not be voted out by democratic means.[1]

The idea of a Nazi or Fascist link to Afrikaner Nationalism was superflous. The Afrikaner community had a long and successful history of self-reification, religiosity and an obsession with physical power and insular values long before Hitler rose to power; the Nationalists needed no demagogic ideology – they had their own. All they needed from the Nazis were the tactics of mass psychological manipulation; once in power they outlasted both the Nazis and the Fascists, and in some respects, I think, applied Nazi techniques far better than the originators.

I have not discussed these developments in detail because they are too well-known. What interested me were the gaps in the generally available literature. I knew that the Afrikaner set up his own institutions, that Afrikaners ruled from 1910 onwards,[2] that the Afrikaners' liberal wing – represented by people like Smuts – was gradually pushed out and the hard core (Hertzog, Malan, Strydom, Verwoerd) emerged all-powerful. What I did not know was how all these things had affected the ordinary people, black, Coloured, English and Afrikaans, and how they had affected the institutions of the country.

This latter was a particularly important point. As I understood it, the Boers had been unable to run their own affairs and had a completely different value structure from the English. How was it possible for these people to run social institutions that looked and sounded and, to all intents and purposes, did the same job as their counterparts in advanced Western societies?

Institutions are the power-houses of democratic societies. Universities, the press, the media, scientific academies, the judiciary, business groups and organisations, welfare societies, all of them act as a check and balance to the power and direction of the central state. The civil service, for instance, is one such institution. As we know it in Britain and America, it acts as a kind of executive arm for the government in power but it is not controlled by elected politicians – they only head the departments; the civil servants themselves act as relatively independent arbiters of ministerial power, backed up if need be by the judiciary, also composed of people independent to the government of the day. Our modern states recognise the need to have a check and balance system, and so try to preserve the independence and separateness of the various state and non-state institutions. At its best it is a kind of healthy self-criticism and is necessary even if the power of institutions is not always what it should be.

All this, historically, had been ignored by the boers. When they chose to go into the psychological hinterland, these are the kinds of notions and values on which they turned their backs. I did not understand how it was possible for them to have developed the ability since 1910 to be properly social, as we in the West understand it. It did not add up. And yet, every South African I spoke to held up the country's institutions – the free press, the semi-free universities, the respected judiciary, scientific and medical communities, the white democracy – as proof of their country's right to be called a Western state. While most of these were English-speaking, a good many were Afrikaans. As one of my colleagues said, 'The government must have some degree of liberality if it has left most of the institutions free – they could easily have been closed down.'

So I had two plans, one loose and vague, one highly specific. In general I wanted to know how South Africa's institutions functioned and whether Afrikaans institutions differed from English.[3] More specifically, I wanted to have more contact with English, Afrikaans and nonwhite subjects for my research in order that I be able to get to know how they functioned and how the psychology of the modern South Africa, black or white, related to the psychological and sociological patterns I had discovered in my historical research.

My initial strategy was to examine the Afrikaner's attitude and prejudice towards the English and see if the relationship between authoritarianism and prejudice held up when the latter was the target rather than the Africans. In pilot studies amongst the few Afrikaans students I had available at the University of Cape Town, this was definitely the case: authoritarianism was much more closely correlated with anti-British than anti-African prejudice. It remained to check this correlation with a large sample of Afrikaans students and so I applied to Afrikaans universities to study their students.

I might as well have tried to go to the moon. From 1969 to 1972, I was repeatedly turned down time after time for one flimsy reason after another. I tried writing, telephoning, even going to see people but always met with the same story: the students were too busy, it was inconvenient, I needed a letter from my own department head (a practice, incidentally, which I encountered in no other field in the same universities); I was too young to do research, or too junior etc., etc. . . . Eventually I was told outright that the Afrikaans universities as a whole discouraged research on the F. Scale, on Fascism, or any research that probed into white or non-white politics.

Once my publications on the F. Scale began to appear in the academic literature, matters got worse; mere mention of my name by my students would result in delays and, eventually, refusals. I tried sending students in to ask for samples and told them not to mention my name but refusals simply came more quickly and more frequently.

The people we dealt with tried to avoid giving direct, blank refusals which might have reflected on their academic status. At first they tried to play on our sense of inadequacy by the old academic trick of citing all the negative evidence to an easily over-awed junior who always imagines that older is better. The junior is then challenged to prove otherwise – indicating that if he does, it will be taken as an act of insubordination and disrespect. My students came back as I had – defeated, depressed and wondering what it was all about. It took me some time to realise that this was a deliberate policy which, if pushed, would be revealed as such; that underneath the academic claptrap was a systematic attempt by the Afrikaans universities to subvert any research project that they found unpalatable.

By persevering, however, and employing deception, I eventually got access to some of the subjects I needed. At the University of the Western Cape, the government's university for Coloured students, at the University of Port Elizabeth and, through a colleague of mine, at the Rand University, samples were discreetly obtained. At Port Elizabeth, for example, I received co-operation but was given to understand quite clearly (they were familiar with my work) that I could not administer an F. Scale; by then, I had learnt and gave the sample an attitude-to-divorce scale in which I had secretly embedded a shortened form of the F. Scale.

Later I tried to get African student samples but this proved to be even more of a farce; none of my letters was answered. With the authorities at the University of the Western Cape, I hammered away as late as 1975, trying various means to get larger samples of Coloured students (to fit in with a later series of studies) but to no avail. I did however get this in writing; the Professor of Psychology tried to make all sorts of excuses, including pressure of work, exams and vacations, but eventually admitted that they would not permit any tests that compared white with non-white students.[4]

In the long run, these barriers proved to be a help. If I had had ready access to Afrikaans and African samples, it is quite possible that I would have gone off on a wrong track and not investigated English whites as extensively as I did. Being quite sure in my own mind that the English had been the prime object of fear for the Afrikaner, I turned to the freely available English student samples at the University of Cape Town to examine their psychology and their role in creating and maintaining *apartheid*.

Historically, English whites had played, until 1910, the dominant role in South African affairs. From 1910 onwards, their institutions had been taken over by the Afrikaner and their kind of conservatism suited the political interests of the majority of English South Africans – they continued much as they had before in the same institutions and, more importantly, they continued to profit by participation in the exploitation of South Africa. I was interested in how this had been done and the kind of effect it had on the English. More specifically, I wanted to know if the English were aware of the Afrikaners' phobia and where they saw their political problems. After all, if the Afrikaners feared the English, it was quite likely that the English would sense this fear because fear is experienced most often as hostility. Did they feel anxiety, I wondered, towards the Afrikaner?

Part of the difficulty I had in conducting research in this area was that most English-speaking South Africans had no idea of what I was talking about. They did not recognise or admit to any anxiety or fear of the Afrikaner; there was no basis for it in politics nor in history, I was told, so it did not exist. If they were scared of anyone, it was of the Africans; my idea that the English whites were themselves a repressed minority was treated as ludicrous, let alone my feeling that they were, in power terms, *the* most repressed community in South Africa. It was apparent that before I could proceed to understand the way the Afrikaners had psychologically controlled the English. I had first to prove my oppression hypothesis.

This was not easy. I could not devise a prejudice-towards-Afrikaner questionnaire: all I would get back would be an expression of political rather than personal consensus. Most liberal whites felt a personal form of guilt about *apartheid* and anger towards the Afrikaner. No one, it seemed, had ever thought of feeling scared of the Afrikaner. What I wanted to do meant that I had to get underneath this outward defensiveness and find out what was going on inside.

A lot of scientific discoveries occur through fortuitous accidents – you look at one thing and, by chance, you discover something else, much more important, buried inside it. 1970 was an election year in South Africa and a month before the general election I decided to test the validity of my sampling by examining authoritarianism and prejudice along political party lines rather than, as had been the custom, comparing English with Afrikaans speakers. I administered the usual questionnaires to a sample of students at the University of Cape Town, had them scored then put them away. It was an unimportant study, I thought. Later, after the general election result was known, I was struck by the difference between the result for the general population and my students' results; trying to account for the difference turned up some very surprising pointers as to the psychological state of English South Africans.

In the voting study, the only similarity between the student and the general population results was the fact that roughly the same percentage of the student sample voted for the United Party as did whites in the general election (34% and 37% respectively); the vast majority of students voted for the Progressive party (55%) in contrast with roughly the same percentage of whites in the general election voting for the Nationalist Party (54%). Just under 11% of the students supported the Nationalist Party and no one voted for the *Herstigte Nasionale Party*. In the general election, the Progressive Party gained 3.4% of the vote and the *Herstigte Nasionale Party*, 3.6%. Even combining the voting weights of the *apartheid*-supporting parties – Nationalist and the United Party – in the student sample still came to only 45% of the whole, quite a marked difference from the 91% polled by these two parties in the general election.[5]

In the student sample there was an apparent psychological continuum between voters of the various parties: Nationalists showed the most prejudice, the most social distance towards nonwhites and the most authoritarianism; then came United Party voters and lastly, the Progressives. However, sophisticated statistical examination of the test results revealed that instead of a continuum, a polarity operated to separate the scores of the voters; that is, United and National Party subjects tended to have the same psychological features on the tests while Progressive voters formed a distinct psychological entity. More important, this polarity was predicted by the authoritarian theory; while each group differed in its degree of prejudice from the other, there was no significant difference in authoritarianism between Nationalist and United Party students.

For the first time, I had clear evidence that the South African white context was psychologically more complex than previous research had established; the bulk of English white students were not good representatives of the South African political system and authoritarianism *was* a key motivating factor in white existence.

Voters seemed to choose political parties according to the prejudice they held, but the real psychological polarity (as opposed to political polarity) amongst whites appeared to arise because of differences in authoritarianism.[6]

The next step was to probe these findings to see if there were any other important characteristics of these voting types. I wanted to know what the relationship between each one of the variables was within each political framework. How, for example, did Nationalists organise their attitudes compared with the Progressives? Was there the same kind of consistency of correlation between F. Scale (authoritarian) scores and prejudice scores? Well, the Nationalist voter tended to have a high correlation between his prejudice attitudes and authoritarianism. The United voter did not; there was, in fact, a lack of consistency. United voters' attitudes were loosely held, indicating not only a possible confusion in attitude but also a lack of awareness of the need to be consistent, which is uncharacteristic of student samples in the Western world. By inference I presumed that these voters – and I include in this, white English voters as a whole – were not as emotionally concerned either with politics or with racial attitudes as were the other white groups.

What was interesting, therefore, was the status of the Progressive Party voter in the sample. I expected a Nationalist student to hold consistent attitudes because he is obviously brought up in an environment that at every level is both authoritarian and keyed to a political ideology. I expected, too, the English white voter to behave as the United Party voter did in the study: to have adopted a disinterest in politics. The Progressive voter was not only in the majority in my study but his psychological make-up was more characteristic of students in ordinary Western societies. They showed a marked degree of political awareness, liberalism and a consistency of attitude markedly in excess of either United or Nationalist voters. Yet such a prominent and powerful psychological force had no role to play in South Africa's political or public life. The Progressive Party which they supported at the time had one seat in Parliament and had polled less votes in the 1970 election than even the *Herstigte Nasionale Party*, a break-away Afrikaner Nationalist group.

I concluded that despite the fact that English-speaking whites had been dominated for over twenty years by Afrikaner values and ideas and had been forced to play an increasingly reduced role in the political life of the country, there remained nevertheless a considerable movement against Afrikaner dogma. What happened then to these ideas and to these people as they grew up in South Africa? How were they contained and how had they been neutralised so that there had been no effective manifestation of this psychological presence in the years of Nationalist rule? How had some English people survived and some, like the United Party voter, developed a form of authoritarianism similar to the Afrikaners'? Was the English-speaking South African's authoritarianism formed in the same way as the Afrikaners'?

These were all grossly obvious questions and because of their grossness, almost impossible to answer directly through research. They were too big, too far-reaching; the answers would have to be worked out, I thought, after the fall of the Nationalist government. In the meantime, I was content to plod along using whatever methods I could to build up the theory I was developing. What was clear was that if authoritarianism is caused by threat and fear, then I now had both historical and empirical evidence to suggest that something odd was going on in South African white society and that whatever it was, the Afrikaners were responsible. However, between 1970 and 1973, studies conducted by myself and my students helped to provide some of the answers to these questions. One series of studies, for example, showed that prolonged exposure to South Africa affected the degree to which our subjects expressed authoritarianism. In one sample of first-year students, those who had spent their entire lives in South Africa were found to be more authoritarian than those who had been in the country for five years or less. Similarly, in another study, those students who had been in the country all their lives showed a significantly higher degree of socialisation than those who had not, the inference being that the pressures of living in South Africa created conformity with the *status quo*.

Significantly, though, this increased degree of socialisation was not a broad scale socialisation but was confined to the kind of socialisation patterns that prevailed in the Afrikaner students in my samples and, by inference, in Afrikaner society at large.[7] Prejudice, however, did not vary significantly with time spent in South Africa, nor did social distance.

Later political events showed the accuracy of these findings and rendered the political study and the authoritarian-fear thesis highly significant because they accurately predicted the reshaping of white political activity after 1970. In the 1974 general election, the Progressive Party gained a further six seats in Parliament at the expense of the United Party, which later disbanded. The Progressives were joined by the liberal wing of the collapsed United Party and formed the Progressive Reform Party. The psychological polarity I discovered in the 1970 study had become an effective political reality by 1977, with the bulk of the white voting population aligning itself with *apartheid* and a small percentage with the liberal policies of the successor to the Progressive Party.

In 1970 though, I was not yet aware of this and at the time concentrated on hunting down the cause of the English whites' fear. I needed to find some clue as to where it lay, how it arose, who (if there was a 'who') was laying it down, how extensive it was and what its effects were. In particular, I was looking for a *style*, a characteristic way of coping with the fear that I knew my subjects experienced, even if they did not!

The evidence, as I think can be seen, was nevertheless there. There was the bulk of my white sample, falling into either of two psychological styles – the United Party type which avoided political or radical ideology (by subscribing to the United Party's helpless and confused policies), and the Progressive types who were *intensely* political and intensely liberal. Both were abnormal responses (compared with students in other Western societies) and both arose as a stylised response to anxiety or fear, the one to avoid conflict and the other to fervently defend a view they obviously emotionally felt was under attack. Further, years spent in South Africa was a guarantee that people would develop the emotional structure willed on them by the Afrikaner (by adopting the same socialisation modes while reacting against the authoritarian style of the Afrikaner) but not necessarily the same political structure (prejudice and social attitudes were not significantly affected by time spent in South Africa) – ample proof, I think, that my white students were under considerable but strangely unrecognised pressures.

To begin with I focused on the Progressive students in a series of studies that are briefly reviewed below. The Progressive student clearly received some support for his ideology at home and at university. What happened after he left both, however, and was exposed to the mainstream of South African life where there was no real outlet or tolerance of this ideology?

I took one of my earlier samples and was able to trace just under half the subjects, most of whom lived in Cape Town. By comparing their scores on exactly the same measures taken five years apart and two years after all but a handful of them had left the university, I discovered two things. Firstly, while the subjects' prejudice attitudes had not changed, they showed an increased tendency to reflect authoritarian attitudes. Secondly, most of them had lost interest in politics in general and in political activity in particular.

In another series of studies I explored the racial attitudes of student subjects and tried to probe them more personally through interviews and through trying to find out how they behaved in reality as opposed to how they wanted to appear to behave. I took the social distance concept of marrying a member of a non-white race and having an African or Coloured around to dinner and translated it into a set of imagery statements such as, 'When you are married there is naturally a high degree of physical intimacy. Try and imagine what it must be like.' Another was, 'Imagine you are walking down Adderly Street with your wife. You are hand-in-hand.' A third was, 'Here comes your child. Imagine your feelings.' I then presented these statements in two series, the first with no reference or mention of race in order to establish a base line. One week later, I repeated the test but this time added the statement, 'Your spouse is a Coloured person.' By comparing the two responses of each person I could then get a picture of the differences between their expectancy of behaviour in general and in a racial context. I selected two sets of subjects, those highly prejudiced towards Africans and those with little prejudice.

In the first week's statements, members of both samples used adjectives such as 'excited, happy, settled, loving, warm, proud' to describe their feelings in the 'marry' context, and words like 'good, relaxed, friendly, sociable, easy-going, pleasurable, groovy' when asked to describe their feelings about having a friend to dinner. The contrast between these statements and those of the following week was marked. The highly prejudiced subjects' responses to marrying a Coloured person were in the expected direction – 'Impossible! are you crazy? Ugh! out of the question. Oh Jesus! Just wouldn't happen to me. I'd kick her out of the bed,' and so on. Their responses to 'friend to dinner' shifted markedly too and included expressions such as, 'OK, well, if I had to I would but . . . ; be really polite; freeze them up; hope they leave early; lock the door; try and cancel; worry about the police.' Talking to these people was in itself an experience: from being relaxed and obliging, they became cold and flippant, tossing off their answers in a kind of 'well, what else do you expect?' manner. After a while, they became suspicious and hostile towards me and began to blame me for making them think of this kind of issue. Inevitably, by the time they left, they had begun to question me about my habits and did I 'entertain Coloureds?' My feelings at the time were that in these interviews, I got a clear demonstration of the very South African phenomenon I was trying to study: the subjects first showed fear at being asked a non-conformist (illegal) question, then hostility, then they 'ganged up' as it were, to turn on the questioner, making me prove my credentials, my right to ask these questions. It was a phenomenon I experienced far more as I got deeper into South African society.

The reactions of the liberal subjects, however, were just as interesting and revealing because in a sense they were caught in the same dilemma but resolved it differently. Basically, what happened in the second week was that they literally winced when given the instructions and then bravely tried to battle through while sticking to their ideals. They used statements such as 'happy but wary; delighted; enjoyable; pleasant', all less positive than those they had used the week before but, more important, everything they said was now conditioned and prefaced by, 'Yes of course, it's only right and if I met a Coloured boy/girl who was really nice . . .' kind of statement. On being pressed they revealed in each case a very similar pattern:

i) This would only happen to them if the Coloured person was really attractive to balance the trouble that would attend such a marriage, that is, make it worth their while;

ii) never even a possibility in South Africa – unthinkable!

iii) there was always some third party, usually a parent, who would have to be appeased first, placated;

iv) a very noticeable fear and anxiety, even distress, about the whole matter.

These subjects' reaction to a friend having a meal was very much the same as the week before, but again a reference was made to appeasing a parent and the whole thing accompanied by anxiety.

The attitudes of these subjects to me and the situation was radically different from those of the highly prejudiced group: because I had posed this kind of question, they presumed I understood the dilemma they faced and they thus treated me more openly and took me more into their confidence than the other group of subjects had done. The main features of their reactions were distress, fear, and anxiety expressed in two ways – either by being aggressively defensive and asserting their right to their ideals or by immediately producing collateral evidence that they had tried to make contact with blacks. All the subjects felt that the situation in South Africa was hopeless and that it would only be a matter of time before a rebellion overtook the country, feelings that Danziger (1962) had found to be pretty typical of English-speaking school children.

This anxiety that attended discussion of politically sensitive issues was a crucial link in my authoritarian-fear theory, so I ran another study to further substantiate it. This time I constructed images of a less intimate nature such as, 'There is a man lying at the side of a road; how do you feel about stopping to help him?' and, 'A beggar stops you; what do you do?' These were administered in interview form to another sample of prejudiced and liberal students at one-week intervals. Before doing the actual testing, though, I asked them to rate how they felt on a straightforward ten-point anxiety-discomfort scale. This was repeated immediately after the test. In the first week's test the sufferers in each situation were clearly identified as white; in the second week, as urban African.

There was no difference between actual recorded responses – that is, both experimental groups reacted the same way whether the target was black or white – but considerable and significant differences were recorded for both groups in before-and-after anxiety scores: the prejudice group felt moderately anxious before the first test while less anxious after it, but more anxious after the second test while less anxious before. The liberal group felt anxiety in much the same way but showed extreme anxiety after the second test.

What was important was the way in which liberal and prejudiced subjects coped with politically sensitive situations which I therefore presumed, in the South African context, were also potentially threatening. People expressing liberal sentiments were deeply troubled by the problems involved when it came to actually acting liberally. They made use of a large number of qualifying statements which indicated a reluctance to, or a fear of, behaving liberally. Let me give an example: take the incident of finding a man at the side of the road. The first response of the liberal subject was, 'Of course I'd pull over and help, black or white.' But if I pushed him and said, 'Now, be realistic – imagine this takes place in Newlands [an English suburb of Cape Town] and the man is black.' Then a note of wariness crept in: 'I'd go and see if he was OK but, you know, the chances are he's probably drunk or has been in a fight, you know, something like that. You could get hurt.' Then there was a classic, 'Well, I'd go and see if he was hurt but if he wasn't – say if he was drunk – then I'd just leave him. You see, if I called the police, they'd beat him up and if he hadn't got a pass, he'd probably end up being shipped back to the Transkei.' If I asked what a subject would do if the same situation happened in Belleville or Parow (Afrikaans Nationalist strongholds and suburbs of Cape Town) they showed concern and anxiety, wanting to know if it was day or night – day was dangerous, people might see you, the police would pick you up – whether it was in a back street or on the main road. At this point they would inevitably tell some story they had heard of Afrikaners beating up English whites who had tried to help or stand up for blacks. Despite this obvious personal fear of the Afrikaners' physical violence, it did not occur to the subject to relate this to a general fear of the Afrikaner. The moment I talked about Afrikaners in general, they relaxed and became articulate, highly verbal, even expansive; they knew how to *talk* about Afrikaners but not how to relate to them personally.

Each experimental situation produced similar reactions. Being approached by a white beggar, for example, produced articulate and humanitarian, intellectual sentiments such as: 'I wish this wouldn't happen; this is a societal problem; society shouldn't let this problem arise . . .' When the beggar was black or Coloured, subjects typically felt a welter of feelings arise, all upsetting – misery, pity, distress, helplessness. My impression was that the personal experiences of these young people had so traumatised them that dealing with non-whites in general was a highly upsetting and incapacitating experience. It was much safer and easier to deal with them through safe political avenues that removed the personal element and the need to act. It was clear in reality that they actually *avoided* racially sensitive situations because they were too upsetting. To me, this was strange; human tragedy should not cause more distress in those who should be helping than it does in the actual sufferers. Here, I felt sure, I was getting close to understanding how white English South Africans could turn a blind eye to the racial injustices and unfairnesses they experienced daily. Perhaps young students turned to the Progressive Party as a means of seeking help in coping with the underlying and puzzling anxiety and fear that they clearly experienced but did not recognise or understand? If this was the case, it was a dangerous sign. Schizoid behaviour almost inevitably is the result of trying to cope with personal problems through ideological or overly intellectual means. Help for problems should be at the level that the problem arises – in this case, in the experienced existential fear of the Afrikaner – not in some abstract, removed, intellectual and, inevitably in South Africa, ineffectual political programme which simply obscured the existential base.

Prejudiced subjects had none of these problems. They felt little discomfort in dealing with black 'victims' and exhibited (in the circumstances) strangely normal behaviour; their actions were accompanied by sensible and reasonable statements, and they said they felt no difficulty in relating to blacks at this level. The impression I gained was that they would go out of their way to help – even beyond normal limits: in the case of the beggar for instance, two female subjects said they would actually phone a social work agency to help and, moreover, see that it was done.

Where the problem arose – and what obviously caused the elevated anxiety score for these subjects – was in dealing with white subjects. Here, very much the same kind of feeling arose as the liberals had had with blacks. The highly prejudiced subjects expressed a degree of embarrassment and pity when confronted with this kind of situation: 'If I were to be honest and I had the chance, I'd cross the road to avoid him.' They also expressed shame and disapproval for that type of white person who 'lets himself go like that'.

Remember these were all white English-speaking subjects – not Afrikaner Nationalists. The two clear styles corresponded closely with the psychological poles I had defined earlier: English whites experienced anxiety and fear which they all coped with by conforming to the *status quo* to some extent by being prejudiced. The highly prejudiced went further and adapted all their attitudes and behaviours to Afrikaner ideology. The others, the liberals, did not. They retained an independence at a cost of fragmentation, distress and the need to use intellectual means of coping with their fears. The prejudiced subjects in my studies quite clearly had no problem with racial issues – they behaved in accordance with government policy – Africans were inferior, needed whites to help them and so on. In personal situations, the prejudiced subject felt no fear. He or she did not expect to have trouble with the authorities or the Afrikaner. They behaved like confident normal citizens – normal, that is, in any other society – despite the fact that they were highly prejudiced and authoritarian. In choosing the Afrikaner mode, they chose to eliminate fear and anxiety and to disengage themselves from political or intellectual involvement with racial issues.

I know I am going on a bit here but you must understand that these findings were not easy to make in the face of cultural as well as academic antagonism. The symptoms I was unearthing were subtle, forming only part of the behaviour of the people who were denying the reality I was positing. I did not know how much weight to give them nor how significant they were – that only came later as the whole picture gradually emerged. I needed at this stage all the evidence I could get.

In another study I took a group of subjects, South African-born English whites, and asked them to rate first Afrikaners, then Africans, Coloureds and Indians on a set of descriptive adjectives which they thought applied to each group. This gave a set of stereotypes, that is, a view of how English subjects generally saw their fellows. Within the list of adjectives used I had embedded an index of adjectives linked to fear or anxiety so that if, for example, a subject checked items such as 'overwhelming, frightening, oppressive, foreboding', and so on, it was possible to establish the degree of relative fear or anxiety associated with each different group.

Afrikaners were seen as 'strong, proud, immovable, granite-like, cold', and so on; Coloureds, as 'lively, foolish, noisy, amiable, drunken, unreliable'; Africans as 'quiet, ordered, self-contained, foreign, proud' – all conforming to the set of stereotypical myths that help to maintain the kind of *status quo* favourable to *apartheid* in South Africa. Strengths had been reified and weaknesses moderated into clusters of explanatory systems. There was little evidence of anxiety associated with any particular group. I then compared how South Africans described Africans, Coloureds and Indians with how people from Central Africa (Zambia, Malawi, Rhodesia) and the Congo (Zaire) described them, and found the latter tended to use a far broader range of adjective choices – they avoided the 'halo' effect and good and bad adjectives were far more mixed in their stereotypes.

In the second part of the study I changed the context of the questionnaire task from the general to the specific. How did these subjects feel about Africans or Afrikaners they actually knew as opposed to the stereotypes they held? Presumably the stereotypes were gained from exposure to the government-controlled media, whereas their specific feelings would be from direct experience. The same sample of whites was tested a month later. This time they were asked to name specifically five people whom they knew in each ethnic group and using the same adjective list, to rate these five. By comparing this second assessment of the race groups with the overall stereotypes, it was possible to see if any shift had occurred.

The results were extremely interesting. Africans were rated at about the same level, that is, the stereotype operating at the general level was the same as at the personal; Coloured and Indian stereotypes improved – there was less use made of derogatory statements and favourable adjectives such as 'sensitive' and 'thoughtful' were added. Ratings of the Afrikaners, however, worsened significantly. Halo traits such as 'strong, proud, courageous, independent' dropped out altogether and adjectives such as 'isolated, frightened, stubborn, bullying, dependent, crude' were added. Anxiety and fear-based adjectives now crept into the ratings of the Afrikaners while remaining absent for other groups.

What was even more disturbing, however, was that many of the subjects could not list a single African as an acquaintance, indicating how little contact whites had with Africans. Interviews established that non-white acquaintances were not *friends* as such but people the subject had come into contact with, such as shop assistants, grocers, students they had met casually on campus, etc.[8] The interviews brought out another factor: Afrikaans-speaking friendships tended to occur at a separate level from the English-speakers' other friendships. This was not a finding that our subjects told us directly, they were not aware of it; it was picked up because Afrikaans-speaking friends did not take English friends into their homes and there was little parent-friend contact or sharing of girl- or boyfriends. One typical comment: 'It was as if they can be friends at work or at varsity but they don't take us home and they are wary of being seen outside with us – not by other students but by their parents. The whole impression I get is that their parents live in a different world which I'm not allowed into.'

What relationship did this fear or anxiety bear to the organisation of the English-speakers' cognitive processes? One response to a pervasive but unrecognised fear is to cover over the feeling by clouding or confusion. At the simplest level people tend to 'explain' anxiety – or, indeed, any feeling that they have – by reference to the immediate situation; they look for a reason, usually a simple one, to explain things. And, of course, they tend to accept the most convenient explanations. This was the strategy of Goebbels and I think it became the strategy *supreme* of the Nationalist propagandists who, through their control of the media, were able, by and large, to control the nature and range of available explanations.

It was clear to me that English whites 'explained' their fear in terms of some of the propagandist choices available to them. In particular, by adopting a fear of Africans and by adopting some of the Afrikaners' values purely and simply because they were current and seemed to be accepted by most people in South Africa. Further, fear of breaking the law, of incurring the wrath of the Afrikaner and his repressive measures created a feeling of anxiety about these areas which had no obvious referent. That is, the English person felt fear but had no social means of being aware of it. There was no body, no referented part to say it. It was not against the law to oppose the government. Yet because the law was so vague, power and authority vested in ministers and the police so apparently arbitrary, no one knew where opposition ended and punishable radical behaviour began. In this fog, the anxiety and fear associated with defying the Afrikaner and of his vagueness were explained through the lack of clear evidence of the Afrikaners' oppression of the majority of whites by the only publicly viable alternative – fear of Africans and of what they might do.

Because the Afrikaner has rendered the English white politically impotent, the latter is forced to watch and listen to whatever the Afrikaner says and does even though he may disagree with it. The trap is thus closed. The English person is anxious and is made to believe it is because of Africans. The only people who can effectively help him are the Afrikaners who hold power. So we get the English-speaker politicising his emotions in two ways: an anti-government stand at the rational, conscious, overt level with whatever behaviours (protest, writing to the newspapers, and so on) he is permitted to engage in and which do not threaten his security, while in reality he is forced to become acutely obsessed with whatever the Afrikaner does. Like a frightened child scared of his parents and dependent on them for his safety, he watches. Hence the obsession of all white South Africans with race, with power, with things Afrikaner.

He begins to adopt ideas that Afrikanerdom wants him to: its explanations of history, its views on race, religion, ethics, etc. – its interpretations of events and facts (like the Russian threat, the Black threat, and others . . .). For the uneducated or uncommitted English white, it is a simple matter to accommodate. As I well knew from my own background, it was far more important to make a living than to concern oneself with whether or not the government was cheating.

This accounted for some of the students in my samples. What of the rest, the majority? Faced with both anxiety and the need to reject *apartheid* propaganda, I anticipated that they would cloud the anxiety and seek some satisfactory 'cause' or 'reason' to explain the fear, to make it understandable. This, I felt, was why so many English-speakers tended to see the Afrikaner as a repressed minority; this allowed them to 'understand' and see the acts of the power they feared in a more sympathetic light while the same acts by others who were not threatening to them would not be so sympathetically judged. If they had had to look deeper into the Afrikaners' psychology, they would have had to face up to their own personal fear, the fact that their so-called democracy was a sham and, ultimately, that the Afrikaner was pursuing a destructive and potentially suicidal path for all of white South Africa.

To get at the answers to these questions, I used open-ended interviews to study liberal students who had spent all their lives in South Africa; they were asked to talk about life in South Africa, their attitudes and fears. Political processes reflect the structure of a society, and in South Africa this means, or has been made to mean, Afrikaner society. To be Progressive in South Africa means to be against the whole social framework. What did this mean for the liberal whites and how did they and their families cope with it?

Several central factors emerged. Firstly, a clear-cut problem had arisen within each student's family revolving around the various family members' attitudes to politics and political action. As the subject had grown up, he or she had shared their parents' liberal attitudes to South Africa and their parents' condemnation of the government. However, in late adolescence the question of taking some overt action arose. At this point, conflict occurred because the parents were afraid of the consequences of their children's actions. Parents began to manifest previously repressed anxiety and fear about the government and especially the police. The parents of our subjects *constantly and routinely* urged their children *to avoid politics of any kind*, indeed, action of any kind *that might bring the attention of the authorities and the police*. The word 'police', incidentally, was the single most recurring term used in every interview.

Secondly, there appeared to have been a noticeable shift in attitude held by the parents. Nearly every subject reported that they could remember times when their parents expressed open hostility towards the government, open condemnation and an open belief in multiracialism. Yet, as time passed, parents stopped talking in company and adopted more moderate and evasive attitudes. This resulted in conflict because their adolescent children challenged their inconsistency.

Thirdly, the subject matter of home debates and arguments indicated that the fears and anxieties I suspected operated covertly in my subjects shaped to a large extent the form home arguments took. Thus children accused their parents of being cloudy, foggy about South Africa, of avoiding the obvious, of being unrealistic, insensitive, blind to injustice, and so on – precisely the hypotheses that my research was investigating. The parents' stock arguments were that they were older and more responsible, they had to look after themselves and their families first, and that they were afraid.

Fourthly, neither our subjects nor their parents apparently realised the fundamental importance of these debates and issues. Subjects regarded them as adolescent hassles not to be taken seriously: 'Everyone has hassled with their parents – it happens overseas. Basically my folks and I agree about South Africa, we just need something to argue about.' They could not relate these arguments to their own perspectives on South Africa because in a fundamental sense they had no obvious reason to:

'I feel sorry for people in other "bad" places. You see, in South Africa we have a free press, free universities, free speech. The government doesn't like it but they can't stop us. They threaten and bully but we're not scared, we can really say what we like because – unlike you foreigners – *we* are South African and they can't just dismiss what we say or bump us all off – they need us. They are short of whites and they have to put up with us.'

Few of the people in the sample had any direct contact or experience with either banned people or people being intimidated or detained by the police. So they had no direct cause to be so afraid. It was bad, they said, but they did not feel that they had been indoctrinated or unduly propagandised; they felt their attitudes and rejection of the government's values were sufficient to have rendered them above the situation. This feeling of aloofness was a consistent theme through all the interviews.[9]

The above study seemed to indicate that anxiety was pervasive and far-reaching. Certainly it was to be found in parents, but there seemed little indication on the surface that student subjects showed the obvious pathology one would normally associate with people who have to live under stress for years. Perhaps there were other factors about life in South Africa that cushioned the English and helped them avoid the effects of their fears? After all, they were not in the front line, they did not suffer direct hardships, injustices and cruelties as did the Africans. They lived well, had a high standard of living and held a privileged position in South Africa. Perhaps I was dealing with a subtle far-reaching form of psychopathology which was peculiar to the situation?

The subjects I interviewed seemed normal enough, but I was by now (early 1971) quite aware of the limitations showed by academic psychologists in recognising pathological mental states. In December 1970, I had taken an intern post at Valkenburg Mental Hospital in Cape Town to train as a clinical psychologist and had begun to get interested in the tests for clinical pathology used by clinicians. Quite by chance, I had become interested in a new test of clinical functioning then unpublished – and I administered this to some of the subjects in the above study to see how they fared on it.

Nor surprisingly, they scored more highly on scales measuring obsessionality and social anxiety than did prejudiced subjects. At the same time, I had recently completed another study on student drug use in which I found that there was a significant correlation between social anxiety and degree of drug abuse; subjects high in social anxiety used drugs more frequently than those moderately high, and those low in anxiety used drugs infrequently. It seemed possible, therefore, that maybe there was a link between the social anxiety I had found in the low authoritarian subjects and drug use. So I carried out a study on a sample of students comparing social anxiety and obsessionality with frequency of drug use.[10]

Students do tend to use drugs. This was especially the case in 1971–1972 when the drug craze was at its peak in Cape Town. The question was then, was drug use any more frequent in English-speakers who were in conflict with their circumstances – that is, experiencing the hypothesised fear and anxiety arising through contact with the South African system – than it was with those who were less so troubled?

The results confirmed the hypothesis: the more liberal a subject was, the more he or she tended to use drugs. Significantly too, liberal, low-prejudiced subjects tended also to be engaged in Transcendental Meditation. Drug use and Transcendental Meditation are often related and were associated at the time with hippy ideology and values – with which many of my subjects were undoubtedly imbued. Young people generally tend to express whatever problems they may be having with their society by using sub-group fads currently in vogue. The difference between how this occurred in other countries and how it occurred in my student sample was that *prejudiced* subjects of the same age, the same culture and at the same university did not behave in the same way. I was sure that drug use in my sample arose out of a fear-anxiety base peculiar to the political divisions amongst the English white group. Elsewhere, drug use is generally a youth-rebellious phenomenon, not a political one.

The drug and DPI studies showed the first signs of the English personality psychological stress I was later to study in more detail. Again though, they were subtle findings, the significance of which, without the historical perspective, I would almost certainly have missed. It was only later, after I had trained as a clinician, that I was able to probe deeper into these symptoms of cultural psychopathology. Before that, though, I had a chance to investigate at close quarters two institutions – the university and the mental/medical institutions I worked at. I had several appointments at the University of Cape Town, and through them was able to see how the supposedly free universities operated in reality and I gained some understanding of how English institutions cushioned and absorbed the English whites' anxiety and fear.

Through working in mental health institutions, I had my first experience of how an Afrikaans institution functioned.

Earlier I suggested that English whites' fears were allayed because they could turn to their familiar institutions for comfort. They were free – that is, not Afrikaner-controlled – and they appeared to be the same as those found elsewhere in the West. It seemed to me highly unlikely that the Afrikaner whose view of institutions and how they should function was diametrically opposed to those of the English would allow free English institutions to exist and pose a potential threat to Afrikaner domination.

I had already demonstrated how anti-black propaganda played a camouflaging role, obscuring the accurate *cognition* by English people of the *cause* of their fear and anxiety. What was the status of their institutions? Perhaps the Nationalists had taken a leaf out of the Nazi book and kept the appearance of English institutions – thus gaining a 'respectability', a favourable overseas image and allaying English whites' fears – while in reality effectively neutralising or controlling them?

Such a thesis was staggering in its implications. Apart from anything else, it would account for the ineffectiveness of the English in South Africa – the way in which they were unorganised in opposition, helpless to appreciate what was being done to them. Perhaps if English institutions were neutralised and no longer serving the true needs of their community, that is, directing and shaping social action, then it was possible that they served a pathological function quite different from the role they played in other countries. This needs some clarification.

The troubled students in my samples expressed themselves politically – thus satisfying their consciences and their pride – and engaged in the English university community's sub-culturally approved activities (drug-taking, Transcendental Meditation, student politics, etc.) to alleviate fear and anxiety. At the same time this gave them a feeling of identity with young people in Europe and America. I surmised that their parents did the same but had simply substituted other sub-group tolerated behaviours varying in their political or social commitment according to the needs of the persons involved. Thus golf, youth clubs, charities, lodges, Saturday afternoon bridge games, country clubs, political activity, and so on, I saw as analogous to drug-taking and Transcendental Meditation. They all served the same function in South Africa.

This identification with overseas trends served another function because they were inevitably *condemned* by Afrikaners as immoral, communist-like activists. This combination of events doubly helped to insulate the English-speakers from their fears and the realities of the situation. What the English whites failed to see was that the acts they engaged in only resembled the overseas trend in *style*. The youthful rebellions and adult movements that took place in Europe and America did so in different contexts and for different reasons. Identifying what was done in South Africa with what was done elsewhere compounded the English South African's dilemma.

Most countries depend for their survival on their institutions being able to direct and shape the energies of their young and creative people. Without youthfulness being blended into the old system, new challenges and new changes cannot be faced (Merton, 1957). Rebellion and institutional activity helps this. South Africa had an elite English-speaking young white population that I had shown to be healthily against the *status quo*. If their institutions were irrelevant and neutralised, if they and their parents were in a fog about what was happening to them, then what happened to this activity, this psychological motivation? Where did it go?

I have already described the machinations of the authorities at Afrikaans universities and Afrikaans-controlled universities where subtle and not-so-subtle means were used to prevent me and my students from obtaining the subjects I needed. Far more sinister procedures were used on English universities to keep them in a safely neutral state.

What I want to specify is how the behaviour of staff and the direction research takes in the social sciences is controlled. I base this information on having worked in three different departments – Sociology, Psychology and Psychiatry – and being well-acquainted with the functions of a fourth, Philosophy. These are generally the most politically sensitive departments at universities, being usually in the forefront of investigations into society, politics, and human motivation. And yet, strangely, at Cape Town and at other English universities in the country this was not the case. At Cape Town, it was left to the departments concerned with African Affairs – Social Anthropology, Comparative African Government and Law – to produce not only the most vociferous opposition to the government but also a steady stream of research and technical reports about *apartheid*, South Africa and the effect of the system on Africans.

South African universities receive subsidies from the government often to the tune of 70% of their costs. One way the government forces university councils and administrations to control the activities of their students and staff, and to control research, is to withhold or reduce its subsidy. The existence of this ever-present possibility makes the university administrators nervous and wary – in the words of one administrator: 'We know the government wouldn't hesitate to close us down in the event of a major confrontation and so we tread a thin line to stay "free" while keeping our subsidy. The universities are caught in a pincer movement between the government and the students and those staff members who demand university autonomy.'

This anxiety and conflict was passed down in turn to the Deans of Faculties and the Heads of Departments who, being tenured, were naturally caught between looking after their own careers and the pressures brought to bear by their radical staff members. So, at no cost to the government, three basic conflict points in university life were created by the use of a simple threat: debate at council level between academic, non-academic and university administrators, debate at faculty level between heads of departments, and debate within the departments.

The pressure on departmental heads at English universities is considerable. How most cope is to engage in two activities which are contradictory: token anti-government stances (attacked by government officials *but nevertheless allowed*) and an obsessional immersion in internal university processes. In other words, academics, like other English whites, use university institutions as a means of avoiding facing up to reality. University life is full of overt political activism, while in reality nothing substantial is being done except by those in the departments that are in direct touch with African reality and who are in a position to know at first hand what the government is doing.

To direct attention away from the main task of a university, that is to expose the follies of South African society, academics busy themselves with internal debates and power structures. Professorships are awarded and taken away in accordance with these games and these and the machinations of power groupings dominate the lives of every faculty and every department.

There was a second and more obvious method of control.

Anyone who attracted too much negative attention, or who disturbed the government too much, was simply banned or had his work banned. The section of the University of Cape Town's central library concerned with special collections is full of works on or about South Africa which have had to have pages torn out or whole paragraphs scored through with black pen as now this author, now that, has been banned. Sometimes pressure is brought to bear on heads of departments to contain and restrict the activities of their rebellious staff members. This was often done in the 'interests' of the staff member concerned; sometimes it was done to avoid trouble. Either way it acted as a form of self-censorship.

What is normal about university activity in other countries becomes dangerous for university life in South Africa. Radical and progressive elements in overseas universities usually provide the impetus for change and inject new ideas, while conservative elements add a valuable check and balance; both operating together allow the best in a university to emerge and are both reflected in, and arise out of, the research and teaching which a university does. This is the value of a university; it should not threaten the existence of that university.

These same characteristics in South Africa, however, have different meanings because the social context is different. Radical and progressive becomes rebellious and revolutionary and, therefore, in the South African context, dangerous. By the same token, conventionality and conservatism become identified with government wishes and directives. In South Africa, the latter have dominated and the result is the continued existence of the university at the cost of continual and considerable inroads being made into its academic status.

Universities in South Africa are fighting for their lives. Normal activities lead to survival or elimination and are therefore not anxiety-free as they are in other societies, and so academics cannot attend to normal university interaction and activities, especially in the areas which may increase the already considerable pressure on them. Hence the lifeblood of the social sciences, societal research, simply does not get done.

As far as I could see, under these conditions the following sort of things happen. Department activities tend to be conservative or radical according to the stance taken by the head of their department and the length of time he or she has had tenure. Thus, in my opinion, the Sociology department was conservative, having had the same head (when I worked there) for over thirty years; little modern research was being done and staff appeared to be selected on a basis of their ability to fit into this pattern. The Philosophy department was split into two factions: those who studied ethics and those who studied political philosophy. The former, in my opinion, served a normal function, having a fine balance of radical and conservative staff. The political philosophy section, which should have been the most investigative and dynamic of all, was run by a South African who, until his retirement, prided himself (so he told me) on using the same notes for his lectures now as he had when he was first appointed in the 1930s. This chap also served on the government censorship board, was an adviser to both the South African and Rhodesian governments, and gave evidence as an expert in communism at certain trials. His advanced courses in political philosophy were apologistic, purely South African and dealt extensively with concepts of political pluralism. The department improved markedly after he retired, but for some thirty years it had had its effect of nullifying any possible threat it and its students could have posed.[11]

In the time I was with the Psychology department, of the three it was the most radical in that its staff members actually took part in student and staff protests, and political and racial issues were often and extensively discussed at all levels. Its research output on South Africa, though, was negligible; staff talked about South Africa but few were prepared to conduct active research. Those who did had forbidding obstacles to overcome to get anywhere.

The Human Science Research Council is the government institute that organises research in the country, gives out grants and so on. Its funds are considerable and, as in other countries, any big research effort requires the financial support of this institute if the university and outside help is not available. Predictably, they turn down applications for grants for any study that is in any way critical of South Africa. The universities' own resources for funding are small and again tend to be awarded for 'safe' studies. There are also risks attached to attracting attention to yourself as a researcher into South Africa: you are inevitably warned by sometimes well-intentioned colleagues about police spies and so on, and of the dangers involved.

While I was on the staff, three teams were doing research into South Africa – mine, Orpen's and Van der Spuy's. But the way the principals in the other teams operated struck me as strange. The three of us never once got together to co-ordinate what we were doing, to discuss the work or our findings. As the youngest and most junior member, I thought it was because of my status. Odd things happened: we all knew of each other's work and students working from one or another team would often pop into my office to borrow the scales I and my colleague, Andrew Colman, had constructed, but quite apart from never discussing the work, the other two, to my knowledge, never referred to it in their publications; what is more, when scales of ours were used, they were never acknowledged or referred to in the published articles – so much so that Andrew had once to write to a journal to point this out.

How I understand it now is that doing research into South Africa created such anxiety in South Africans that they treated the work as if it were a secret to be carefully guarded. I also realise now that combining and systematising our work would have created a far more obvious and thus more threatening research group, with a corresponding increase in personal anxiety.

This approach, I was later to discover, operated at all levels in people who wanted to *act* in any way against the government; they became so tense, anxious – even disturbed – that their behaviour towards others became strange. What was significant though about the three teams was that each suffered a different fate, entirely predictable from the differences in origin of the leaders: the English-speaking South African gradually stopped this line of work and concentrated on industrial psychology; the Afrikaans-speaking South African who had returned to South Africa from overseas left again as soon as he could. I, the foreigner, continued to run overt research until 1973, and then did covert research on a more extensive basis until my flight in 1978.

This was the start of my explorations into South Africa's institutions. If I had been disturbed by my experiences of university life, this was nothing in comparison with what I uncovered when I left the ivory tower and went into South Africa proper. Universities still retain some of their healthy and proper functions; it was still possible to do research into South Africa, for example. At Valkenburg Mental Hospital, for the first time, I found out how *government* institutions functioned.

Chapter Three

Apartheid and Mental Health Institutions

If a relatively independent institution like the universities is controlled and its character changed by subtle and devious means, then what was the case in those institutions more dependent on government and, above all, Afrikaans institutions – direct creations of the Afrikaner Nationalists? In December 1970, I decided to train as a clinician and was soon involved in these kinds of institutions.

Mental Health services in South Africa take four basic forms: Department of Health mental hospitals and related services such as outpatient clinics; provincial hospital services, which took the form of the services offered by a general hospital's department of psychiatry; private practice and private nursing homes and, lastly, the services offered by non-government institutions such as private clinics, university, church and welfare agencies' services, and so on.

I eventually had experience in all four areas, working first at Valkenburg, a Department of Health hospital, then at Groote Schuur (a provincial hospital), then at the University Child Guidance Clinic (a private university unit), and lastly, I ran my own clinic in private practice. Each brought me into contact with a different type of patient and attracted a different type of professional.

Private practice, because it costs money and because of the societal structure, is restricted almost entirely to whites; blacks cannot afford it, and it is only in big cities like Cape Town that private practitioners accept black patients, even if they can pay. There were, to my knowledge, no black psychiatrists or psychologists in private practice. There were certainly no training facilities for black or Coloured psychologists that I knew of at the time because I was once approached by an African psychologist working in the Psychology department at the University of Cape Town for help in getting an internship. I went into the situation fairly thoroughly; no one was prepared to take the risk of employing a black. In another case, a Coloured student was accepted at Cape Town for a Master's degree course in clinical psychology, but halfway through the course, could not find a state hospital to accept him for the practical intern year. As far as I know, there were only two non-white psychiatrists in the country – one Coloured and one African, both in hospital service. Consequently, the bulk of the black population is treated in state or provincial units by white doctors, psychiatrists or psychologists.

In Cape Town, people who do not go to private practitioners go first to Groote Schuur Hospital (casualty or out-patients) and are treated there either as out-patients or in the hospital's small in-patient (and segregated) ward. Serious, unmanageable or long-term patients are referred to Valkenburg, which has two patient compounds, one Coloured and one white. African patients are also seen there and the hospital has its own out-patient department as well. It is, like Groote Schuur, a training hospital and trains social workers and occupational therapists as well as psychologists and psychiatrists.

As far as I could ascertain, conditions in Cape Town – at Valkenburg and Groote Schuur – are analogous to those elsewhere in South Africa. I know my experiences were typical of other trainees because I remained in close contact with nearly all the trainees in psychology at both hospitals for over three years after I left.

The organisation of the hospitals is pretty much along the lines found in most countries. Patients are admitted, assessed medically, psychiatrically and, if necessary, in the event of complexity or doubt, psychologically, and then diagnosed. Treatment is prescribed by a psychiatrist and consists of the normal range of psychiatric treatments – shock therapy, drug therapy and occupational therapy. When I was there, social work was also done and, at Valkenburg, very rarely, psychotherapy. The psychologist was called upon when I first arrived to administer psychological testing to help in diagnosis and very little else.

Not very different then, on the surface, from any large mental hospital in Britain or America. In fact, on two occasions, I showed visiting psychologists from overseas around Valkenburg and just such sentiments were expressed. Again, Valkenburg is an institution that *appears* to operate just like other comparable institutions elsewhere.

Of the two state-run services, those offered by the Provincial government were more independent at that time from government control, and so working at Groote Schuur and at the Child Guidance Clinic was very much like being back at university with approximately the same concern for academic issues and responsibilities; problems and deficiencies were recognised and nearly everyone I came into contact with was eager and willing to learn. Moreover, the usual hierarchy of medical specialities was sufficiently flexible to permit interaction between staff members of different disciplines, so allowing people to learn from and understand one another.

The in-patient ward at Groote Schuur was a brave attempt to overcome the problems of trying to offer a sensible service irrespective of colour. Legally it had to be segregated, but this was very loosely structured although patients of different colours had to sleep and eat in segregated areas. Periodically, though, we were warned to be on guard and tighten up because the hospital administrators were constantly checking up on whether mixing was taking place or not. They would have used, I was told, any excuse to close it down, but thanks to the efforts and perseverance of the head of the psychiatric department this was avoided. But only just.

The greatest effect of this loose system was that Coloured and white staff interaction became, in working hours, almost completely desegregated. We shared ward rounds, discussions, tea-breaks – nowhere else in all my time in South Africa did I come across this kind of situation. You came to know and interact with professionals from the other side and, if you chose, you could get to know about what was going on in their lives and how they felt.

There was one problem, though. Racial issues and the problems of *apartheid* were even more studiously ignored than at the university despite the fact that the staff as a group of professionals were more in touch with the issues and the people involved than most.

Like my academic colleagues, white clinicians avoided their dilemmas by obsessively focusing on the internal power and personality structures of their institutions. They spent their time worrying about expressing their interest and concern in safe, institutionalised protests while studiously ignoring the immediate manifestations of *apartheid* on their own doorstep. No research was done into racial issues and little or no group discussion took place about them.

Relating this avoidance of racial issues to the research I had done earlier, I saw contact to be a disturbing and conflict-producing situation for whites because it introduced new and threatening existential data about, for example, Coloured people ('they are human', 'they get hurt' and 'angry too') that created in white staff members a desire to behave differently and to think differently about Coloureds. For the first time in their lives – for many of them – they had real contact with non-whites. Through a loophole in the government's strategy, whites mixed with non-whites outside those areas stipulated by the *apartheid* doctrine and it created conflicting stereotypes for both sides. I began to explore this and to try and uncover the kind of psychological processes at work.

One of the side-effects of the structure of English institutions is that because they are made to feel that they are continually fighting for their right to exist, their cognitive efforts are shaped by both this and their need to oppose the government. Mental health institutions have thus little time to deal with the issues that institutions should deal with – in this case, alleviating mental suffering. The behaviour of whites and blacks in these institutions when faced with a politically sensitive problem provides ample indication of this; white therapists (psychiatrists, psychologists and social workers) tend to react in one of two different ways to cross-racial problems, depending on the context in which the interaction takes place. Thus, where a therapist has cross-racial contact in private practice, the reactions of the therapist seem more free-flowing, self-critical and lead to deeper involvement with the patient – often in South Africa to the detriment of both doctor and patient. Where a therapist interacts in a group context, as for example in a hospital, then the behaviour of the therapist shows a tendency towards limiting contact, blaming the patient for the difficulties experienced. Contact with the patient becomes superficial and isolated. Either way, interaction of this kind is always problematic, leading to hostility, bitterness and frustration on both sides.

Therapists varied simply in terms of how they coped with the difficulties. In my experience, problems with Coloured patients were blamed inevitably on the patient using respectable academic labels. It is a common practice amongst clinicians – especially those in training – to blame patients for their own lack of insight and inability to help. If a patient does not improve, simple – they have no motivation, etc. Sophisticated therapists often erect whole explanatory systems about the incurability of some patients and then attribute their own lack of progress to this. If you go through the literature, just about every mental disturbance has, at some time or other, been called incurable by some eminent clinician as a means of obscuring important failings in therapeutic programmes.

A favourite device used by clinicians is to call a difficult patient 'character-disordered' – the implication being that a person with such a disturbance cannot be treated by psychotherapy. A disturbance in personality or character, so the argument goes, is too fundamental to be modified by psychotherapeutic interaction. In South Africa, rather than use racialistic stereotypes, this device is used by liberal clinicians to 'explain' problems with Coloured patients. Character disturbances *are* difficult to treat, but I found that difficult Coloured patients were more often so labelled than difficult white patients. The same liberal therapists were more prepared to see their difficulties with white patients in terms of their own personal problems than they were with non-whites. Liberalism was for white patients but not for black.

Ward rounds and staff meetings tended to revolve around academic sounding discussions in which staff tried to pin the right label onto a problem Coloured patient. Clinicians supported and comforted each other with sympathy rather than attending to the realities that therapy was bringing up. To deal with and bring up these issues would have meant exposing the fabric of the social structure of *apartheid*. So patients paid the price and were 'managed' out of the ward or out of therapy.

Clinicians who did not operate in group contexts had different types of problems. Many of the clinicians I studied were quite capable and did not give up on their Coloured or African patients easily – they persevered and worked through the patient's resistance to insights and interpretations about themselves. For most of them, it was their first real contact with non-white people and they behaved as if they had generations of guilt on their shoulders. Helping their patient was a way of alleviating some of their own guilt and anxiety about the situation, and they would often throw themselves into the job, working long hours, getting intensely involved in one or two patients. In this, they began to lose touch with reality and disintegrate because, like many patients, their threw up every trick in the book to 'explain' their problems – blaming other people, circumstances, anything but themselves. So, within a few sessions, you would find your intern taking on the *apartheid* system singlehanded. Suddenly the patient's world became his and *vice-versa*. Special relationships began to develop that united both against *apartheid*.

All this is fairly typical behaviour for new trainees. Carefully supervised and managed, the new therapist's energies can be channelled into learning about himself and his own needs as well as learning to help his patient more realistically. But because of the embargo on the discussion and recognition of things *apartheid*, this necessary and healthy supervision and redirection does not take place. Supervisors and group milieux tended to steer clear of the problem either because of their own distressing experiences or because of their political commitment. One of my supervisors described to me, quite unethically, the behaviour of another intern involved with a Coloured patient, as 'sick, neurotic – he's totally over-involved'. Yet, a month later, he accepted the same behaviour in the same intern towards a white patient as evidence of creativity. My supervisor was Afrikaans and a Nationalist. Other supervisors or group milieux did the opposite: they reified the trainee's behaviour, encouraged it, used it as an entry permit into a closed society of 'committed' professionals. They gave status and sympathy instead of guidance and criticism because they themselves were caught in the same dilemma and had tried to resolve it unaided and without being made aware of the problems.

The results of this neglect for the individual patient were tragic. Clinicians who chose a committed mode found themselves rather than the patient undergoing a transition. In South Africa this kind of choice has always been dangerous. Choosing to be with your patient against *apartheid* involves enormous potential risks; ostracism, loss of your job, the attention of the security police, arrest, torture, death even. Few choose this. Most become the classically impotent therapist, protected by their professional community.

Some use radical ideology and become committed white liberals; they 'help' the patient by words and not by the promised deeds. The patient, dissatisfied, wants more evidence that he can trust the therapist and believes that therapy can alleviate his *apartheid* suffering. The therapist cannot provide the promised relief so he starts avoiding the issues or he gets involved up to the point specified by his white support group. A cycle of disappointment and frustration begins. Guilt and impotence in the therapist turn into an obsessive ritualisation of the appearance of relating, of dealing with *apartheid*, of being a friend, of seeking new ways of proving his or her good intent without getting too involved in the dangers. It is only a matter of time, then, before the game of liberalism, played in all English institutions, begins. Therapists begin to form new life-styles based on their new commitments, speaking to and seeing only their 'committed' friends. Slowly, over two or three years, they become tightly organised and ritualised as they close around themselves to deal with the anxiety and fear caused not only by *apartheid* but by their contact with black persons. Trapped in their fear and their responsibility, they pose no threat to Afrikanerdom.

Other clinicians, once involved, stop short when they realise the dangers and what the cost of friendship could be. They take the academic 'out' I have described earlier and retreat behind jargon and technicalese. The damage done to the patient is immense: after having hopes built up, he or she is dropped and becomes freshly hurt and angry, reliving all the old hurts gained over years of exposure to the *apartheid* system. Some break down after an experience like this and become, for example, alcoholic and, in some cases, suicidal. Clinicians seldom venture into the area again, and over time they gradually begin to lose interest in non-white problems and again use jargon to justify this.

There were other therapists who refused to be drawn into this area and they dealt with their patients purely as psychotherapists. They would attempt to pinpoint psychopathology and separate it from *apartheid* issues so that they could deal with the problems they had been trained to and not those that they could not help with. Usually, these therapists' patients did not stay long; it depended on the therapist and how he demarcated the two problem areas. Many patients rejected a therapist no matter how skilful or how pleasing, if he or she did not deal with *apartheid* problems first and foremost. Hostility here was usually much more open on both sides and each blamed the other. It takes a really skilled therapist to let a patient hate him or her and so let the patient have at least *one* experience where they can hate and win (hurt) without being annihilated. Sometimes such an approach worked; more often than not it did not – patients under stress plus *apartheid*-stress cannot be expected to stay around; they have no precedent to behave otherwise. In their minds, things sooner or later go bad.

The difficulty with this approach – that is of separating *apartheid* from the patient's own problems – is simple. It is just not possible in South Africa because it imposes an unrealistic demarcation on the patient's appraisal and experience of his or her reality. The therapist's golden rule is that the patient's world (objectively and subjectively) is paramount; you have to start with that, not impose a false order on it. Skilled clinicians start with each individual's framework, no matter how similar it is to someone else's, and derive structures from it – not lay them on it.

The form and direction an individual's pathology takes is to some extent shaped by the unique geographic, social, economic and cultural conditions exigent in his or her society. Likewise, the methods used to remedy the situations. Most of the models used today to conceptualise mental pathology as well as normality and treatment have been derived from highly homogenous societies, such as Britain and America, where institutions and life-styles are similar.

These models presume a model of political function based on an acceptance by the majority of the citizens of the state of the values and the aims held by the political institutions that exist. Communities form institutions to attend to certain basic needs of the community, and debate within institutions revolves around the best way to attend to those needs. There is agreement about what constitutes the needs and thus the political constitution.

In South Africa, the institutions do not serve the basic needs of the community nor is there free movement of opinion within the political institutions. People whose needs are not attended to or not recognised because they are outside the frameworks set up for the white system, of necessity have different levels of normality and pathology. Consequently, treatment systems derived from non-South African societies have little or no bearing on the life-styles of non-white patients.

Treatment modalities accepted unthinkingly by clinicians in Europe or America as obvious and correct become, in the South African context, modalities that could compound a patient's pathology and possibly even bring him harm. Encouraging an inadequate and unconfident Coloured person to be assertive could lead to his dismissal from his job for insubordination; teaching an African to stand up for his rights could land him or her in jail. In one case I knew of, helping a Coloured alcoholic school-teacher to stop drinking as a means of avoiding his problems, led to his suicide because his fragile new development was broken by a police raid during which his brother was shot and killed. This kind of thing does happen occasionally in other societies; in South Africa, all of these examples form a daily and routine part of doing therapy with non-whites.

Let me show how, at the simplest level, the very act of doing therapy can cause more problems than it solves. Early in my practice I treated a middle-aged nursing sister who suffered from migraine and who, under normal conditions, would have made an excellent candidate for psychotherapy: she was intelligent, well-educated, insightful and willing to work hard. More important, she had a helpful family, which is rare amongst migraine patients. We began treatment and I first conducted a clinical investigation taking a case and symptom history, all of which usually took two or three months. After four weeks, she began to behave oddly in her interviews: she was listless, unhappy and masked. And yet her migraine had begun to clear up (it often does in this part of treatment due, mainly, to the extra interest the patient gets). She had settled down well at first and seemed at ease in my office but gradually I could feel that things were not right. I had put no embargoes on what she could talk about either and she had freely expressed anger at the way she was treated in the hospital where she worked.

Gradually, however, she began to tell me what she thought was the matter. It involved the way she had responded to the treatment situation, not to the treatment as such (there had not been any). For years, she had daily experienced a certain type and level of relationship with white people – doctors, nurses, hospital staff she came into contact with. This involved learning a certain expectancy towards whites, an expectancy designed to shield and cushion her from being hurt. She had got used to protecting her dignity by being cold and hard and aloof from all whites without being insubordinate or hostile. People liked her and found her friendly because they mistook her aloofness for inoffensiveness and her coldness for submissiveness. As she put it, 'You have to get used to being ignored by doctors, to being treated as if you didn't exist; if you are in the way you'll literally be walked on. Anyone, if they're white, can order you around. Nobody cares and nobody protects you. You don't exist.'

For her, exposure to the therapeutic situation had been a shock which she had struggled to contain over the weeks. It had exposed her to a form of interaction (that is, normal politeness, normal interest) which she had never experienced and which she did not know how to deal with. She had no referent and so the therapeutic framework had been like a traumatic injury:

> 'I haven't been able to work properly. I weep all the time. My husband complains that I'm bitchy now, and hard. I can't cope. You've made me worse and I have to stop.'

And stop she did. The situation had exposed feelings of bitterness and anger, resentment and frustration that had long been repressed and controlled. Her therapy with me had given her a target for those feelings, had made her hate me as the first white person who had ever treated her ordinarily. Hating me made her guilty because she had sufficient insight to know that her feelings were a product of the system. She was better off without treatment and I had to agree with her.

Many patients do not have this insight. They goad and push the white therapist then pour out resentment in one final act of vindictiveness and self-destruction, aware that even this is futile. I know one chap who saved up to pay for two consultations each with three different white private practitioners; with each one he gained their sympathy, let them think they were getting on well, got them to commit themselves to anti-*apartheid* stands, then informed them he was a special branch agent and that he was going to report them. He said it was worth it just to see the expression on their faces as they rapidly tried to retract and explain that it was for the good of the patient, that they did not really hold those views, and so on. After a while he told them who he really was then got up and walked out.

Doing psychotherapy with non-whites is for most therapists a little like putting your finger in a fire: it always burns and it always hurts. Little wonder, then, that over time English-speaking units developed institutionalised ways of helping their staff and patients to avoid being constantly traumatised that obscured and befuddled constructive awareness of the issues involved. Because clinicians are more exposed to the system and thus more traumatised, they have in the main an even greater level of anxiety and fear than their academic counterparts.

This combination of circumstances creates a population of clinicians who are more easily controlled and coerced by the government and its agencies than their academic counterparts. They are vulnerable through their exposure to the hostility and violence existing in racial contexts, and tend to avoid hurt and pain, to close off without understanding it. Thus closed, the guilt and fear remain *personalised*. The therapist thinks it was *his* fault and retreats into either of the two poles described earlier – both of which help him to avoid a proper understanding of what is going on.

The fuzzy thinking of English-speaking students and academics absolves them from a personal sense of responsibility. The academic can say 'I've done my bit' and get on with his life. For the clinician exposed to non-white persons, this is not possible because his day-to-day living does not permit him to 'get on with life'. Every day he is reminded of his *personal* responsibility and the need for a personal commitment. To be *removed* or to be *involved* has to be got out of the way before you can live. If you choose to be removed then you have to stay removed, disinterested, heartless, cold, clinical, to deal with the daily anxiety. This is why I found callousness as much institutionalised in some quarters as commitment was in others.

Both groups sought relief from the guilt and anxiety and did so while ensuring that they: a) took no effective action with their patients; b) made no political fuss, and c) allowed themselves to be controlled by the government with little or no resistance. Imagine the kind of problems that would arise for the government if South Africa's English-speaking clinicians united to expose the situation, to protest about how their patients are treated, to expose the way government agencies treat Africans. Imagine if they had gone on strike or set up alternative systems. Mental health practitioners have privileged access to South Africa's blacks and could provide highly damaging evidence against the government. But they do not.

The result of all this is, for the patient, to make him or her prefer dealing with Afrikaner clinicians – even given the maltreatment they suffer – because, in the long run, experiences with them are less traumatic, more realistic and situation-orientated. Afrikaner therapists know this and use it as evidence of their superior knowledge and ability in dealing with non-whites. This completes one of the many cycles of experiences I came to recognise as determining the maintenance of the *status quo* in areas which could have been highly threatening and dangerous for the government.

This was my experience with mental health services in English-speaking units. It was, whatever its faults, infinitely more humane and tolerant than my experiences of Afrikaner-dominated state departments. In Afrikaner institutions, the same problems are dealt with completely differently and the institution of mental care take on a meaning that is at variance with ideas of acceptable practice elsewhere in the world.

It occurred to me that if I had been interested in how English-speaking psychologists and psychiatrists dealt with their non-white patients, because it was a rare example of racial contact outside *apartheid*, then surely the Afrikaners – far more alert to possible breaches in their system than I was – would almost certainly have realised the importance of this earlier. Research revealed, in fact, that they had. Clinical psychology was in its infancy in the English-speaking universities and medical schools but had been in existence for years in Afrikaans institutions; most of the patients in South Africa were black, nearly all these were treated at state institutions whose staff psychologists were Afrikaans. Further, few psychiatrists in the country as a whole did psychotherapy – most did counselling and drug therapy – psychologists did nearly all the therapy going, especially in state institutions. The government had made sure that the people who dealt with non-whites were Afrikaners. The creation of the departments of Bantu Affairs, Bantu Education, Coloured Affairs and Indian Affairs, and the massive enlargement of the predominantly Afrikaans public service since 1948, was entirely devoted to achieving this end. African-white contact in the area of mental health in South Africa, therefore, is, like in all other respects, in the hands of the Afrikaners.

Valkenburg Hospital provided me with an inside view of how Afrikaans psychiatry and psychology function. I spent eight months there from December 1970 until August 1971 and in that time learnt a lot.

The hospital is situated in an isolated part of Cape Town (as are all government mental hospitals) and it is completely segregated at several levels, the white building at one end and the Coloured at the other. You have to travel over half a mile by road over a bridge to get from one side to the other. White patients never go to the Coloured side, but teams of Coloured patients are daily put to work servicing, gardening and labouring on both sides. This is their 'occupational therapy' and is justified on the grounds of their status on the bottom rung of the social ladder. White patients do not have this form of occupational therapy – they have art classes and the usual run of things to busy themselves with. The more retarded patients are used to bottle preserves, the fruit and vegetables for which are grown in the huge hospital grounds and sold in home produce stores at a tidy profit. There was a tiny non-white occupational therapy unit when I was there, used mainly for show and for patients likely to complain or make a fuss.

White conditions were poor, the buildings were old and in a poor state of repair, inadequately heated (doctors' offices were heated but not the wards) and the food was unpalatable – although one always hears this about hospital food. They were, however, neat and orderly and, above all, not overcrowded. The Coloured side was several times worse and, above all, overcrowded, and ill-kept; the food for non-whites came from a separate kitchen and was based on a separate and inferior diet. This is government policy in all state hospitals; Coloureds and Africans have different standards of living and therefore receive different diets, Africans less than Coloureds. What makes this worse, though, as I discovered at Valkenburg, is that a much tighter check and control is kept over white diets than over non-white diets. As a result, non-white patients often receive far less than even their discriminatory diet stipulates owing to kitchen staff taking the dietary ingredients and the unsupervised nursing staff taking their food. The effects and implications of this state of affairs are considerable; not only do non-whites have no way of complaining (there was a complete disregard for non-white complaints against the staff) but as mentally disturbed patients whose only contact with doctors is infrequent and brief, their conditions are completely irremediable and compound whatever pathology they suffer from.

There were many such examples reported to me by my patients of material discrimination in general medical practice; white patients always get their wounds dressed in new bandages, non-whites are dressed in old bandages removed from whites, washed and sterilised. Staff are permitted to use a new bandage on a non-white only if there are no old ones. Due to overcrowding in maternity wards, black women are encouraged to leave as quickly as possible, to make room. They are told this is medically sound and will help them recover quicker.

Non-white patients received no psychotherapy at Valkenburg, only drugs or shock therapy. I examined some of their files and found huge time gaps in entries indicating that, in some cases, patients had not been seen for years at a time. I found similar things much less frequently on the white side. Physical abuse of patients by staff and other patients was prevalent amongst non-white patients and virtually absent among whites. I witnessed, on occasion, male nurses smacking heavily dazed and drugged non-white patients brutally in the face for being in the way. I was informed that this was routine and 'the only way to deal with them'. It appeared to me to be a popular pastime amongst the male nurses who kept it from the doctors who, so they told me, saw nothing. None of the doctors I spoke to liked working on this side and spent as little time there as possible.

You may wonder how I obtained this information. The answer is simple but requires an understanding of the segregation practised at Valkenburg. It was the policy of the hospital to segregate each type of profession. Thus psychiatrists, medically trained doctors and registrars had the highest status, their own common-room and their own offices in each ward. They were completely separate from all other forms of professional life. As a psychologist, one was not allowed into their common-room, neither was one permitted to use their offices in the wards. Thus one had the spectacle of psychologists and social workers conducting interviews and doing testing in little corners of the ward while being denied the 'privilege' of using the empty doctor's office. No privacy, no seclusion and sometimes no roof – once to get a patient to concentrate on a test, I had to sit under a tree outside his ward, it was so noisy inside.

Next in line came the nursing staff followed by social workers and occupational therapists. Last and least came the psychologists. Each group had its own common-room or area and they seldom mixed. The nursing staff were superior in this hierarchy to us because they were considered to be medical. As a consequence, they treated us as nonentities. In particular they treated me – who spoke little Afrikaans – as the lowest of the low, paying me little attention, covering up nothing and in the process, telling me everything I needed to know.

Basically, the psychology department was there under sufferance and it took the role dictated to it by the hospital's psychiatrists. During my time, the multi-complex function of clinical psychology was reduced to the level of a misused testing service. Ordinarily, when a medical doctor asks a psychologist to test a patient, it is because he is puzzled and needs clarification for diagnostic or management purposes. Doctors at Valkenburg requested psychological testing in virtually every case they saw – purely in order to avoid the task of having to spend time with patients. Psychiatrists in the hospital resented the presence of psychologists and grudgingly withheld the 'plums' of the profession, such as group therapy and individual psychotherapy for themselves or their trusted, Afrikaans psychologists.

My first personal complaint was that there was no training programme. Not only were we not permitted to do psychotherapy but there was no training in the administration, scoring and interpreting of psychological testing. The situation at Valkenburg in this respect was appalling. Testing was done by literally anyone. A nursing sister attached to the unit had, for years, been administering, scoring and diagnosing intelligence without any kind of formal training in test theory. Students in their third year were shown how to administer and score the standard IQ test in a hour and then sent to do routine reports without supervision.

No test was used with its handbook, and these were often discarded. Incredible as this may seem, I sometimes found brand-new handbooks that had been brought with the test equipment discarded in their plastic wrappings at the bottom of the test cupboard.

The work of a psychologist, in short, could have been done by a clerk.[1] You were supposed to learn, therefore, from the senior psychologist all the interpretations and skill you needed. Diagnoses generally followed the standard classifications of mental illness where possible. But since so much routine testing was required to assist in diagnosis, considerable pressure was thrown on the instruments used rather than on the skill of the psychologist using them. Several malpractices in this regard occurred, all arising out of the way doctors mechanically used tests to avoid contact with either the patients or the psychologist (few doctors wanted to hear your opinions about patients – you had simply to submit test scores).

None of the tests were standardised for non-white populations. This means that cultural and linguistic differences were inadequately catered for. The well-known Wechsler test of intelligence had been standardised – but for whites only. It was not used on non-whites except in certain cases where the psychologist felt the patient was socially up to it. Instead they used a version of the Alexander test – a non-verbal intelligence test standardised in Europe. What was disturbing was the fact that it is generally recognised that the test is not valid for testing at the upper or even average limits of intelligence. No one on the staff knew the range of applicability, but what we did know from experiments we conducted amongst ourselves was that the entire psychology staff of the hospital came out as dull-normal or as borderline retarded on the test. The Ravens Progressive Matrices was another test used. This is a test of non-verbal intelligence and was standardised in Britain in the 1940s and 1950s. The test norms were applied freely to white and Coloured South Africans. Cultural and colour bias were controlled by adding compensatory marks to the score of the patient, but each hospital unit had its own idea of what was to be added: some added 10, others added 15, and still others nothing at all.

Obviously the key to whatever learning was possible lay in the hands of the senior psychologist and there, he was sadly and irresponsibly lacking. What he was good at was keeping the doctors happy and managing the system. So poor was his knowledge that I doubted if he possessed a Master's degree let alone the Doctorate from the University of London he claimed he had. But he was not unusual: the other psychologists were not only poorly trained but made no effort to improve their limitations.

Tests were 'interpreted' in such a fashion as to render the whole concept of psychological testing meaningless. If a person scored highly on certain sub-scales on the MMPI,[2] for example, these would then be listed as symptoms and his or her personality described as such. A person scoring highly on obsessivity and on hysteria, for instance, would be labelled as an obsessive-hysteric or an hysterical-obsessive, depending on which scale he or she had scored highest. Any attempt to perform cluster analysis or the finer points of testing was ridiculed. The errors made using this method were gross. I will mention only two here.

They had in a young boy of fourteen whom the psychiatrists thought was a drug addict. But they were not sure so they asked the psychologists to see him and test him. He was given an MMPI and his scores showed a drug user's pattern which they then triumphantly rushed over to show the doctors. Fortunately, the boy's father was not happy with this and insisted on a re-assessment, so I was asked by the chief psychologist to do projective testing[3] on him on the quiet (that is, without letting the psychiatrists know) and so had a chance to look at the testing they had done first. It was then that I saw they had given him the MMPI and I pointed out that the test not only is not normally used on adolescents – the norms do not apply or have the same meaning – but that adolescents tend to show a disturbed pattern anyway. All this was quite clearly stated in the literature – they had read it but not taken it seriously because they did not have a test for adolescents and could not be bothered looking for one. I went on to discover a seriously depressed and suicidal boy who needed psychotherapy – not the major tranquillisers they were thinking of giving him based on their diagnosis on the invalid MMPI. Needless to say, he had never used illicit drugs in his life.

Test administration is a complex procedure requiring not only great skill in drawing responses from often unco-operative patients, but considerable clinical acumen in both the correct interpretation of the subject's responses and in judging whether or not the patient's responses reflect accurately on his present state. The second example concerns the case of a professional man I tested who had suffered brain damage in a car crash. Because of his prior learning and high level of education, he was able to reach the same score on an intelligence test as he had before his accident. This was because where he was unable to remember what to do, he would simply work it out. Because there was no discrepancy before and after his accident, and without seeing the patient, my supervisor declared that he was clearly not brain damaged. I submitted a second report based on my belief that he was responding to the test on the strength of past functioning in an area in which he was verbally and practically highly competent. The testing session, in other words, did not tap *new* tasks of a different nature and when I administered these (which I had found, incidentally, dusty and unopened at the bottom of the department's test cupboard) his performance showed a clear discrepancy between it and his supposed IQ level. Because of this impasse between my supervisor and me, the patient was sent for re-assessment to the EEG centre where a sub-clinical pattern was diagnosed. Follow-up testing showed the existence of a tumour.

I discovered these malpractices only after I had trained myself and when I was able to get new or up-to-date handbooks. Then I found that some of the tests had been misused in a gross and professionally negligent fashion for years. The worst example concerned the only psychological test for brain damage the hospital used and which consisted of patterned blocks that the patient had to copy. Now, when the original forms that had come with the test had run out, the staff made fresh copies from the original and in the process had left out by accident the last page containing the normative scoring and diagnosis. The effect of this was simple. The test was scored in two parts: the formal scoring for the performance on the task, then the clinician's evaluation of the patient's symptoms during the task. The latter had to be subtracted from the first score before checking the final score against the norms. This would then tell you whether or not and by how much the patient was brain-damaged. The author of the test states quite clearly and categorically that the second score is the most crucial and reliable and could even be used without the first but on no account and under no circumstances is the first to be used alone. The psychologists at Valkenburg had been making just this mistake for seven years.

Disturbing though this was, the reaction of my colleagues to my discovery was even more disturbing. I at once told the head psychologist of my findings and explained how we were using the test wrongly. My interest at the time, being quite aware of my tenuous position as an intern, was purely to correct procedure and not to blow the thing up. I made this quite clear. The reaction was unspectacular and typical. He asked me for the book, took it and read it and did nothing. I taxed him about it the following day and he said he had thought about it and if we changed now, the Superintendent and the doctors would want to know why and he would be in trouble. If I made more of it he would see to it that I lost my job and that I would never get another in a state hospital in South Africa.

He kept the book and, I believe, destroyed it. I took the only option I had open to me: I told him that I was not prepared to use the test in the fashion he had indicated and that I was going to make it clear in my reports. Further, I intended using a separate battery of brain damage tests and not the concept of testing used in the hospital which was nearly twenty years out-of-date. I also determined to remove him when and if I could since I considered him to be a danger to his trainees and to the patients.

The core of the problem in the psychology department at Valkenburg lay not so much in the person of the chief psychologist nor in the fact that shoddy and dubious practices were allowed to continue for so long, but rather in the fact that they were never recognised as such. What was incredible to me was that these activities were the norm – that is, it was I who, in trying to improve the service I personally offered, in criticising constructively and through the usual channels, was severely attacked psychologically – in what I can only describe as an insensitive and vicious manner – and was considered to be 'arrogant, rebellious and a troublemaker'. I was wrong, they were right. This, I later learnt, was in fact a typical pattern in South African institutions, especially those run by or connected with the government. You did things the way those in *power* did or said. No other way was tolerated. There was no morality, no academic right to be objective. Afrikaans interns were quite familiar with this authoritarian stance having been brought up with it and taught to obey it unquestioningly. For me, it meant trouble.

Malpractices were not limited to the department of Psychology – those committed by the medical staff were far more serious and were the result not simply of individual carelessness or error of judgement but of sheer ignorance and routine negligence. They were widespread and common to both white and non-white patients although, of course, the latter suffered more.

The major malpractice I discovered was the overdosing of patients with psychotropic drugs. From the Superintendent down, I was frequently informed that Groote Schuur's psychiatrists did not know the first thing about dosage and that whenever difficult patients came to Valkenburg they were soon controlled by 'the method' used in the hospital. This 'method' was to administer huge dosages of drugs far in excess of the safety limits prescribed by drug manufacturers. It was normal procedure to administer a drug, watch its effects and then, if it did not appear to work, to escalate the dosage – often two or three times the maximum advised by the manufacturers – rather than to try another drug, question the diagnosis, look for psychological causes or even try psychological means of helping.

What used to happen to patients who were in distress or who were violent or depressed was that under the weight of their medication they would become zombies, literally drugged out of their minds. But this satisfied the hospital staff because firstly, like this, they were no trouble and secondly, they no longer showed symptoms. It was no use protesting that they also no longer showed *any* normal human behaviour because this was dismissed as irrelevant. Yet patients like this (and they were in the vast majority) sometimes could not talk or had to be led around; they would bump into tables and chairs or sometimes be found standing, staring at the wall. And these were not long-stay patients who, it can be argued, usually exhibit this form of behaviour through a combination of drug damage and withdrawal from human contact; these were people who just days or weeks earlier had been outside in the world, as capable of reading, talking and thinking as the next person.

Registrars who came to Valkenburg from other hospitals and who discussed this aspect with me later were as distressed by the phenomenon as I was but they had to conform and they justified it by saying that it did 'seem to keep the patients under control'. They showed no appreciation – neither did Valkenburg staff – of the work done on the very real and dangerous side-effects of prolonged use of psychotropic drugs, let alone prolonged over-dosing.[4]

A second malpractice was the use of shock treatment. Most mental hospitals and units continue to use shock treatment often in large quantities and for prolonged periods of time, and this occurred too at Valkenburg. It is also a matter of considerable controversy amongst mental health professionals. So what I have to say about its use at Valkenburg is limited as a criticism of a specifically South African practice. What is not open to question, though, is the manner and frequency with which it was used on non-white patients at Valkenburg.

One of the limitations of having white doctors attend to Coloured and African patients is that most whites not only have little or no contact with non-whites but have very specific stereotypes and prejudices about them. The prevailing attitude at Valkenburg was one of disinterest and gross prejudice. Coloureds were all 'lazy, drunken and troublesome' and Africans 'just plain stupid' – they believed in witchdoctors, magic and witchcraft and were thus 'dumb and ignorant'. An intelligent or sensitive, educated, middle-class non-white was seen as a real headache; I quote from a conversation two doctors had during a ward round about a Coloured school-teacher who had collapsed and behaved hysterically and was brought in by the police:

First: I can't take these educated Coloureds. (The other nods) Why can't they just behave like the rest? She was drunk, wasn't she?

Other: Of course she was; won't say, that's all. Denies it. Says she's upset – her boyfriend's left her.

First: Oh yes, I've heard that before. You'll see, she drinks.
Or takes drugs. Lies too.

I heard this kind of conversation countless times.

White doctors 'explained' non-white mental disturbance in terms of the stereotypical denigrative attributes they thought non-whites possessed. Where these did not fit, doctors attempted to coerce the patient verbally. Where this failed and the patient did not improve, then drugs were used. More often than not, though, shock was used straight on the grounds that 'a shocked *hotnot* [a derisive term Afrikaners use for Coloureds] doesn't cause any trouble'. Patients were threatened with shock treatment as a punitive measure and to coerce them into 'agreeing' with the doctor's diagnosis. Here is an account from one of my private patients who describes the way she was shocked at Valkenburg in 1971. She was twenty-eight at the time:

'I'd lost my job and couldn't cope. My mother, whom I lived with, called the house doctor and he sent me to Valkenburg. I was weeping and crying a lot and I was in there with this white doctor. He never looked at me once. All he was interested in was whether I drank or took drugs. I explained that I was a Seventh Day Adventist and didn't smoke or drink. I tried to tell him that I thought the problem was my mother. I needed to leave home and she wouldn't let me go. But the doctor wasn't interested. I was in there five minutes. At the end he looked at me for the first time and said, "Look, when you tell me the truth, you can go, OK? You're a drinker, see. *I* know." I became very upset and tried to argue with him and I suppose I must have got hysterical again. He lost his temper, called some orderlies and they grabbed me and took me to this room with equipment in it. They stuck something in my mouth and then I felt these things on my head, pain and I lost consciousness. I was terrified. But this was only the beginning. The next day, the Coloured staff told me to apologise to him and say I drank even if I didn't and they'd let me go. Naturally I refused. How could I tell him something that wasn't true? So they gave me shock again. This went on for ten days. It was unbearable and eventually, I gave in – told them I drank and smoked grass and they let me out. I only saw that doctor twice in all that time.'

This report is entirely typical. No attempt is made to understand the complexities of the patient's situation. Instead a hospital's decision is forced on them like a rubber stamp at a factory, creating a nightmare experience that bears no relationship to the patients' conditions. The woman in question avoided doctors thereafter for several years, regarding them in the same light as the police: callous and brutal.

What was more disturbing was that because so many shock treatments were administered to non-whites, premedication was not given as a matter of policy. Shock treatment, quite apart from whatever damage it may or may not do to the patient's brain, is dangerous if the patient is not properly relaxed and tranquillised; they can make involuntary movements and can cause considerable damage to themselves, such as breaking their limbs, banging their heads, and so on. Black patients were shocked on the basis that 'the first shock knocks them out anyway so why bother putting them out'. White patients were, of course, not exposed to the same logic.[5]

I must digress here briefly. On the only occasion that I knew of where anyone wanted to do research on aspects of the black patient's dilemma, it was not to help pinpoint problems but to make use of the discrepancy involved in their treatment methods. In 1972, I was approached by a senior psychiatrist on the staff of Groote Schuur and Valkenburg Hospitals to help with some research to be conducted on non-white patients. His research team was taking advantage of the fact that the medication procedures on non-white patients receiving shock treatment permitted black patients to return to consciousness more quickly (because of not being previously medicated) to study disturbed thinking in bilingual subjects. Great care was taken to point out to me that this was a rare opportunity to study this phenomenon since it occurred nowhere else in the world. I declined the offer to participate on the grounds that they were exploiting a situation that I considered to be irresponsible and discriminatory towards black patients and instead of putting it right, and drawing attention to it, they were using it for their own ends. The team easily recruited the services of another psychologist and the project went ahead without me and, as far as I know, with the co-operation and approval of the Superintendent and Head Psychologist at Valkenburg Hospital.

The person who originated this study and some of the other researchers involved in it were not South Africans, and this conformed to a pattern that I unearthed in other areas of medical or paramedical research. South Africa, while in many respects attracting highly competent and humane researchers, has from time to time attracted also some who have taken advantage of the little attention paid to research ethics to conduct studies that are not permitted elsewhere. Many of the doctors I later treated in my practice complained on many occasions of research studies that exposed patients to levels of medication, surgery and radiation that they considered to be dangerous.

This attitude of punitiveness as therapy was not confined to non-white patients. A white nurse who attempted suicide was permitted to leave only if she apologised to her matron. Tranquilliser drugs were used but no other therapy and no other issues were considered. I had to give the girl psychometric testing (she was in fact one of my first cases in the hospital) and reported that she needed extensive psychotherapy as she was highly depressed and dangerously suicidal. I was disciplined by the Superintendent and ordered off the case – simply for saying this. I never saw her again and she was eventually discharged after apologising. I heard of her again in 1978 when she shot an ex-patient of mine and then killed herself in a conflict over a man.

An elderly woman whom I also tested was not allowed out on much the same grounds. She had disagreed with the Superintendent who said she was schizophrenic and she said she was not. They argued about her diagnosis for six weeks and about nothing else. In despair she came to me to ask if I would help her to get out – the Superintendent had told her that simply accepting his decision was not enough. He would not discharge her until her MMPI profile showed that she was schizophrenic. In an effort to comply, she had done the test twice in the past week and there was no hint of schizophrenia (there never had been). Would I not tell her what to answer so she could leave? Being quite familiar with hospital policy and its insanities, I checked her case file and decided to help her. I explained how to fake the test to show schizophrenia which she did and she was promptly discharged with great satisfaction by the Superintendent, who congratulated himself on being right all the way along.

The point about these malpractices is that they were the symptoms of a deeper pathology present in the institutions. What I have described is not in itself unfamiliar. Mental institutions everywhere manifest some of these traits but not to the degree and frequency of South Africa's. Moreover, they are known to be wrong. People in hospitals I visited everywhere – in the United Kingdom, in the United States, in Austria and Switzerland – were active in trying to eliminate these kinds of occurrences and to improve things for patients. In South Africa, they were standard, tolerated practice, part and parcel of the training given to psychiatrists and psychologists.

White and black patients were treated as so many cattle to be herded around and contained. Blacks suffered most because they had the least rights – even if they had influential or wealthy relatives or friends on the outside, they were of little use because there was no one to take it up with, no one to listen to their complaints. They were, too, in the most unfortunate of all positions. Prejudice towards an outgroup with whom you do not have much contact is one thing – prejudice towards a troublesome, emotionally disturbed, weak and helpless outgroup whom you are supposed to care for, become in South Africa institutionalised carelessness and brutality. *Apartheid* ensures that most aspects of a non-white's life are controlled by whites. *Apartheid* in mental institutions means that every single aspect including life and death of the Coloured or black person's life is controlled by unsympathetic and prejudiced whites. Because of this and because of the truth in the maxim that power corrupts, power in the hands of white professionals at Valkenburg became, in some respects, institutionalised corruption.

Through lack of control, lack of interest and the disregard for human life, practices in Valkenburg became ways of life. Let me detail some: Patients were sometimes treated as commodities amongst the staff members – especially male nurses. Patients who were inside for drug offences could buy whatever they needed including cannabis, LSD and a wide range of medical drugs including hypnotics, amphetamines, barbiturates, and so on. Certain doctors and nursing staff would steal drugs intended for patients and sell them outside. There was, I believe, a huge and profitable market in drugs such as mandrax, major tranquillisers, hypnotics, barbiturates, and in fact anything that was going. Patients were also, in some cases reported to me, used by nursing staff as 'personal assistants' and, on some occasions, were 'sold' or lent to other nurses or patients for homosexual or heterosexual purposes. This happened on both the Coloured and white sides. Patients could also approach certain members of staff to buy their way out of the hospital and from closed to open wards by using money or by offering themselves as favours. Some patients were used to smuggle drugs into and out of the hospital, others received special attention from certain nurses and doctors in return for relationships after discharge. Attractive patients, for example, were seen outside hospital and office hours for 'therapy', a practice I later discovered to be rife in certain mental health units throughout Cape Town.

By far the most serious of these transgressions, though, was the use made of Valkenburg by the security police. If a Coloured or African person not attached to a known political group came to the attention of the security police for acting more or less independently, then instead of going to the trouble of arresting and charging the person, they would bring him or her along to Valkenburg for 'treatment'. The thing was carefully handled, though. The police did not simply pick up a person and cart him off to Valkenburg – they tried to do everything legally to avoid suspicion. They first administered a drug at the police station or in the police car then called a co-operative district surgeon to certify the 'troublemaker'.[6] An ambulance would be called and the 'patient' would travel with a policeman to the hospital. Once there, he would be drugged and shocked – with the policeman giving the duty doctors the kind of 'facts' they needed to know. Few such 'patients' recovered from this process fully. They were frightened, dazed and, as far as the police were concerned, of little trouble afterwards. If they were, the whole process was simply repeated.

In 1977, I learned of new buildings being put up in the grounds of Valkenburg. In preceding years, the non-white section had been effectively walled off from the outside; now within the compound, a building some 200 feet square with a wall 15 to 20 feet high, along the lines of a maximum security prison, was being erected. This building is 'intended' for Coloured and black psychiatric 'problem' patients. But I learnt from a reliable source that this was to be used for an expected increase in political dissenters and was to serve the function of a rehabilitation centre along the lines of the hospitals in the country for psychopaths. The latter were originally built for psychopathic people and drug offenders and the like, but have apparently been used increasingly to 're-educate' Africans committing offences under the pass laws.

Given the approach that I found in 1970 towards Africans and Coloured patients, as well as the fact that the South African police have made use for some time of certain Afrikaans universities' medical departments to help them experiment with and develop appropriate combinations of psychotropic and punitive drugs to deal with politically problematic people (not just patients), there is little doubt in my mind that the practices I have described here have been extended thoroughly and that certain state-controlled hospitals are co-operating with the police to provide facilities for managing certain 'problems'.

It was a long time before I could make too much sense out of my experiences in the hospital, but I acted the following year to try and at least take the minimal steps I knew would bring some improvement. After I left Valkenburg, and after waiting until I was fully qualified – and could not be touched – I decided to check on the qualifications of the chief psychologist. I wrote to the University of London and discovered that he not only had no Doctorate from them but had never been registered as a student. I let this fact be known to certain people and an investigation was begun at the hospital.

My efforts were successful. The two people I felt were most culpable for the travesties in the hospital – the Superintendent and the head psychologist – both suffered as a result of this enquiry and the chief psychologist was asked to resign; the Superintendent, I believe, retired soon after. However, my hope that justice would be done was shortlived. Not only was no enquiry launched by the South African Medical and Dental Council but the chief psychologist was immediately placed in a senior position in another state organisation, the railways, at a higher salary than before, in the same job and with increased status. Later on, I learned that this practice of obtaining false higher degrees was quite prevalent amongst certain sections of the Afrikaner professional and academic community.[7]

The same problems that reduce the efficiency of English-dominated mental health services became, in the hands of government units, means of controlling and coercing not only difficult patients but any potential danger that arose. Government institutions are in fact *organised* around this axiom. Where they appear similar to overseas mental institutions lies purely in the fact that similar-sounding people use modern techniques to achieve a very different end. Mental health institutions have an important role to play in any society. They help break down barriers because they deal with the very things most people hide from one another and from themselves: fear, guilt, anxiety, anger, and so on. The psychotherapist deals with emotions, problems of living, problems of love, working, families – everything that forms the psychological life of a person. Little wonder then that Afrikaner academics and government officials realised early the importance of psychiatry and psychotherapy.

It was a fairly simple matter to set up effective *de facto* control. How they set about tightening this control, as English academic and medical services expanded and thus became a potential threat to their domination, was informative. Working in co-ordination with the Afrikaans universities, the government began, from 1972 onwards, to tighten the existing practices. It set up a commission of inquiry into mental health and began to centralise mental health affairs under the Department of Health.[8] All psychiatric and psychological units not already under its control were taken away from the Provinces and placed under the Department's jurisdiction. Then the government limited the right of non-registered practitioners (some psychologists, social workers, lay and religious counsellors) to practise any form of psychotherapy and psychological service. Then it began to do to English-speaking mental health institutions what it had already done to other English institutions, like the universities: it made them fight for their right to exist by threatening to close them down unless they co-operated.

As the universities had been forced to control and discipline their staff and students, so psychotherapists were placed under the same pressures until, by late 1977, the government and its agents were firmly in control. So effective has this been that barely a word of public protest by the professionals themselves has emerged, although I know of considerable anxiety expressed in private by clinicians and academics.

All of this has been done under the guise of improving matters. Forcing psychologists to train and register was advocated as simply bringing South Africa into line with accepted practice overseas. But close examination of what has been done reveals that control of this registration is in the hands of the South African Board of Psychology, dominated by the psychological and psychiatric faculties of Pretoria University, which has taken a leading role in the direction of mental health in South Africa. This board is largely comprised of government nominees and it has stipulated that training has to be done at State and university hospitals. Afrikaans universities speak for themselves; English ones are busy fighting for their existence.

The biggest deception of all, though, occurs in the way in which Afrikaans professionals have used developments in Western psychotherapeutic thought to cover up and justify their domination. It explains, incidentally, some of the phenomena I experienced at Valkenburg where the status of psychotherapy was minimal and, as practised by Afrikaans university-trained people, entirely in favour of the system.

Basically, Afrikaans psychotherapy draws its main theoretical base from the popular American psychologist Carl Rogers. Rogers' approach, 'client-centred therapy', stresses the non-involvement and value-neutrality of the therapist; the psychologist or psychiatrist acts purely as a mirror for the patient, reflecting and dealing only with the material that the patient brings up, helping him to find a solution to the difficulties that he himself experiences. The goal of this therapy lies in getting the patient to be happy with his existential lot.

In America or other Western industrialised countries, this doctrine has many advantages, not least that it encourages the patient to take responsibility for his own existence. Rogers' approach is part of the 'Third Force' in American psychology, the other two being psychoanalysis and behaviour therapy; it is humanistic, that is, concerned with man's humanity to man and it has arisen out of the existential psychology and philosophy that has so dominated much of European thinking, art and writing since the end of the First World War (Rogers, 1951; 1961). Existentialism and phenomenology are essential features of the doctrine – it cannot be understood without it. It stands for a belief in the basic rights of man, in human decency, and its aims and views of personality stress equality, individuality and benevolence in human relationships (Rogers, 1955; 1956; 1957).

Strange, then, to find this doctrine the moving spirit behind Afrikaans psychotherapy which, in reality, stands for the very opposite. At the simplest level, as is found in opinions of the apologists of

SABRA,[9] client-centered therapy was latched upon in the mid-1950s to provide a neat 'out' for the question of responsibility in psychotherapy that faced Afrikaans psychologists. Unlike medical personnel, whose duty to save lives and to help patients live comfortably does not involve him in social issues, psychologists and psychiatrists are charged with duties that do. As experts in human emotional functioning, they are expected to identify and make public dangerous and disturbing trends in society just as a doctor is expected to report incidents of dangerous diseases so that the community can be protected.

Client-centred therapy in its South African context has provided a perfect excuse for avoiding this key aspect of a therapist's responsibility. It reduces the role of the psychotherapist and restricts him purely to helping the patient adjust to his situation, whatever that may be. Thus, the American has to live with the demands of an American situation and the South African with his.

A South African black has to deal with the demands of the *apartheid* state. The therapist's task is to help him appreciate the limits imposed upon him by the whites, not to question the system or point out the errors. Happiness and mental health in this context are achieved by the black conforming to the system: fighting or bucking the system creates psychological problems. Within this framework, Afrikaans psychotherapists pride themselves on doing a considerable amount of work helping the patient either by explaining the system or making sure the system is applied accurately. Let me quote from a patient of mine who was a psychiatrist working at Stickland Hospital near Stellenbosch:[10]

'You see, take a Coloured bloke who is depressed and unhappy about his situation at work. I can do a lot to help him. I can make sure that he is getting the right allowances by law and that his family get their allowances. We have a lot of bureaucracy in South Africa, especially in government departments and when a patient has a just complaint, I help him with it. Often, because I am a doctor, I can get things going, get through the red tape quicker than he ever could. And I am an Afrikaner; if I phone up the Department of Coloured Affairs on his behalf, they'll listen and jump to it. And of course, I do the same back for them. The patient is naturally impressed and grateful; to him, I'm like God because I can move the Coloured Affairs Department and he leaves happy and at ease again. If the Department hasn't been fair to him, why, I give them hell for him. He can't do these things and I can – that's my role: I help him to see how to be happy. Now, there's another type of Coloured – what we call the criminal type; he wants to change the world. He doesn't like the Afrikaner and he causes trouble. He is a psychopath and is a job for the police or for those new psychopathic hospitals just coming in now. We therapists can't help him.'

This is the doctrine and this is how it works: everything that does not fit into the situation and may cause distress or problems is irrelevant to the Afrikaners' view of client-centred therapy.

The use of the term 'psychopath' above is important and significant; it is one that occurs often in discussion with Afrikaans clinicians and in the Afrikaans literature and it is another example of taking a well-known part of contemporary abnormal psychology and bending it to fit the situation. 'Psychopathic' refers to anti-social behaviour (also called anti-social personality disturbance) and refers to people who are of a specific type – who show lack of emotion, lack of social responsibility and lack of guilt. It is also a term becoming today less often used because of the problem of specifying anti-social behaviour. Homosexuality, for example, used to be considered anti-social but this has caused controversy and is no longer so regarded.

As I understand the term 'psychopath', it is probably more correctly used today to refer to near-criminal acting out behaviour characterised by a style that shows a lack of remorse, etc. In the South African context, however, the term retains its old connotation used to characterise people who behave anti-socially in South Africa, that is, against South Africa's view of social behaviour. Thus, pass offenders, revolutionaries, protesters; anyone who actively fights the system – irrespective of style – is labelled as a psychopath. Back to my psychiatrist patient:

> 'Everyone knows psychopaths are incurable so you've just got to be tough and hard on them – they'll never change. Put them away somewhere – in prisons – or shut them up in hospitals so they can't do any harm.'

I found this kind of attitude expressed towards English-speaking student protesters, troublesome schoolchildren and members of opposition groups. One of the psychologists under whom I trained at Groote Schuur hospital prided himself on curing student agitators: 'They come in rebels and go out Nationalists,' he joked. Often. This was his view of successful therapy.[11]

To cement this link with American and continental psychology and psychotherapy, in 1971 the University of Pretoria brought J. H. Van den Berg, an eminent Dutch psychiatrist-philosopher, to South Africa for a year to help motivate and publicise the founding of a South African Institute of Psychotherapy. Van den Berg travelled around the country, giving lectures, seminars and helping promote the new institute. The Afrikaner academics behind this project made subtle and effective use of Van den Berg's international and respected status to cash in with English-speakers and create the impression of continuity between overseas movements and South African ones. The institute and its plans have of course progressed considerably since then and it requires little imagination to conceive of the time in the not-too-distant future when the whole of clinical psychotherapy training in South Africa will come under the direction of this institute.[12]

By using set-ups like these, by working slowly and methodically and in co-ordination with the Ministry of Health, by using ideas and terms derived from overseas and by cloaking itself with the pretence of responsibility and professional respectability, Afrikaans professionals in the Mental Health field have succeeded not only in controlling clinicians in South Africa and their access to non-whites but they have also created the necessary organisations to serve a very nefarious function in the present and future control of South Africa's white and black citizens. Laws now make it possible for a policeman to detain anybody he feels is behaving in a mentally abnormal way – the policeman has thus become the arbiter of public mental behaviour. Further, the Department of Health is busy centralising and computerising all the functions of its mental health professionals and services; I have already detailed what this has meant for the training and control of professionals; what is not so well known is that a computer is being programmed to form a central memory bank containing data on every person in the country who receives mental treatment. This will include case history data, diagnosis, treatment history, and so on. All practitioners including those in private practice will be forced to contribute to this, which will mean that at any time the government will have data available about any single person who has seen a doctor. With this system, the government's control over the mental functioning of its population will not only be greatly extended, it will, with the increased encroachment of the army into civilian life, achieve a level of information about its citizens hitherto unheard of.

One last point. In 1976, the South African government passed a law making it an offence for anyone to publish any 'false' information concerning the 'detention, treatment, behaviour or experience' in any mental institution of anyone, past or present. This, in effect, means *any* information because who is to judge the falsity of a report but the very people who are perpetrating the malpractices and cruelties. I myself was threatened with this act for a paper I had published in America in 1975. 'If,' I was informed by an anonymous government official on the telephone, 'you don't stop publishing these articles about our institutions, you will be charged.'

Afrikaans psychiatry reflects the same concerns in maintaining Afrikaans power and dominance as other Afrikaans institutions, and is organised accordingly. Quite early on at Groote Schuur Hospital, I found the test library in ruins and bits and pieces. Checking, I discovered that this was not through lack of effort on the part of the staff. I put in an urgent application for stocks of tests (there was no proper set of tests for assessing brain damage, for instance) and when I left nearly two years later, it still had not been filled. Yet at Valkenburg, the department of psychology had so many tests it did not know what to do with them. I also knew that the Afrikaans psychology departments at Afrikaans hospitals and universities were astonishingly well provided with everything they asked for – and any amount of money. They were into clinical psychology and psychiatry in a big way.

Chapter Four

The Psychological Effects of Apartheid

Nothing could have referenced my theories about *apartheid* more than working in an Afrikaner institution that dealt largely with non-whites. At one and the same time, it showed me personally how the Afrikaner actually applied *apartheid*, what sort of people the institution's officials and professionals were and how frighteningly real their brutality could be. My reactions to working at Valkenburg were typical of the average white English person; I was shocked and concerned. My protests, completely justified academically and rationally, were smashed, my career threatened and so, like a good English South African, I ran away as quickly as I could to Groote Schuur and safety in the form of the English establishment there.

I had penetrated a reality that I should not have; I had found out how Africans were treated (as irrelevant and ignored) and how bad their mental health care was. Worse, I had naïvely tried to do something about it through the normal channels. You see, the Afrikaner has ensured that he alone deals with non-whites – for a reason: he cannot trust the English to do so because they become squeamish and upset, unlike the *ware* Afrikaner who would never dream of questioning the *status quo*. I realised that part of the design of *apartheid* was to separate the English from the realities of South African life; too much exposure would undoubtedly have been dangerous for the Afrikaner; he feared more than anything the capacity of the English to act on their emotions – especially their revulsions – without regard for political consequence. The attacks on me personally took me completely by surprise; their way of dealing with me was to completely ignore the general points I was making and to frighten me sufficiently so that I would not take it further. This, I realised, was the iron fist that the English were afraid of. It was this kind of individual personal onslaught that obviously created the tension and anxiety I discovered in my student samples and their families. The Afrikaners, by threatening and controlling English institutions, by removing any English political base and by isolating the individual and personalising attacks on him, ensured that English opposition and protest was never effectively organised. It is a subtly conceived, brutally effective programme that shows an acute awareness of the psychological and social needs of the individual. As I will show later, the formalization of this programme after 1948 and its effectiveness was due to the expertise and skill of H.F. Verwoerd – once, as I have said, a Professor of Applied Psychology and of Sociology.

I emerged shaken from my first direct contact with the Afrikaner; my clinical colleagues avoided reality, the students in my samples were tense and anxious and overused things like drugs, Transcendental Meditation, cerebral politics; their parents and my academic colleagues filled their time with endless, ineffective rituals in institutions that were shells of the real thing. These all helped to substantiate my theories and to back up the empirical studies I had already done.

But a question-mark remained over my work. I had survived Valkenburg, the English survived, work and life went on. Nonwhites may receive excessive ECT in hospitals, but they were not dying or being tortured there, as far as I knew. At this stage, for those who support South Africa, there will be a puzzled shrug – 'So what?' they will say. 'These things go on everywhere. Mental patients aren't treated too well in any modern country; universities in America or Britain have to serve the community, don't they. . . ?'

In short, I needed more proof. I had, apart from anything else, to prove to my own satisfaction that I was not just being hopelessly naïve and unsophisticated – a country boy, barely out of his adolescence, just discovering the Big Wide World outside.

In 1971, I set up a small research team to study the psychological effects of *apartheid*. All of its staff were either clinicians, clinical trainees or students who were interested in clinical work, and the main tools we used were psychometric tests such as the MMPI, Projective tests like the Ink Blot and Thematic Apperception Test, and clinical interviews. What I wanted to establish was firstly the *style* of reaction to *apartheid* of the various groups, that is, how the various groups coped clinically, and then to establish the contextual meaning of their coping mechanisms. Put simply, all I knew at that stage was that some liberal students used drugs to cope with their anxiety – I wanted to know if this was the tip of a psychological iceberg or if it was mere speculation on my part. Surely, I reasoned, *apartheid* must have some deleterious effects psychologically? At least, if not on the English, then on non-whites? I could appreciate that the English, if they lived in the psychological cage I thought they did, would have a more subtle kind of problem than Africans, for example, had. If you cannot see who is frightening you and if you do not realise that you are being frightened, you cannot hit back. No such problem confronts Coloureds or Africans. They know they are being ill-treated and by whom. The oppressor is clearly white and Afrikaans. What happens to Coloured and African people? What are the effects of *apartheid* on those it affects the most?

To begin with, I turned again to the literature to see what studies had been done and what other people had found. There were many studies which spoke of the poor conditions in which non-whites lived, of the hardships and repressions they suffered, and of some of the corollaries of being discriminated against.[1] Most of these condemned the situation and most had been written by white sociologists, social workers or anthropologists in direct contact with non-whites and so in a position to know. But there was no *psychological* evidence to back up these arguments. Far from finding that *apartheid* created diminished levels of functioning or even mental disturbances in those most affected, the studies that had been done found little clinically wrong.[2]

The only study that I could find to report any psychological distinction between Coloured and white, for example, found that Coloured clerks and manual workers showed greater 'externality' than their white counterparts.[3] This meant simply that Coloureds tended to believe that their personal actions were more in the hands of *external forces* than in their own hands – not a greatly startling finding.

So I was faced with the incongruous situation in which researchers had been unable to prove the existence of any deleterious effects of *apartheid* while my clinical experience was completely to the contrary. Moreover, research had been conducted, by and large, on the very group in which I suspected problems were more likely to be manifest – namely adolescent schoolchildren and students.

In one study, for example, a group of researchers in Cape Town found no difference in anxiety or neuroticism between young whites and Coloureds, but did find that their samples as a whole did show more anxiety than overseas samples.[4] The corollary of this was that it did not matter whether you were being discriminated against or doing the discriminating: neither seemed to cause overt mental pathology or substantial disturbance in personality.[5]

In many ways, though, I was fortunate to be living and working in Cape Town. There were still areas in which Coloureds and whites lived alongside each other. These areas were mainly old and established where Coloured communities had lived for years; now they were gradually being uprooted and moved out in terms of the Group Areas Act. There were other less well-endowed areas in which Coloured people and poor whites had formed a single community for decades; areas which lay on the wrong side of the railway track and so were left unappropriated and often free from official attention. Thus, in some cases, there were complete multiracial communities which continued to function as they had for years, affording insight into the nature of black and white contact in the country outside the framework of *apartheid*.

Furthermore, Cape Town is the home of the Cape Coloured people. These people of mixed race – descendants from white-black interaction in previous centuries and from Malay, African, Madagescese and Indian inhabitants of South Africa – are discriminated against like all non-whites but they share the same *lebensraum* as whites. Moreover, the majority speak Afrikaans – sometimes referring to themselves as 'brown Afrikaners' – and share the Afrikaner's cultural values. Apart from the Malay-Moslem community, who form a separate entity, the single largest church in the Coloured community is the Afrikaans *Nederduitse Gereformeerde Kerke*. Now, in any research that has cross cultural interests as mine had, such a population is like the answer to a prayer, unlike African-white comparisons, those between whites and Coloureds are relatively free of cultural disparity. Thus any difference found in testing can be attributed to *apartheid* policy and not to cultural differences or difficulties with the languages.

In early 1972, I instituted two empirical studies to try and find out more about how South Africans reacted to discrimination. I used, in my opinion, better techniques than had hitherto been used and I studied a broader range of people including those in the little multi-racial communities I have described above. Further, with the help of several assistants who collected the data, I was later able to gather information on the most elusive (to study) non-white people of all, the urban African.[6] In the initial study I used the MMPI on a sample of second-year Coloured students from the University of the Western Cape which one of my students obtained for me. I also used it on a sample of Coloured and white nurses working at Cape hospitals who applied to do psychiatric nursing at Groote Schuur. Later, I was able to make use of samples of Afrikaans students obtained by the same student from the Rand Afrikaans University to further extend these comparisons.[7]

The MMPI (Minnesota Multiphasic Personality Inventory) is perhaps the most well-known and widely used measure of personality and clinical functioning in the world today, and has been for the past thirty years. It is a scale that has been extensively researched and used both academically and clinically so its strengths and weaknesses are quite well-established and known to users of the test. I had learnt to use it at Valkenburg and chose it because it assesses the presence of types of clinical pathology expressed as psychiatric symptoms by asking detailed and extensive questions of the patient. In short, it makes available a set of symptom-scales showing in which areas, if any, a person is experiencing difficulty. Outside the clinical area, it shows how people in society, normal or otherwise, defend and protect themselves from problems they experience in life.

I also used the MMPI in several different ways to provide a sociological perspective as well as a measure of personality-functioning. But I used it initially to assess clinical dysfunction. There are cut-off points on the scales used in the MMPI which indicate the presence of marked clinical pathology when the subjects score above or below those levels. The degree of clinical disturbance is expressed both through elevated (peaked) scores on each scale and number of peaks. Each scale taps a different clinical dimension and these include Hysteria, Hypochondria, Depression, Psychopathic proneness, Masculine-feminine inversion, Paranoia, Schizophrenia,

Obsessive-compulsive symptoms and Intraversion. These scales, I think, speak for themselves but where they do not I will amplify as we go along.

Not only did clear and distinct patterns of functioning emerge for each group (English, Afrikaans and Coloured) and in both sets of subjects, that is, students and nurses, but I was intrigued to find that there was clear and statistically significant evidence that the development of the Coloured personality was severely handicapped through experiences with *apartheid*. Further, there was clear evidence that the anxiety and fear I had discerned in English-speaking South Africans was present in far greater depth than my previous research had shown.

Among the student samples in this study, English males peaked on the masculinity-femininity measure and came close to peaking on psychopathy. Coloured males did not peak on any scale but came close to peaking on the schizophrenia scale. Afrikaans student profiles, male and female, stayed well within the normal range, showing not only the absence of overt pathology but little evidence of psychoneurotic dysfunction as well.

So. The most clinical distress was shown by males, not females, with English-speaking and Coloured males showing the most, and in this they were clearly and significantly distinguished from Afrikaans males. The fact that English males showed their pathology on Scale 5 indicates that the masculinity-femininity measure has sociological as well as clinical significance. Scores on this scale are generally accentuated in college and university male students and are taken to be an indication of the presence of a certain degree of creativity which, in sociological terms, is a valuable factor in the role young educated people take in society later.

New movements, growth and the development of sound and realistic adjustments to the changing demands on any society require that a society's educated elite, its new generation of leaders in politics, business, academia, the arts and so on, be well-endowed with the kind of healthy creativity that this scale taps in university students.[8] To score highly, therefore, is to be expected. What is significant here is that English males scored pathologically highly and Afrikaans and Coloured males showed no elevation on this scale at all. In other words, for the last two groups there was a notable absence of the kind of important psychological characteristics deemed necessary for societal continuity and progression.

At the clinical level, the high score of the English-speakers indicated that the subjects tended to be obsessed to a marked degree with aesthetic, political and altruistic values. Scale 5 deals with masculine-feminine interests in such a way that high scores on it indicate a lack of interest in overt masculine pursuits and styles of behaviour that one typically associates with 'macho-ness' in males – the denial of feelings, insensitivity to social and political issues and atmosphere, and so on.[9] In the South African context, English males tend to be concerned with and aware of sensitive social and political issues while Afrikaans and Coloured males are not, the implication being that these issues and this style of relating tend to dominate their emotional and intellectual lives.

Clear evidence of the problems experienced by Coloureds and English-speakers showed up when we compared the pattern of personality-functioning and the manifestation of symptoms of the various samples with American and Australian students.[10] Afrikaans male and female students showed no obvious symptom clusters and there appeared to be no evidence of any type of disorder among these students. In marked contrast, Coloured males and females scored significantly higher on the scales measuring depression, schizophrenia, obsessive-compulsive functioning and hypomania. I also discovered that Coloured male and female profiles were very similar to each other, unlike those of their English and Afrikaans counterparts.

This is unusual. Males and females exposed to Western cultural values tend to develop different personality profiles according to the sex-typing demands made on them by their communities. Coloured males and females showed a similar level of defensive functioning and style of personality. Normally, males tend to develop defensive habits around a range of life-expectancies. The same applies to females. Because Coloured males and females had essentially the same patterns, I inferred that their personal development and thus their defensive patterns were *not* shaped according to sex stereotypes. It was clear to me that this was one direct result of living under *apartheid*.

So severe were the effects of the overall stress under which these Coloured students lived that their normal personality development (determined by biological sex and society's reaction to it) was subordinated by the Coloured community's over-attention to the demands of *apartheid*. It was as if gender-induced personality differences had been wiped out – I was examining profiles of people who had been branded in such a way that the structure of their personalities had been irrevocably changed without overt manifestation of the damage done. I had never come across anything like it in the literature and had to work out the above hypothesis blindly. But there was more to come.

Two of the three scales that Coloured students scored highly on fall into the severe category, namely the scales measuring schizophrenia and obsessive-compulsive behaviour. Now the precise meaning of this has to be carefully interpreted. One cannot simply say that Coloureds tend to be more schizophrenic and obsessive-compulsive because they score highly on these scales. An examination of the literature on this subject suggests that this pattern is best interpreted as a manifestation of extreme stress barely contained by the type of personality organisation possessed.[11] No such pattern was evident in Afrikaans or English students living in the same geographical area, of the same socio-economic background and status. The pattern, it was clear, arose because of *apartheid*.

Outside the South African context this pattern is common to psychiatric patients. If these results were to be coded and examined purely at the level of clinical functioning, profiles such as these would be labelled schizoid or borderline psychotic. I concluded that the South African situation creates the conditions in which psychotic-like levels of symptoms become *normal reactions*. The Coloured subjects in this study were not psychotic or even borderline but they were deeply stressed. As a result of prolonged exposure to *apartheid*, they had had to develop ways of coping that in any other culture – and even amongst the whites in South Africa – would be regarded as psychotic or borderline.

Psychosis or severe personality disintegration occurs when a person develops unrealistic fears, anxieties, tensions and the like, born out of a pathological assessment of reality. He or she imagines people are plotting against them, they see or hear things not there; they live in a state of inordinate tension and anxiety in which obsessions, phobias and compulsive acts repeated endlessly are the only means they have of dealing with their fears. This is because – and this is the crux of the matter – they cannot admit to their fears publicly because everyone recognises that they are imaginary (and so do they). When a psychotic person has a breakdown, it is because stresses have become so acute that he or she has to create 'voices' and the like to explain their irrational behaviours. Recent research had established that the psychotic reacts to real stress found in his or her home situation which he or she continues to carry around with them outside the family. The stress is subtle but nevertheless real; few people, including researchers and clinicians, can see these immensely powerful and subtle influences because they are below the level of most people's 'social awareness'. You have to be in a schizophrenic situation or to know one intimately to detect them.[12]

There is only one reason why the Coloured students did not become psychotic or borderline: their assessment of reality, their terrors, fears, anxieties and suspicions were *to be found* in their reality. More than their English counterparts, they showed an accurate and insightful appreciation of the dangers facing them in the normal course of leading their lives. To *ignore* these perceptions would have resulted in psychosis; to attend to them led to survival but at the price of having to maintain a chronically disturbed personality organisation.

English students appeared to be less deeply affected by the pressures of living in South Africa but they still showed evidence of considerable disturbance in the organisation of their personalities. They manifested a degree of ill-directed rebelliousness, indicated by the high scores on psychopathic deviancy and hypomania scales. They had energy, insight and active creativity but no means of directing it – precisely what I had found in the authoritarian studies. The high psychopathic scale in the South African context I took to indicate a penchant for expressing frustration by anti-social acting out – a finding that accords well with the earlier evidence of drug-taking behaviour in liberal students. This is significantly more marked in English males than females.

Females in all the samples seemed less affected by the system than males, especially amongst white students; they showed less pathology. Afrikaans women as a whole seemed to be the most normal, both by ordinary Western standards and in terms of the Australian and American samples I compared them with. Afrikaans males had flattened profiles which indicated a tendency to respond to self-analysis in a defensive way and to deny personal problems.[13] All the South African groups responded to the questions in a far more guarded and defensive way than their overseas counterparts.

South African groups as a whole differed from both overseas

samples in several other key respects. The active hostility indices of English-speaking and Coloured male South African students differed significantly from Australian students in that they were far higher, with English-speaking students showing more hostility than Coloureds. Afrikaans student indices were comparable with Australian students'. Coloured female students showed significantly more hostility than Australians, but Afrikaans and English-speaking females did not.

On an anxiety index, Coloured and English-speaking males showed extremely high levels of anxiety while Afrikaners showed less anxiety than Australians. Coloured males scored extremely high, being over four times more anxious than Australians. While there was no significant difference in the anxiety indices between Australian females and white South African females, Coloured females showed more anxiety. English-speaking females were less anxious than Afrikaans. Finally, calculation of a passive-aggressive index showed that all South African groups, male and female, showed higher scores than Australians, with English and Coloured males showing three times more passive-aggression than Australian males and Coloured females showing four times more. English-speaking females were the least passive-aggressive of the South African groups.[14]

In the second study of this series, a group of nurses was given a battery of tests to complete containing the MMPI as well as two projective techniques, the Rorschach Ink Blot Test and the Thematic Apperception Test (TAT). Coloured, Afrikaans and English-speaking nurses were then compared on these three measures and the results helped to further substantiate the finding of the first MMPI study, namely that Coloureds were not in fact psychotic but had psychotic-like personality styles caused by the pressure of living under the *apartheid* system.[15]

The Rorschach Inkblot Test is just what it says – a series of ink blots, many in black and white, some in colour. I had used the Rorschach quite extensively both in my practice and at the hospital to do research on schizophrenia and I believed that it would go a long way to substantiate the findings of the first study. The TAT, a series of black and white pictures, and the Rorschach are depth tests which help a trained tester check the validity of a person's overt statements; when you are shown a blot or a picture and asked to interpret it, you do not know what the psychologist is looking for in the same way as you do if he asks you questions.

Afrikaans nurses showed very much the same patterns on the MMPI as the Afrikaans student females of the first study did, except that the gap between Afrikaans nurses and English-speaking and Coloured nurses was much greater. Again, Afrikaans profiles showed little disturbance, remaining in the normal range. If anything, they appeared to have a tighter personality organisation than student females, who showed a slight elevation on mania which was absent in the nursing sample.

Coloured nurses showed a pattern similar to students in the first study, but significantly they peaked, on average, above the cut-off point on hypomania and schizophrenia scales. Active hostility indices of Coloured nurses were extremely high while anxiety and passive-aggression indices were not significantly different from white nurses'.

The MMPI results of white English nurses were spectacular, showing marked disturbances in hypochondria, psychopathic deviancy and obsessive-compulsive tendencies. They were also highly anxious and exceptionally hostile. The overriding impression I got from these profiles was of people whose discomfort and fear was expressed as a definite confusion and disorganisation of personality. They were in trouble and used depression, acting-out, hypochondria and the like to express it. The Rorschach and TAT findings of English nurses supported this interpretation. Their TAT stories were full of fear, dread and unresolved anxiety, while those of the Afrikaans nurses reflected a high level of contentment and tranquillity.

Coloured nurses tended to explore the TAT in order to focus on themes of oppression, victimization and helplessness. They actively sought out any underdog in the pictures and built up oppressive forces against him or her. They showed a marked degree of communality and a tendency to express anger through the use of collectively approved passive rituals rather than through any notion of individual anger and hurt. There was no evidence of schizophrenic disturbance in Coloured nurses; on the contrary, their style of perceptual functioning was acutely accurate and factual.

Something emerged, however, which concerned and disturbed me: I could find little sign of adult emotional maturity. Most of the Coloured nurses seemed to be caught in early adolescent modes of thinking and feeling, indicating that personality growth had been 'frozen' at a given point. There appeared to be little potential for movement beyond it. There was a kind of tunnel-vision approach to the test cards with the nurses tending to see only conventional and socially approved material: there was no flexibility, spontaneity or desire to explore beyond the obvious.

On the Rorschach, the English nurses tended to show disintegration of personality; they just were not able to organise the material and were explosive and impulsive. It was clear that emotional demands made on them were managed fragmentally and inconsistently. There were occasional and spontaneous bursts of creativity and insight with an overall tendency to make no use of their intellectual powers at all. In other words, their responses were either flat and dead or alive and hypomanic. Over half the subjects suffered from depression. Again, the personality organization of these people was labile and reflected a high level of anxiety.

Ordinarily, in my experience, people who show these levels of anxiety and personality disintegration have histories of mental illness, yet less than 5% of the English nurses had such histories. Somehow these people were getting sufficient support from their environments to ensure that their personalities did not disintegrate in the face of chronic high tension. The central disorganization was somehow contained by strict conformity to the psychological framework of their daily lives.

I found this puzzling. There were in these people two levels of personality organization – a superficial conventional 'crust', as it were, in which the subjects showed an ability to perceive stimuli appropriately and normally. Inside this were the explosive labile disorganized processes I have described above. This pattern was not new to me. I had seen it before – in psychoneurotic and character-disordered mental patients. What was surprising was that I had never seen it in such large numbers of 'normal' people, people who managed to contain, somehow, the two parts without major evidence of overt pathology.

Normal people have three levels of personality organization. If you like, on one level demands are made on a person by society, and on another level the person is subject to his own infantile or personal needs; the unique personality of the person emerges through the interaction of these two pressures. This interaction creates a third level of personality which shows how well and in what way a person had adjusted to the demands of his daily life. If his third level is missing or is only marginally present, then something has interfered with the normal process of growth.

The only way such a person could survive without becoming overtly mentally disturbed would be if the society itself were organised in such a way as to tolerate such personality organisation and also to offer more support and acceptance than is normally the case. Mental illness and symptoms only occur when a person comes into *conflict* with his or her experience of reality. That is, when a person behaves in a way that brings negative results in significant areas. Under the pressure of this punishment, normal people either adjust to the new demands or they decide to leave the community or the context because it does not suit them. Mental symptoms are signs of *stress* and they happen when, for some reason or other, the person cannot leave the situation *and* cannot adjust.

Since the personality structure of these people showed high levels of stress and disorganization and they did not collapse, it followed that their society reflected this structure in its own organization. The intriguing question was how was this support given? Students and academics get support and security from working in a closed, ineffectual system; academics are supposed to be critical – let them criticise harmlessly and they do not think they are being repressed. What did people who do not fit into this kind of community do? Obviously each social layer in the English, Afrikaans and Coloured communities provided its own support system; but how? It was some time before I was able to answer these questions properly, but I knew that the answer would lie in the way the functions of apparently normal institutions were being bent to support the pathological life-styles of the people I studied.

On the Rorschach, Afrikaner nurses showed distinctly different profiles from either the English or the Coloured nurses. Their anxiety levels were very low and there was little evidence of stress or conflict. These Afrikaner women tended to have neat, ordered minds, characterized by highly conventional and uniform patterns of functioning; their emotions were integrated in an orderly fashion. Developmentally, these subjects had lived lives that had allowed their personalities to form in much the same way as anyone living in a normal country. If there was any anxiety at all, it was related to minor infringements of the social rules; worry about conforming, for example; not anxiety about *not* conforming or the consequences of rebellious acts, but anxiety about whether or not the person had conformed enough. There was a strong need to please, to do exactly what was expected.

In one way, though, the Rorschach profiles of these Afrikaner nurses, when compared with profiles recorded in other parts of the world, were not normal. Although all my subjects were adults, their personality profiles were not the protocols of fully functioning normal adults. There was so little anxiety and so little conflict as to constitute, in fact, a pathologically low level of functioning. Most normal people need a degree of conflict and tension in their lives to act as a means of creating frustration so that tolerances and perseverance, for example, can be learned. This lays the foundation for a personality based on the demands of reality rather than on the kind of artificial reality that children face. These women showed no creativity, no energy, no evidence of non-conformism – no sign that they thought or acted or experienced emotions beyond the confines of the expectancies laid down for them by their communities. In Coloured and English subjects, even though there was no outlet for these tendencies, they were at least there.

The Afrikaner nurses' personalities had been shaped by their community to such a degree that there was almost a lack of individual personality. So effective was the cocoon in which they had been brought up that at all levels these people thought felt and acted *exactly* as they had been told to. So conventional and so similar were their profiles that I rechecked them and rescored them several times to be sure.

This kind of protocol is usually found in normal societies in young people between the ages of ten and thirteen, where the demands made on them by school and home are so all-encompassing and so singularly focused that no reference is made or expectancy given to other levels of functioning. So you get conventional, conformist responses to Rorschach cards related to the most obvious shapes seen in the card. For example, Card One looks like a bat. Children see a bat; it is simple, conventional and obvious. Older children, adolescents and adults give this response first and then go on to 'play' with the card, trying to see what else there can be in it. In fact, most people enjoy the Rorschach because it is an opportunity to let loose and be creative.

Creative young children and adolescents are able to find other things in the card, conventional things such as a mask, a fox, but as people get older they tend to develop personalised responses with each person seeing things according to how his or her personality has developed. The cards are structured so that any one of a hundred responses is possible to any one card. Normal adults and adolescents give a wide range of responses – some see furry animals, some use depth and see a valley, for example; others turn the card up-side-down and see mountains. There is no correct response and this is where the cards have their value – they allow a person to show you the whole range of his or her functioning.

Now, when a whole batch of adults whose average age, incidentally, was twenty-eight, score in the same way as pre-adolescent children do, then it is clear that their society has had the same effect on them as ordinary societies do on pre-adolescents. In other words, my Afrikaans subjects functioned as if they were in school. No more was demanded of them than is demanded of schoolchildren. It explains why their personal development was focused purely around the cultural expectations imposed on it. It is as if these people were permanent children in a permanent schoolroom being watched by a permanent teacher. The development of their personalities was geared exclusively to the teacher and to the other 'pupils' – no hint of trying to reject the teacher or of ever wanting to leave the classroom.

Intrigued and startled by this finding, I took a small group of people whom I knew and who were Afrikaans and gave them Rorschachs to do. It was not a formal study, the groups were not closely matched; they consisted of university and hospital staff members, students, patients and friends. I wanted to see if this style of functioning really was common to Afrikaners as a whole. I wanted to see what would happen if I 'tested the limits'. Let me explain: if I gave you a Rorschach card, you would first respond *characteristically* – and this is an important level of functioning – which I write down. This tells me how you normally react in situations. If I wanted to know more about what you *could* do, I would push you: 'Come on, what else can you see?' Then, 'OK, can you see this? What about that?' I would point out hard to see things to see if you could spot and hold them perceptually. This is 'testing the limits'. When we had finished, I would go over the material and see how you reacted to being pushed – whether it was difficult for you, whether or not you pushed yourself, whether it upset you and whether you learned to do it yourself (that is, if I pushed you on Card One, did you push yourself on Card Two or did I have to push you again?), and so on.

All this would help me form an accurate picture of your personality.[16]

In this study, I found males and females functioned in much the same way as the nurses did. When I tested the limits, I found that some of them, the more creative, could produce alternative responses, but they only did so if they were pushed. Most of them did not learn to test on their own and when I pushed them they seldom came up with creative or subtle answers. They simply produced more obvious and conventional shapes. They could see subtle and complex things if I asked them, but they never learned to look for them on their own. English subjects on the other hand, responded well to being pushed and related well to the things they saw. For instance, a normal adult when pushed can see a small furry rabbit on Card One and normally exclaims with pleasure and goes on to tell you how they love or hate or fear furry animals. Then they go on to find other things buried in the card. Afrikaners did not do this: if pushed they'd say, 'Yes, there's a rabbit' – and then stop.[17]

The results of the various studies confirmed what I had suspected; Afrikaners were not deprived developmentally of mature perceptions or sensitivity – they were there in their personalities – they simply formed no part of their cultural perspective. They did not show sensitivity or depth perception because they *did not know how to*; in their experience of reality, there was *no need*. At the time, I was struck by how similar this culture appeared to how one writer earlier had described the Dutch settler community – isolated, insular and not interested in art, education or science, neither wanting any of those things or producing any. While the twentieth-century Afrikaner is undoubtedly educated and has made use of science and the arts, it occurred to me that few Afrikaners have applied the learning and insight gained from these disciplines to crucial social problems or, indeed, to the art of personal reflection. In the arts, the only material of any substance has come from Afrikaans writers who are in rebellion and who are frequently ostracised and, in some cases, even exiled.

These studies told me something about the personality styles and clinical pathology of students and nurses and assorted others, but I still had no idea of the kinds of attitudes and values held by the average Coloured or African person. Coloured students were obviously deeply effected by the processes of *apartheid* and nurses even more so, but because the studies had had to be done discreetly and covertly, I had not been able to probe too deeply into their feelings – what I uncovered was, as I have said, a structure of personality, not a content. In my clinical work and, especially after March 1972 in my private practice, however, it was much easier to get people to talk. Actually it just poured out.

Coloured people organise themselves around two polemic attitudes which apply irrespective of sex, social class and education. At root, this revolves around whether the person is in favour of the existing Coloured way of life or in favour of rejecting it; whether a person could see through what was happening to the Coloured people or not.

Within the framework of South Africa, the Coloured people have always had a somewhat privileged position amongst the country's non-whites, largely arising out of their familiarity with white customs and languages. When the Afrikaans Nationalists took over in 1948, they set out as part of a deliberate (and little-appreciated) policy to duplicate the pattern used to separate white from black, amongst all the non-white groups. A policy of systematic differentiation was established whereby the non-white groups were organised hierarchically so that Coloureds and Asians would in all practical matters be better off than Africans. Coloured education, Coloured wages, pensions, allowances, facilities and the way a Coloured person is treated differ hierarchically from both Asians and Africans, who in turn differ from each other.[18]

One result of this is that there exists a secondary form of *apartheid* between those who are most like the whites, namely the Coloureds and Asians, and those who are not. Added to this has been the subtly propagated idea that the Coloured has a special relationship with the Afrikaner (language and culture) that puts him at the head of the non-white group. The government has actively fostered this type of thinking not only by discriminating between its treatment of the different non-whites, but also by encouraging various Coloured leaders to express this view openly.

The issue for the Coloured people I studied was whether or not they were prepared to live with this ideology. I knew the Coloured people were bitter and resentful towards the whites; what came as a surprise to me was discovering some of the reasons why this was so.

Fundamentally, Coloured people who are grouped around the first pole mentioned above, resent being treated as inferior. Fair enough. This is especially the case with educated or skilled people who feel they possess the necessary qualifications. It is also to be found, for example, amongst labourers and shop assistants who object to discrimination in public places, on buses, and so on. But the reason why this is objected to is because it excludes them. They do not object to discrimination *as such* but simply that *they* are discriminated against. I asked my subjects how they would ideally like to see a future South Africa. They paid lip-service to altruistic aims like a 'free multiracial' South Africa, but on being pressed they inevitably adopted a 'pragmatic' stance and saw their future with the whites as partners in ruling a South Africa from which Africans were excluded.

This attitude was thoroughgoing. My Coloured subjects showed the same kind of social distance towards other non-white groups as I had found among whites. They would not marry an African and only under exceptional circumstances would they befriend one. This was in 1973, long before Soweto and the riots in Cape Town in 1976 had united Coloured opinion more realistically. Few of the subjects had regular contact with Africans and most had less contact with Africans and Asians than they had with whites. Contact with an African was to be avoided in case, I was told, neighbours started thinking you had African relatives.

Not only was there far greater prejudice expressed towards Africans than whites but fear of Africans was frequently and readily offered as an excuse. For the Coloured, lumped with the African in the day-to-day public reality of his country, the blacks posed far more of a threat to him than they did for whites. Whites were organised, powerful, educated, they had an army, they could control the Africans, whereas Coloured people felt they could easily be swamped by them. In some respects, Coloured people were glad of the Group Areas Act. Even if it did deprive them of their traditional homes, it did at least keep Africans out. And job reservation kept their jobs safe for them.

Asked about their feelings towards whites, most subjects said they preferred dealing with Afrikaners than with English people: 'At least we know where we stand,' was a typical response. 'The English, we don't respect, they are hypocrites. The Afrikaner does exactly what he says – there's no social games, no pretence.' The more educated the person, the more fervently he or she expressed a sense of being white-orientated. This was expressed in terms of notions of full equality associated with white status in such countries as America or Britain. But within South Africa, it was clear that, at all levels, subjects preferred dealing with Afrikaners rather than English whites. In the long run, the Afrikaner brought less trouble and less disruption to their lives.

In a fundamental sense a deep mystique was attached to the Afrikaner, who was seen by many of the people I interviewed as strangely powerful and omnipotent, even when they disliked or hated him. Many had personal experiences of Afrikaners that encouraged them to believe that, inside, they were not quite the tyrants they were made out to be.

To these people, the Afrikaner was an immovable presence firmly imposed on the present and future of South Africa. They were the framework around which the Coloured person had to build his life. And, not surprisingly, the Afrikaners were seen as the focus, obsessively so, of Coloured life and activity; 'English people are weak, easily duped, phoney – the Afrikaner runs rings around them.' Consistent contempt was expressed towards English South Africans by Coloureds from all strata of society. The psychology behind this is important. The English are used as a communally approved scapegoat in a matrix dominated by Afrikaner skill and power on the one hand, and the threat posed by the African mass on the other. Caught between these two poles, the Coloured person conceives of three possible courses of social action: a revolution in which they are engulfed by the Africans; they join the Afrikaner and become part of white South Africa; and English liberalism (and through it, the humanism of the outside world) provides a peaceful reasonable alternative. By 1973, when the bulk of these interviews was done, the last of these three possibilities had long since been discarded. A quote from one interviewee:

'The United Nations, the Americans – nobody has ever done anything to help us. Talk, yes – and a few really useless things like boycotting South African sherry. What have we got to hope for from the white English in South Africa? The Afrikaner has taken the country over completely from under the *Engelse* noses. How many countries in the world win wars and then give back what they have won to the enemy? No. The English are too comfortable here. They'll never help us so we have no choice but to turn to the Afrikaner.'

The feeling of inadequacy and self-hatred experienced by a Coloured person, the humiliation of not being treated properly, at being dominated by the Afrikaner, are not faced as a reality, as *major personal* problems. Just as the English use their institutions to cushion themselves from their experience of fear and anxiety, so the Coloureds institutionalise this by a projection outwards. It is 'they', the English, who are fooled by the Afrikaner, who run around like the Afrikaner's servants, who believe all the Nationalist propaganda and so on. English-speaking whites are sneered at and condemned as a means of preventing the Coloured person from having the same feelings about himself and his community.

This institutionalised projection fitted closely the theory I proposed earlier in this chapter about the structure of Coloured personality. I noted then that the functioning of the Coloured students and nurses was psychotic-like but without the kind of disintegration in personality normally associated with mental patients. I suggested that they therefore in some way must be supported by their communities, that their communities tolerate and regard as normal what elsewhere would be considered abnormal. Projection is a device used by psychotic and paranoid people to cope with their stress. The institutionalised projection of Coloured society thus could be a psychotic like device that has become a normal means of avoiding facing a disturbing reality. Just as English whites busy themselves abnormally in normal institutionalised rituals based on fragments of reality, so Coloureds use projection. Both are pathological means of keeping anxiety from breaking into full consciousness and so acting as a motivation for change. This psychology has been encouraged and abetted by governmental agencies who have effectively isolated, emotionally, the Coloured community. By using sophisticated psychological techniques and by controlling the information and education available to Coloureds, they have ensured that the average Coloured person devotes his energy to keeping his or her 'identity' separate, focusing all the while on the Afrikaner and Afrikanerdom. The English watch the Afrikaner out of fear and anxiety about what he might do next but basically not wishing to belong to the Afrikaner community. The Coloureds in my study watched the Afrikaner for signs of their being accepted into the ranks of Afrikanerdom.[19]

The system in which Coloureds live is structurally repressive and creates psychological problems but it is applied in such a way that the daily content is not overtly oppressive. Thus it is possible for a Coloured person, once he or she accepts the limits of the system and provided they do not break the rules, to live a kind of a life on the tit-bits of contact and status that whites permit. These processes serve to narrow the quality of life expected by a Coloured person while at the same time not closing down access sufficiently to prevent a hopelessness occurring. If it did, it might allow the deep depression underlying Coloured behaviour to penetrate their narrowed consciousness enough to make rebellion a viable alternative.

A truly repressive regime sows the seeds of its own overthrow by closing all outlets and contacts between the rulers and the ruled. In South Africa this is not the case and this factor alone has been instrumental in the way Coloured communities – and by inference, the black communities – have been shaped and controlled. In addition, though, this fine balance of repression and contact is put to another use by the government. I interviewed a middle-aged man and his wife who were active in formal politics as members of a delegation protesting about conditions through the services of a liberal white MP. Despite the Coloured couple's deep conviction about what they wanted to achieve, their contact with the government and its agencies together with the special attention they were given (they proudly talked of being 'watched', for example, by the Special Branch or of being fetched for a meeting in a government car) had become objects of status in their own community, this despite the fact that their delegation was being hopelessly circumvented and ridiculed.

The man confided in me that the minister himself had spoken to him privately, given him his own personal telephone number and asked him to get in touch any time he felt like it or if something should come up. Over time, this 'arrangement' became an accepted part of the couple's life, as it did in many other such couples in the same position. Unbeknown to them, however, they were being used as part of a highly effective and thoroughgoing plan developed by the Department of Coloured Affairs to gain regular and accurate information about the feelings of the leaders of the Coloured community. At the same time these people passed information for the government back to the Coloured community enabling them to ease situations or to incriminate and discredit potential threats.

All these contacts were monitored by the Special Branch of the

South African police, and in fact formed the basis for a successful security operation which the police have conducted over years. The experiences of my subjects were typical: contacts they formed with officials were carefully nurtured and maintained in accordance with the social demands of the situation. The authorities knew precisely how to behave, who to use and who not to use to manipulate and control the community. So you have a situation where potentially dangerous people in delegations were snubbed, never given the status the authorities know is vital for the individual's psychological survival in the community, while 'safe' Coloureds were set up as 'leaders'. 'Confidential' information was given to make these selected people appear more effective in the eyes of their community than they were.

At no cost to the government, and with minimum effort, the authorities set up a leadership core to whom the Coloured community listen. The process is never discussed – it just happens. Smoothly and effectively. As time went on, my subject and his government contact exchanged information regularly. He was made to feel as if he and this contact were working together and:

'Since we both want the same things, you know, peaceful change, gradual multiracialism – we were united, you know, against the real roughnecks, the rebels who want it all now. So of course they help me and I help them. When J . . . was beginning to get quite big in the community, I got worried. I knew it would lead to trouble. So I mentioned it to my "pal" and he agreed with me. So I told them what I knew, everything, even the gossip. It was an informal chat, man, nothing serious, you know. Nothing they didn't know.'

The people I studied had no apparent idea of the role they played in helping the authorities – they genuinely believed in the sincerity of their contacts and the profundity of their role in helping the Coloured community. The subjects who worked with the government were made to think that their contacts were accidental, just chance happenings; their contact was inevitably 'just passing' or 'just happened to pop in' to the Coloured Affairs building at the right time. This gave the subjects the impression that it was not an organised and official link – to them it was 'personal', friendly. But in studying the frequency of these 'chance' meetings with white authorities, there was an obvious difference between the number of 'chance' meetings made by these 'safe' Coloureds with white authorities and the number of contacts with 'unsafe' Coloureds made by white authorities. The study showed these 'chance' meetings to be methodical, thorough and well-organised.

Over and above this informal network, there is the structure of formal political organizations with more overt and direct lines of contact between the authorities and the Coloured community. But these structures are of little value because they are not tied to Coloured feeling, they are not subtle – they are too obviously show-pieces and the Coloured people who take a leading part in these structures are too obviously bought and paid for. The very antagonism the bulk of the Coloured community feel towards these formal institutions has helped the efficiency of the informal networks precisely because the people involved are used subtly and informally.

As I mentioned earlier, there is a second pole around which the Coloured people are organized. In 1972 and 1973, when I first studied it, it was very much less prominent, less important than the pole I have described above. I refer to the completely anti-white and anti-West pole that I found in some students, well-established in adolescent school pupils and in some professionals such as social workers and teachers.

I encountered it initially in a sample of Coloured prematric pupils at several schools run by religious denominations in Cape Town. It was then not a definite political perspective but it was a sullenness, a moodiness and unresponsiveness that I had never before encountered in Coloured people. In interviews, the reasons emerged loud and clear.

For a start, they mistrusted anything that was connected with or even remotely white. This included Western notions of freedom, democracy, humanitarianism, even music in some cases if it was associated with establishment South African whites. This was understandable in a community which was highly culturally orientated towards white values and white ideology – the only way not to be compromised by Afrikanerdom was to reject everything that was. Thus these adolescents were anti-religion, anti-drugs, anti-alcohol, anti-cinema, anti-fashion, anti-makeup, and so on. They identified closely with the Africans and their sense of reality was perhaps the most aware of any group I had studied because they mistrusted the artefacts on which their parents had built their community.

They mistrusted and despised their parents and their parents' values – they trusted *only* one another. And in this lay their strength. They turned their adolescent fervour, creativity and energy into being properly and thoroughly rebellious in a way and with an organization that no ordinary adolescent usually achieves. There was no coercion, there was simply a communal spirit shared by all. Thus these adolescents' dreams and fantasies, normally left behind as they grow up or lost in some cause, became directed and energized in reality. They formed organizations and action groups that accurately and effectively helped them rebel against the reality they faced.

They did not argue and confront – they rebelled quietly and safely amongst themselves; they used passivity and sullenness; as time went on, they became better organized, learnt to shift their leadership so that they could not be infiltrated, and they chose to act in ways that were effective yet safe. They formed in fact the only healthy community I came across in South Africa. Amongst these people I could find little evidence of the psychopathy, anxiety or fear that characterized their parents.

By and large, these people were Marxist-orientated; they were communal and behaved accordingly by rejecting the trappings of both 'imperial' communism *and* Western society. It was the first time I had seen a communal system operate that was not based on a unifying personality, that was not a personality cult. Hatred for the Afrikaner and for the English had galvanized these people into a realistic appraisal of the situation and they saw their survival in terms of a slow methodical rebellion which protected them and yet gave them a sense of purpose and direction other than that postulated for them by the authorities and their parents.

The first manifestation of their intentions was in their dealing with whites and those in authority such as parents and teachers. They behaved passively with them and avoided contact far more so than the average teenager; they formed extra-mural study and action groups which they used as little communities of their own. There was no sex discrimination and no age discrimination – anyone could voice an opinion and a direction. They planned outings and the like designed to strengthen their sense of separateness and isolation from both whites and their parents. Much of this was loosely organized and informal. And in 1973, there was nothing that could be remotely identified as a common policy or a political programme – what existed was a consensus of opinion.

Later, though, this rebelliousness achieved astounding results because it was this very organization and spirit that ensured the temporal success of the uprisings in the Cape and in Soweto in 1976.

For three years, between 1967 and 1970, I lived in one of those pockets in Cape Town in which a kind of multiracial society flourished. I studied these people more by accident than by design, and yet it was an experience that gave me a valuable insight into the kind and level of contact that occurs in South Africa between black and white when *apartheid* is absent.

The first thing that characterized this community was the absence of racial discrimination; the common problem facing these people was one of survival, earning enough money to live comfortably. The community was comprised of a mixed bag of Afrikaans and English poor whites, Coloured and Malay shopkeepers and assistants and labourers. At the end of the street lived the 'enemy' – a small contingent of predominantly Afrikaans policemen and their families as well as a small group of young middle-class English whites living in renovated houses that had formerly belonged to Coloureds. The actions of the 'enemy' were the focal point of interest. The English community avoided and ignored everyone else, complaining all the time about the way the blacks and Coloureds were encroaching on the area; the only contact I had with them was when one came round to ask if we would sign a petition to have a proposed bus terminus moved away because it would increase the number of blacks in the area. The policemen's children terrorised the neighbourhood and the policemen were resented because they beat up Coloured troublemakers but not white.

The second characteristic was the easy interaction between families in the neighbourhood. While most families were either white or Coloured, some were both. Contact between the races was social: men drank together, usually in the *shebeens* (illegal liquor outlets). A 'dealer', usually a marginally more affluent white, would buy demi-johns of cheap wine, for example, and sell it by the glass to non-whites and others. Political issues by and large were irrelevant to this community and cross-racial interaction occurred along the lines which one would expect to find in any single-race community, based on inter-family squabbles, gossip and the conflicts that families had with the authorities.

Whites and Coloureds in this community showed no racial prejudice towards one another. However, both expressed fear and prejudice towards Africans, mingled with curiosity. Children mixed
freely and played together. What was crucial was that this community united within itself against the authority figures. The most
bitter and vociferous complaint was directed against the police who
caused many problems but not for the obvious reasons.

The police in the area went to exaggerated lengths to *avoid*
trouble as we would normally understand it. If members of the community went in to make a complaint of rowdiness or drunkenness,
they tried to dissuade the *complainant* from 'causing trouble' or
from 'being a nuisance'. Sometimes, they would pretend to investigate or pretend to write complaints into the chargebook; if you
went in later or the next day, there was no entry and no one knew
anything about your complaint. The officer who had been on duty
was never available, and so on.[20] However, should a complaint be
made by a passer-by or by one of the affluent English, police intervention was swift and effective – particularly if the complaint concerned racial mixing. I witnessed this phenomenon on several
occasions. Robbery, sexual assault, rowdy *shebeens*, stabbings,
drug abuse, muggings all took place with little or no police interest.
But a complaint about a multiracial party or a white passer-by being
accosted by a Coloured brought the police to the scene promptly.
Twice as quickly if there were Africans involved.[21]

The result of this was that while the area contained no racial fric-
tion that one could readily identify, the level of unchecked criminal
activity was relatively high. And a substantial degree of criminal behaviour was brought into the community by whites from outside.
Several housewives, for example, complained of being proposi-
tioned by white men who walked or drove through the area over
lunchtime. Certain of the white shopkeepers who worked nearby
were the subject of complaint by several Coloured employees in the
area. Some examples: A white shopowner employed several Coloured female shop assistants and approached the one he wanted to
sleep with by threatening to fire the girl if she did not accept the conditions of her employment. In other shops employing African
females, to whom the same conditions of employment applied,
there was more than just the threat of being fired. If an African did
not possess the infamous pass allowing that person to live and work
in the area, he or she faced arrest. So failure to comply with her

boss's demands would result, at worst, in being shipped back to the 'homelands' through being reported to the Bantu Affairs Department; at best, it would result in the loss of a job.

Many African women had to comply. The risks of not doing so were too high. If these things were reported, the police tended to show an interest only if a complaint was made by a white woman despite the fact that a white man who propositions a Coloured woman is breaking the law – the Immorality Act. Other complaints concerned the way policemen and shopowners (white) used violence at the slightest opportunity. If an African made a mistake, he was hit; if he protested, he would be taken outside, round the back and beaten up by his white employer.

Another object of complaint was the behaviour of policemen towards Coloured shopkeepers and barrow vendors. Some policemen would threaten to arrest a vendor or shopkeeper on some pretext or other, then let him go but 'confiscate' those items of merchandise that they wanted – usually fruit and vegetables. The procedure was routine and accepted, albeit reluctantly. A Malay shopkeeper, for example, was once caught smoking *cannabis resin* with three friends in his back yard by a policeman. The policeman did not charge him but threatened to unless he provide him with a regular supply of the drug.

What was important was the level of corruption that this community accepted as normal. Racism was *used* as a commodity to be traded in the area; they were exploited, sometimes brutalized, always victimized because they were vulnerable to racism and because they were unable to protect themselves as a white or Coloured community could. The fact that they were not organised racially as everyone else was, was seized upon and manipulated. It also proved that white and Coloured could live amicably side-by-side without the conflicts or the kind of anxiety and depression that I had encountered in segregated South Africa. Race for these people was not an issue; corruption and the misuse of power was. One of the significant social effects of *apartheid* is that it permits exploitation by anyone in power – any minor official, any white, a shopkeeper, Coloureds towards Africans – all behave in ways that would not be accepted in other communities.

I come finally to the Urban African community. Most of what I have written about the Coloured people applies to these people but there are some important differences. When young African school-children and students rose up in the six-month confrontation that started in Soweto in 1976, they were reacting not only to the cruelty and oppression of the government's African Affairs departments but also against the way of life that their elders had adopted. If Soweto came as a surprise to the government, it came as a double surprise to many Africans and other non-whites who live and work in locations around white cities. The government was surprised because it had not even conceptualized the possibility of trouble from that direction; urban Africans were surprised because their young people broke the rules and turned the *game* of rebelling that many African engage in into an *actual* revolt.

Let me explain: earlier in Chapter One, I described how a labouring African population had arisen as people flocked to the cities in search of employment and the wealth offered by South Africa's growing industrial sector. Over time, this urban black population expanded enormously and, with it, the kind of black infrastructure that it needed for its own existence and support. Within the framework of historical separatism, the Afrikaner slowly extended this until it became the system of *apartheid*. Great care was taken, however, to ensure that these urban systems developed in such a way as to ensure the maintenance of the *status quo* whereby blacks served the role required of them by whites.

The boer, fully familiar with the ways of his own Africans, systematically applied this system to the rest of South Africa's non-whites. For a start, the Afrikaner recognised that the need for the Africans to have their basic requirements met overwhelmed all other concerns; he needed employment, wealth and prosperity long before he needed education and rights. Give him a little at a time and he will, like an animal being tamed, be satisfied – but not sufficiently to make him want the secondary needs of education and rights. Giving him not quite enough leaves him still hungry for more without being desperate. Keep this process up, add services and an education system of poor quality and little value, give him plenty of harmless outlets and all his apparent needs will be met. Let him see the white's wealth and he will demand and want it – not his education or his rights – because he thinks he already has those. He has no real *leisure* time to sit back contented with his lot and think about his children's future. Give him little by little a share of this wealth and he will be satisfied. But above all, at all times, this wealth must be minimal so that he never gets into a position in which normal middle class values can develop.

Afrikaans governments since 1910 and especially during Verwoerd's era (remember he was in charge of African Affairs for over sixteen years) have carried out this policy to the letter. The psychology behind it is cunning: people demand better things for themselves such as political and human rights only when they have their basic needs met – that is, their standard of living is high enough to allow them the luxury of planning ahead, thinking of their children and generally thinking beyond their immediate day-to-day circumstances. The Afrikaner state took two steps to control this while appearing on the surface to improve things for the African.

First it ensured that the only middle class that developed in South Africa was one that did so entirely dependant on the *apartheid* system. It eliminated businessmen and shopkeepers outside the framework by means of the Group Areas Act and ministerial directives that made it illegal or difficult to work outside a black area. Then it allowed Indian and Asian traders, who form a very small percentage of the population of non-whites, to fill the gaps left behind – a far more manageable and more easily controlled group. Within the African and Coloured areas it then permitted the indigenous middle class to flourish and to lead very profitable existences far better than they had outside their areas and at a level far above that which they would have had in the open market.

The authorities also protected these traders, allowing them to form monopolies, raise prices and to make excessive profits through corrupt and devious business practices. Such a middle class becomes highly dependant for its existence on the system of *apartheid* and, moreover, it is almost guaranteed to support the system. The only people who get rich or who are permitted to raise their heads above the poverty line *have* to be, therefore, *apartheid* supporters.

Secondly, the government also ensured that the standards of living in African and Coloured communities remained low *even while their apparent incomes rose*. The government knew that it would face trouble if non-white wages remained fixed below the level necessary to make a living, so it had to make gradual increases and yet keep the black inhabitants suffering in relative poverty. It did this by deliberately manipulating and creating economic circumstances that suited its own self-protecting policies.

To start with, the government set about controlling the companies and industries that provided for the basic needs of the major non-white communities. Through *Broederbond* co-ordinated action,[22] it controlled in time the Dairy industries, the bread industry and the industries providing the buses and transport to and from the townships.[23] While this was being done, the government was effectively eliminating black trade unions.[24] Finally, it was in a position to allow the wage increases necessary to keep non-whites quiet but only because, *for every increase in earning capacity*, it could effectively *restore* the necessary poverty balance by increasing the cost of staple foods and transport. Also, if it had to, it could reduce the level of subsidies to the industries providing the staples thus forcing them to increase costs.[25] The final link in the chain were the beerhalls and liquor stores that tranquillize and entertain the workforce. These are government-controlled and operate at huge profit.[26]

The result of all this is that the urban African communities that have emerged in South Africa are of a certain kind: like the English and Coloured communities, they are fully integrated into the *apartheid* system and, in large measure, have become corrupted by it. I was not able to measure the effects of all this as I was with whites and Coloured people but I did manage through interviews to establish one psychological pattern that resulted from the system.

The predominant concern amongst the lower class African people is, as per government design, with survival, coping with crowded conditions, poor services, poor pay and the high cost of living. Where any person rises above these conditions, he does so because he is either of the established middle class or is able to profit in some illegal, emotional or material way out of *apartheid*. Either way, both are dependant on the system. Some people do become genuine radicals and revolutionaries but very few. Most adopt one of two broad methods: they either support the system and get on with their own lives, or they become apparent radicals but use various means to avoid taking firm action or having to think clearly.

The latter use a very subtle form of self-deception. They play on the fact, well-supported inside and outside South Africa, that whites have created and run the system of *apartheid*. With the blame apparently well outside their own sphere of responsibility, they then use this as a means of excusing any responsibility on their part and as a right to behave with an inverted morality. The result of this has been to create a community which is in its own way as corrupt as that of the whites. Let me give some examples: African intellectuals, artists and professionals who remain in the country tend to do so because they need the situation to function properly. Their position allows them to be permanent victims without having to do anything about it – they usually make some contact with whites as a token of their rebellion and then proceed to institutionalise their 'victim' status by playing on the whites' guilt, sympathy and need to commit safe rebellious acts, sometimes engaging in petty instances of law-breaking.[27]

Some creative Africans fall in with this, sometimes genuinely, but often as a means of venting hostility in a safe and irresponsible way – sometimes in order to take revenge by psychopathic acting out and sometimes to make a profit. Some take revenge by exposing white radicals to the police; some by supplying them with drugs and some drift into engaging in robbery with white accomplices and others into shoplifting – a very lucrative, well-organised and extensive occupation in some areas.

Shoplifting in the big white shops in Cape Town, for example, supplies the African townships around Cape Town with a steady black market of luxury – not utilitarian – goods, mainly in clothing. This shoplifting is an important and unifying act of aggression; complete strangers will often help one another to steal such items as fashion boots, leather coats, exclusive-label suits and outfits:

'I was sitting in that luxury shoe shop in Adderley Street looking at this beautiful leather bag. Real leather man. R105. Across from me was another African woman. Big, fat, with big shopping bags. We both looked at the bag and at each other; she smiled and nodded, I went over and sat down next to her. "You want?" she said. I opened my eyes wide and grinned. "OK. You take and I'll move it for you." I got up, looked at the bag then put it next to her while I looked at another. When the assistant came over with the "buy something or leave" bit, I just shrugged, put the one I was looking at down and left. I waited outside. About five minutes later, she came out with her bags. "This one," she says, "just under the top packet." She'd hidden it there while the assistant was kicking me out. I thanked her and that was that.'

Abnormal values thus become highly valued. People who use the system to profit become heroes and hold high status in the community. Crass materializm is to be clearly seen, especially among the young African middle class and amongst certain classes of women. Successful criminals have a status quite unlike any I have found elsewhere; not only do they beat the system and make a profit, but amongst the women in the townships they are highly eligible because they are the only ones able to keep up the high standard of living that the materialism latent in the *apartheid* policy encourages.

I have talked thus far about those who use the system and who play with it. There are others, ordinary people who, like the young schoolchildren who provided the motivation for Soweto and like those who live in multiracial corners, have tried to avoid dealing with the system of *apartheid*. Let me give one example of some of them and how they are treated.

African contract labourers are not permitted to bring their wives or families with them to Cape Town. Many choose to live in the dormitories provided by the government and spend most of their free time in drinking, gambling and prostitution. These are encouraged by the authorities who both turn a blind eye and as I have shown provide the beerhalls because they do not want to encourage family life and all it entails.

Some contract workers, however, have rebelled against this, brought their families with them illegally and set up home in shanties around Cape Town. In these camps, the Africans have organized themselves, set up communal health centres, schools, committees, etc., all without the help of the government. They live rudimentary and poor existences but at least they have their families. This is the main reason behind the government's attempt at demolition of squatter camps. Not only do they provide a family life for the contract labourer and make him thus less likely to go back to the homelands, but they help break up the degenerate pattern of existence of the contract labourer. Further, it is well known that the squatter camps are the only African communities in South Africa which operate anywhere near to the normal idea of a community.

The squatter camps are, for the government therefore, a direct threat to the structure of society that has been set up for Africans in urban areas: within the squatter communities, normal human existence, normal human growth and, above all, a sense of normal communal conscience is possible. In destroying the camps, the government is trying to destroy the seeds of normal middle-class development and, in the final analysis, the seeds of revolution.[28] This is why such a fuss is made about the camps and why the government is slowly trying to bulldoze them down. They are crucial focal points and the government would be embarrassed – and shown up for what it is – if too many people became aware of their significance.

What I have tried to show in this chapter is not only the kind of psychological disturbance that *apartheid* creates but how the ordinary people who oppose the system – such as the schoolchildren, multiracial communities, the squatters – are crushed by it systematically and deliberately. The latter three are not guerrillas or revolutionaries, nor are they ideologists or radicals or student activists, nor do they want power or support a political grouping. They are ordinary people who spontaneously react to an inhuman system.

The chapter has also drawn attention to another central and significant fact: each of the ethnic groups studied suffers from a specific form of psychological disturbance. Outside of South Africa, I was convinced psychological systems such as these would collapse. No one in the modern world could survive with the kind of massive schizoid weight the average Coloured person carries; the English appear constrained and explosive while the Afrikaner . . .? I had trouble imagining how an average Afrikaner, transposed from Cape Town to a similar social position in New York or London and without a South Africa to run to when things got too much, would cope. These were all people who needed their societies to help them survive. Just as the Afrikaner needed his system, so I saw that the Coloured and African people *needed apartheid*. It had become so much a part of their lives, their status, their personal psychology, I felt sure that they could not live without it. Their energies, their creativities were all directed towards the system; manipulating, bending but always using it. In place of trying to *see* clearly, they preferred, I think, to be part of it.

Remember, I investigated the ordinary everyday lives of average citizens, not people who wanted to do away with or who were rebelling properly against *apartheid*. Not people bought by the government, nor committed revolutionaries. The people I spoke to wanted *theoretical* change but not if *they* had to do anything to get it.

Life, in many respects, was *too* comfortable, too safe and too familiar. In the words of a Coloured doctor:

'If you don't join radical movements, keep your nose out of trouble, you can live. I hate *apartheid*, I hate the Afrikaners but they don't harm *me*: I live OK.'

He had a good practice, drove a Mercedes, sent his children to private schools. This was the other side of the psychological picture – living a psychotic-like existence had its advantages and its rewards.

Chapter Five

The Legitimisation of Corruption

Most of the findings reported in the last three chapters were made in the space of a two-year period and so they came to me rather *en masse*, a confusing impact of sometimes conflicting ideas that needed sorting out and comprehending. It was, I remember, a very emotionally perplexing task, trying to sort out the data and relate it to the theories and structures I was developing. I had started off, I suppose, hoping to find a simple single-factor framework to explain and account for *apartheid*, and once I had exposed the myths of the Afrikaners' history, discovered the English South Africans' deeply embedded anxiety and what I thought were the crippling psychological effects of *apartheid*, I thought I had discovered my predators and their victims. But it was now turning out to be a far more complicated affair. Some of the victims did not behave like victims at all but like eager and active participants in the system, accepting their inferior status and all it involved for the chance to participate in the carve-up of the country. It was like a massively indulgent game in which all suffering was relative, all psychological hardship irelevant – the act of playing the game of *apartheid* was stimulation and excitement enough to make life worth living.

I could see this most clearly in the Coloured and African people I studied, possibly because at this stage I knew more about the kind of lives they led. The young white students I was familiar with were not yet actively involved in adult white society. The Africans who lived off other people's sufferings, who had channelled creative energy into a *demi-monde* of institutionalized petty crime or who prided themselves both on condemning and cheating the system, could not see anything wrong with their life-styles. They were not to blame for the system, the Afrikaners were. If *they* took advantage of others weaker than themselves it was not their fault: if the suckers did not like *apartheid*, they could revolt. The Coloured social workers I interviewed, who likewise hated the system but accepted government grants to go to university, could work for Coloured Affairs because the pay was good and treat the people under them – their coloured cases – with a brutality and indifference that made their white supervisors wince.[1] These were not atypical examples.

What I could not easily come to terms with was the way psychopathology had become institutionalized at each and every level. The victims survived because instead of reacting with upset, concern, shock or fear, they *institutionalized* callousness, indifference and the ethic of manipulation in order to insulate themselves from their inner feelings. Like the psychotic who lives with his own paranoia or hallucinations, it was *unreal*. Moreover, there was an inverted sense of unity and charity. There was always an underdog, someone else lower down on the social scale who could be the victim, who was worse off. I detected no unifying victim status amongst the people I studied, no sense of upward-directed anger; it was always someone else who caused it and someone else who paid the price.

The prevailing ethic of manipulation was derived from the cultural values of the Afrikaners; 'if you are not cunning, manipulative and ruthless,' I was informed, 'you are weak, a failure.' Normal human emotions of sympathy, concern and fairness were foreign, laughable – signs that you could not belong in South Africa. In their place you were expected to express your hurt, anger, dismay or whatever by one of the many *institutionalized* rituals available – 'drink yourself mindless, drive and cheat recklessly, bunk school or work, fuck indiscriminately, beat someone up . . . anything but show the proper emotions, the proper shock, or recognize the ungodly mess that you live in in the first place.' I had entered, it was clear, into a brutalized society living on its wits and on its nerves.

All this was much clearer to see in Coloured and African communities where the schisms were raw and exposed, more so than in the white English world in which I lived. I was easily able to relate the psychometric findings, the MMPI and Rorschach profiles, to the indifference and institutionalized psychological and physical *violence* that predominated in the lives of my subjects. They were clearly unstable even when trying to be calm and detached; the unreal was forever present.

The clinical evidence indicated that of the three groups studied, Afrikaans, English and Coloured, the Coloured person's personality structure was the most fragile, the most in contact with reality, albeit in a muted, psychotic way. They knew and understood the reality imposed by the Afrikaner because, I thought, they had more contact with it. The English did not and instead sensed, intuited if you like, the threat and the reality as it filtered down to them through their institutions. The Coloured person's creativity, his ideology and his survival are acted out in a far more fundamental physical world. If he behaves, he can live in peace. The situation is not hopeless and he can see that. Life for the non-white as defined by the Afrikaner is a simple equation; his avenue to normal living is to take part in the kind of ordinary pathology I have described. If he does not the options are clear, brutally and immediately clear. The personality profiles reflect this simple life or psychological death choice.[2]

What was far more difficult for me to understand, because until 1974 I did not start to get proper information about it, was white society. What avenues of life had the Afrikaner mapped out for the English? Theoretically I knew the structure should be the same. South Africa is an Afrikaans state through and through; wherever I had looked I had found values, ideas, social systems – even personality systems – that were direct copies of the Afrikaners'. I presumed that what I had seen in Coloured and African societies were the manifestations, peripheral and muted perhaps, of the Afrikaners' own social psychological structure. Africans and Coloureds had much more contact with the Afrikaners' executive reality than had the English and so were more likely to be accurate reflections of the structure of *apartheid* than those I could see occurring in the English sector.

What happened to the English rebellions? To their sensibility? To their progressive ideology? Were they content to play institution games, content to appear normal? If everyday Coloured and African creativity was absorbed into the psychological demands of the *apartheid* machine, perhaps, in some way I could not quite see, English South Africans too got something out of it – some pay-off that made it all worth while, the grease that turned the cogs?

There was an inconsistency I could not explain. The English were *the* threat for the Afrikaners and their anxiety and fear showed this. However, they turned a blind eye to what was going on in South Africa and to their own instincts. OK. Earlier I had explained it as a kind of deliberate clouding of issues, a failure to act on their feelings and to penetrate the fog they were enclosed in. But I was too kind, too naïve. As I got to know people better I learnt that people choose to be duped, to be blinded, to be ignorant, only if it gets them something. There was a very good reason why the English played dumb: it was worth their while. They were rewarded in as subtle and as complex a way as they were threatened; on analysis, I found the same structure of inverted manipulative morality to be at work in the English and in the same way as it applied in Coloured and African communities.

Earlier in Chapter One, I described the personality organization of boer communities, how everything was done through personal contact and pull. I wrote too of how the rule of law and the normal stable patterns of institutionalized functions were always made secondary to the personalities of the most powerful members of their community. Later, in Chapter Three, I described my own experience in an Afrikaans institution and how my rebelliousness had been effectively stopped by the way the authorities had *personalized* both their treatment of me and what I had to say. What I discovered through being in private practice was just how extensively applied was this system of personalism in English South Africa and how it worked. It was, I discovered, not only the means of ensuring that the English complied but also how they were controlled. It is the *modus operandi* of the *Broederbond* and of the security police and it was the missing link in my theoretical chain of explanation. In this chapter, I will discuss how the English are corrupted; in the next, how they are coerced and brutalised and then, in Chapters Seven and Eight, how the same principal operates in the Afrikaner community.

The analysis I presented earlier about how English institutions – universities, hospitals, welfare agencies – function, established in me a sympathy for the English people I knew or researched. I believed for a long time that there was no more to it; that the psychologists and psychiatrists I knew, the architects, lawyers and businessmen busied themselves with their rituals but otherwise led exemplary lives. South Africa is a Christian country, highly moral, religious; censorship eliminated such goodies as *Playboy* from our bookstalls, the Beatles from the radio and ensured the mutilation of any film trying to deal with contemporary moral or personal issues. There was not, I thought, much room for the kind of licentiousness one usually associated with corruption.

However, just as I had found liberal students turning to drugs, not as a form of rebellion but as a community tolerated practice, so I found that large numbers of the people I saw in my practice engaged in deviant behaviours that had clearly become an integral part of their existence. Underneath the appearance of institutionalized behaviour, webs of personal contacts were formed – not to promote the proper interest of the institutions' functions (these, as I have shown, were blocked) but to further their own manipulative and exploitative ends just like the members of the other communities I had studied. The English people closest to, or in contact with, the Afrikaner systems exhibited very much the same type of personalism as the Afrikaner, while those furthest away, isolated or only fractionally in contact, developed their own obsessive social pathology based on overseas patterns; the rest of the people I studied fell between these two poles.

I identified three types: those furthest from Afrikaner reality who took overseas ideas or modes of behaviour and tried to apply them in South Africa, developing in the process bizarre and esoteric relationships; those who try to adhere strictly to what we would consider to be normal and conventional codes of behaviour; then those who engage in behaviour that is considered *in South Africa* to be conventional.

Now these three groups differed only in how they coped with the basic white dilemma, which is to act out in reality as the Afrikaner demands – that is, to exploit South Africa and to maintain the *apartheid* game in all its facets – while at the same time appearing to think and behave as if you were acting for other, more humanitarian, more respectable, Western motives. To take out of the system while yet seeming not to belong to it.

The choice was, as I saw it, to join the Afrikaner, play his game and drop the pretence – which the third group did; to pretend to not be in South Africa – to live your life *à la* Europe, which is the lifestyle of the first type; or to be drawn into the process and to smother your anxieties by placing your faith in the semblances of normality – the choice of the second type. What I needed to know was how extensive was the third type? And what was life like for the other two? What was the quality of their existence?

It is important, first, to understand quite what I mean by Afrikaner reality and the ethic of manipulating that I posit to be the true nature of social reality and organization in South Africa. Basically, South African society is built on a simple building-block system; at the bottom are poor people, mainly non-white but with some whites. Above them come the blacks and whites who for one reason or another have survived better than those below. Above them the institutions of society, staffed mainly by whites and a few non-whites. Above them come the elite, mainly Afrikaner businessmen, politicians and professional manipulators, but included in this elite are some blacks and some English whites. Each strata operates and functions by the manipulation and misuse of the block below it; the reality is such that the lower blocks cannot and do not reverse the process; the only way to practise the ethic is to do it on someone in an inferior position; there is no power balance or power conflict as such. In Western societies, the lower blocks have competed with the upper blocks and the resulting conflict has given rise to our modern styles of government and social institutions. Rights of the worker, freedom of the individual, freedom of speech, freedom to contest value and worth are the institutionalized manifestations of this conflict. They were not granted by a benevolent elite but were fought for and established as a means of permanent living by a community which sought a stable balance of power between the various blocks of society. This does not exist in South Africa.

We all *use* people and there is sometimes a problem of identifying proper and improper use of people; if someone works for you, you are using that person but this can be proper if you treat him fairly, pay him well and conduct your activities with him in accordance with normal Western modes of behaviour based on equal status in politics and law. When that status is not a reality, however – no matter how much one pretends that it is – then 'use' becomes a one-way process. Worse, you, the employer, can do what you like, in reality, knowing that so long as you 'pretend' to appear to play the game, the worker, your employee, the person below you, cannot really stop you.

Now let me try and explain how this is applied to the behaviour of the three groups.

Turning to the first pattern, this is to be found amongst what one might call the English professional and business classes or amongst the English-orientated Afrikaans elite. Unlike members of other groups, these people are overseas-orientated; they follow trends in Europe and America in fashion, in living, in politics and act and behave as if they did not belong to or live in South Africa. Having made a token political gesture as liberals, they then shut themselves off in little worlds of their own, populated by people who share their ideology. All the latest trends in psychology and human movements are engaged in, and these form the central focus of their existence, dictating their pattern of living.

When people with similar personalities and needs engage in these sorts of *avant garde* behaviour in other countries, they do so to channel some of their energy and to fulfil the entrepreneurial needs of a nation's elite. Some people explore power and politics, others do research and some explore the frontiers of human intimacy. But they are all acts carried out in societies that have a very different reality base from South Africa's (becoming a women's liberation-ist, for example, in America can serve a definite purpose – women's rights have improved and many of the women who engage in this activity feel a sense of pride at their achievements – all of which are essential components of a healthy psychological cycle of functioning). However, when the same activities lead nowhere, as is the case in South Africa, then those involved get bogged down in unfulfilling and frustrating ritual.

Social movements exist to channel energy through institutiona-lized activities so that by working in them and through them person-alities can be developed properly; through having to work at something and fight and think and operate against frustrations, you develop an adult sense of conflict and tolerance; you learn the immeasurable importance of balancing; you learn to value toler-ance. In a simple sense, people who sail through things do not develop much beyond a simple cause-and-effect understanding of reality; accurate ideas about reality, true intelligence, creativity and wisdom emerge through learning how to solve problems.

When social movements do not go anywhere or do anything, then they cease to have a communal function but operate simply as an as-sociation of people using the association as an end in itself. Under these circumstances, there is a tendency for the association to foster its own pathology. It creates a closed group-mindedness in which personalities become involved and obsessed with association itself rather than with the task of working towards some attainable end. Value is then attached to being *good members* of the association, of being approved of by the association; personal development then remains fixed, locked in the need to be accepted by the association. This creates an immediate and false sense of involvement but frustrates proper development.

In South Africa, proper causes cannot exist as they do elsewhere because there is no base for them in Afrikaner reality. Causes thus become associations and the proper development of the members' personalities ceases. Women's liberationists in South Africa stand as much chance of shifting male domination in the Afrikaner community as Africans do of being granted full rights. Consequently, women's groups are associative circles and people *live* for the association rather than use them as a means to effect change. Having their normal outlets frustrated because they have no effect in South African society and through having to cope with pervasive anxiety they are largely unaware of, these people act out in a damaging and pathological way. Here are some examples of this: the drug-use study I conducted earlier amongst students tapped the tip of a drug-taking iceberg; drug-use amongst young professionals, artists, businessmen and academic people, couples and singles, was widespread and endemic. While it peaked in the 1973–74 period and dropped off as a result of new laws and a curtailment of the ease of access, drug-use remained routine and high amongst the people in this group. They used cannabis resin daily on average and LSD and cocaine when they could get it. In other words, the drug habits found in students trying for new 'highs' and kicks was a well-established part of the lives of many of the adults in this group – as part of it as tea-drinking.

Some professionals, businessmen, attorneys, accountants and the like used cannabis as a pick-me-up to start the day, going onto quite heavy doses in the evening. Some psychologists ran group therapy sessions while under the influence – on the grounds that it improved their perception. Others used it to help them face problems at work or in their private lives. Some encouraged their patients and students to use the drugs, often engaging in marathons or week-end T-groups in which most of the participants were using cannabis for much of the time.

Some people who had access to psychotropic medicines – doctors, chemists and their friends – experimented with various types of drug mixes to obtain permanent states of coping-euphoria, while others would mix liquor and concoctions using drugs and take them to work to use during the day. Some doctors had got so enthusiastic about the use of drugs to solve their patients problems that they often created addicts out of not only their patients but of their families as well. For example, a hypnotic drug used as a sleeping pill was the single most addictive drug used in Cape Town when I first went into practice. In time, I learned of three separate rackets extending into several suburbs operated through co-operative and profit-sharing doctors who supplied the drug in large quantities on the black market. One of my patients, in fact, was a dealer in this drug, and he supplied schoolboys at four of the private schools in Cape Town.

In one case, I treated the son of a well-known Cape Town white family, who was importing LSD into South Africa in large quantities; through a network of friends and relatives, this person was effectively and regularly supplying many of Cape Town's select suburbs. Amongst his biggest customers were several doctors and a handful of very prominent and well-known businessmen. They, of course, did not know that he was the importer; some of them were also my patients and they often sat in my waiting-room next to their supplier without realising who he was. His activities were well known to the police, but through his parents' connections – which went to the highest governmental level – he was never apprehended, although his parents did try from time to time to control his activities.

I knew of other cases where doctors had caused severe damage psychologically and, in some cases, physically to their children and wives through giving them prescription drugs in large quantities.

The essential feature of these cases was the way new ideas and developments in drugs or chemotherapy were seized upon and engaged in frantically. We all know that Western societies are 'pill-pushing' societies, but the way this trend applied in South Africa involved sometimes gross and irresponsible over-use and over-dosing of drugs, occasionally by the very people who should have known better. At one hospital, for example, I was told that some psychiatrists and registrars read of a study in America where doctors had tried the psychotropic drugs that they gave to their patients to get an insight into their effects. So, promptly, the staff launched into a chaotic month in which they swallowed anti-depressants, phenothazines, the lot, to see how they felt. No planning, no experimentation and no responsibility. Some fell ill, others took time off work, others got depressed; work suffered. I noted, incidentally, that nobody volunteered to see what ECT felt like.

Instead of *personally* thinking out whether the bizarre actions were right or wrong, each individual in these associations simply asked what the group as a whole thought and then complied; common sense, professional responsibility, academic knowledge were all irrelevant to what the 'crowd' was doing; one person (not a patient of mine) said:

> 'When I saw doctors [in his T-group] popping "goodies", I thought, Gosh they must know what they're doing – so I went along with it. I asked one of them if it was OK. He said he didn't know for sure but "Oppie", his professor, had said it was OK so he supposed so.'

Perhaps this kind of individual avoidance of responsibility explained how it was that patients in Valkenburg were so heavily overdosed and some doctors so unaware of the dangers of side effects.

A second type of pathology concerned sexuality. When a normal person expresses pathology, it is seldom in the form of the kind of obvious symptoms that we associate with mental illness such as the bizarre personal behaviour we see in schizophrenics who experience hallucinations. It usually takes the form of overdoing a normal pattern: people express their anxiety or fear through drinking too much, arguing, fighting, playing too much golf, and so on. One of the most susceptible of these 'normal' symptoms is sexual behaviour. In stressed individuals, one often sees this expressed in some form of perversion. The person engages in his or her particular form of pathology usually secretly and illicitly, taking elaborate precautions to hide it from their spouses or their community out of a sense of guilt, shame and, above all, fear that it will be stopped.

But this is not the kind of sexual pathology I am talking about. In Cape Town, some people did have pathologies like this and I treated a number of them for it, but there was a separate sexual deviancy practised by people who fell into this group. This was communal sexual pathology. As with drug-use, sexual experimentation was used as a means of expressing or acting out anxiety, fear and frustration. I uncovered this when, in several cases, people came to join one of my therapy groups hoping to have the kind of sexual adventures they had had elsewhere and left disappointed when my groups turned out to be ordinary therapeutic groups. It was then that I learned that sexual experimentation was a common practice engaged in by many professionals and businessmen and women in Cape Town.

Basically what would happen was that some people while travelling overseas would get fascinated by ideas about greater permissiveness, greater personal and sexual freedom, and so on, and then they would try to introduce these ideas to their circles in Cape Town, mainly of like-minded friends but also discussion groups, art societies, women's groups and therapy groups. Again, these are valuable developments if they are treated in a thoughtful and responsible way and in the right social context. Again, in South Africa, I found these experiments in new styles of living led not to creative and responsible experimentation but to pathology. Associative groups would start off well-intentioned and then disintegrate into sometimes orgiastic, often overtly promiscuous sexual encounters in which concepts such as 'touch, sensitivity, being honest' were used as a means of coercing people into interpersonal sexual adventures. 'Openness' – a concept which, properly used, means the healthy and fruitful expression of a wide range of previously repressed feelings and problems – became, I discovered, a catch-phrase whereby massive hostility, crippling anger and the reduction of human interaction to sexual preferences were released.

In other societies, these behaviours are supported by the communal ethic in which they occur and can lead to new and responsible innovations in life-styles and interpersonal behaviour. In South Africa, the insurmountable pressures created by the system means that any shift in morality or any change in levels of intimacy exposes the residual anxiety and fear. Since these are buried fears, they are not recognised as reasonable fears and they are blamed on the context in which they occur. A husband expressing anger towards his wife suddenly finds her over-reacting back with a viciousness that surprises him. Nobody realises why because they have not done this sort of thing before and so they presume that it is because the wife harbours deep anger towards her husband. Since no one has compared the American and South African context, people, even the professionals and experts taking part, presume that outbursts like this are a normal part of 'intimate' and 'open' experiences, and so the cycle goes on. Husband turns to sympathetic group member (female) whom he uses to support him; in the ensuing chaos, the marriage begins to disintegrate and a new lifestyle emerges to cover both the breach and the fears. This was a typical pattern.

My patients reported on just how severe and widespread these trends were and how they spilled over beyond the limits of the original groups. Some people joining women's groups found that they were expected to engage in lesbianistic encounters in order to belong effectively to the association. Students complained that they were induced into T-groups by their lecturers and professors only to find themselves embroiled in on-going sexual experiments that so disturbed and upset them that a significant number experienced breakdowns during the course of their group attendances. These inductees often had to face the demands of highly skilful and verbal male and female intellectuals or figures of authority who were quite unable to moderate their own needs or to see the effects they were having. Often patients complained that husband and wife teams made sexual demands on the same person at the same time, inviting their target to form a kind of *folie à trois*.

Having a general psychological practice, I had access to people from different levels of society and to different age groups. It was an easy task to trace the effects and extent of these practices, sometimes in the same suburb, often in the same family. Thus in Sea Point, an affluent white suburb, I knew of several groups of young adult friends who engaged in communal sexual encounters over weekends in flats and swimming-pools. What they did not know was that while they were out at work, their fourteen- and thirteen-year-old children showed *their* pornographic movies after school in *their* flats while using *their* drugs and cannabis. Many of the adolescents in Sea Point, I learnt, had access to cannabis; by far the easiest access being gained from rifling their parents' supply.

Select suburbs of Cape Town, such as Constantia, Sea Point, Fresnaye, Bishopscourt, Hout Bay and Claremont each had extensive 'empires' which engaged in this kind of behaviour. Sometimes inductees were provided for by a well-organised network that could deliver virtually anything, even on occasion reaching across the racial barriers to provide suitable connections. Attractive Coloured women, for example, were transported to homes in white Bishops-court, Constantia and Sea Point on a routine basis. In other areas, groups established for the purpose of some association (for example, gay clubs) became simply outlets and excuses for week-ends of blind escape in which young people would be used as game to be 'played' for. In one set of chess devotees, for example, mara-thon chess games were played with the members competing for select 'experiences'. I must stress that these activities occurred in varying forms at all levels of society.

Clearly these acted as welcome outlets from the kind of stress to be found in English institutions in South Africa. People engaged in these activities and in interdepartmental power games had precious little time left over for studying the situation they were in.

The second type of pattern is characterised by the almost total absence of overtly corrupt behaviour; these people behaved com-pletely normally and, above all, conventionally. If they sought therapy at all, it was for conventional neurotic problems like ago-raphobia, fear of heights, depression or hypochondria. Politically conservative, their morality in so far as *apartheid* went was to remain aloof and uninvolved. 'We prefer,' I was told, 'to lead a normal quiet life and let the government get on with running the country.' Elsewhere, this group would be labelled 'middle-of-the-road', or 'the silent majority'.

When confronted with major crises in the country, such as hor-rendous government actions, riots, and so on, they reacted with shock as if hearing about these things for the first time. While people in the first group tended not to be upset or shocked or sur-prised by extreme government actions, the conventional group showed characteristically labile behaviour. At Biko's death, for example, many wanted to protest and went around in states of despair and anguish for a few days; two weeks later, things were back to normal. These same people had been very frightened by Soweto and went around in the same shocked states extolling the virtues of the government and thanking God that the Afrikaner was tough and that the police knew what they were doing. The analogy of a set of ostriches occasionally taking their collective heads out of the sand aptly describes this type.

I discovered that the behaviour patterns which characterised their particular mode of pathology was that they were not just conventional people going to country clubs or playing bridge, squash or golf, etc., they were totally immersed in these behaviours. Not surprisingly, they were also completely immersed in conventional means of managing psychological problems, anxiety and tensions. And they used conventional psychotropic drugs in the same way that members of the bizarre group used cannabis resin, consuming huge quantities of tranquillizers, anti-depressants, stimulants and sleeping pills on a daily basis.

It was quite normal to discover every member of such a family routinely taking tranquillisers. I found other people in this category taking up to ten different types of psychotropic drugs a day: something to wake up with, something to take before going out to the shops, an appetite supressant to take before lunch to keep the weight down, something after lunch, a drink at five in the afternoon 'to steady the nerves' and two different types of sleeping pills taken with a tranquillizing syrup to sleep. In several cases I found people on over thirty drugs taken daily.

These were not isolated instances, they were commonly accepted practices; to suggest otherwise was heresy. 'It's quite normal in modern society,' I was told. 'After all, don't all Americans go to psychoanalysis every day? At least we don't do that. We don't need analysis, we've got our friends; there's nothing wrong with us; if things get me down, I play golf, have a drink or get Mike [a doctor] to give me something to make me feel better.' The best way to characterise this is to let one of my subjects describe his own family life:

'My stepfather is one of the top professional men in South Africa. If my mother wasn't involved in preparing huge dinners for his affairs, she would be running to and from committee meetings. She was always involved in outside affairs and not giving us the attention we needed. She became the kind, dedicated Mrs –, so involved, doing so much, organizing lectures at the Club, joining this art committee, president of that. She was really into charities and into the "right" liberal politics: Progressive. She used to boast to her friends about how friendly she was with the Big Liberals in South Africa. You should have seen the way she treated the maids. She was always competing with other rich people – who wore the best clothes, who had the best house, who was doing the most. She was always on the go – smiling and putting up a front to everyone. We mattered as long as we could be used to boast to her friends – Michael got five distinctions in his matric; Paul is on AFS this year; Beverley is Head Girl – the rest of the time, though, we were a nuisance.

'The smiles were what she showed outside – inside at home we received the results of all the pretence – migraine attacks regularly, fits of anger that had been built up, the tension of a marriage that had disintegrated – where they hardly said a decent thing to one another and my mother pretending all the time nothing was wrong – even to her own children.

'But they carried on – "But there's nothing wrong – our marriage is as good as any of my friends, he hugged me after the fight last night – really there's nothing wrong."

'Even when I broke down, she still maintained this. Every one in the family is on drugs of some kind. Tranquillizers, antidepressants, migraine pills. Michael was nearly arrested for drugs but they got him off. Every family I know is the same – good conventional people, nothing wrong. That's all I hear – "There's nothing wrong with us."'

The people who suffered in this set up were, of course, the children; parents were just too busy to be proper parents.

This is obviously the sort of complaint that can be found in many societies, but the meaning in this context is not quite the same. The conventional rituals employed by these people were to them matters of life and death; straightening out your golf stroke or entertaining the bridge club were not the activities of the spoilt and the idle rich but of people who *needed* these activities in order to continue living. No amount of argument – even when they recognised what was needed – would convince these people to give up any ritual time in order to spend time with their kids. They were obsessed with and fixated upon these ritualistic channels of behaving.

The result was that many children were neglected emotionally as a matter of course. They were not materially neglected, and in appearance parents behaved normally so no one was aware that at a subtle yet crucial level a whole generation of young people was growing up deprived of proper family life. It was these young people who were so easily led into accepting drug use and pathological and harmful forms of behaviour when they got to university.

They had been conditioned all their lives to accepting convention and social approval as the arbiter of behaviour, so simply changing the direction of these conventions was irrelevant. In fact, it helped them to think that they were rebelling. Meanwhile, they were simply behaving in precisely the same way as their parents, reducing their anxiety through over-engaging in conventional rituals. They could also condemn their parents for these same habits, albeit packaged slightly differently, for drinking too much and taking too many tranquillizers – which they did not. Then they would rush off to the latest protest meeting, T-group, or to smoke joints together.

The third group of people appear to belong to the above group because they do not engage in the kind of group bizarrerie that the first does. But in a deep sense, these are the people who, along with the Afrikaner elite, take the most out of South Africa. Their working lives are organised around professional and business malpractices and it is in this area (unlike the other groups, whose pathology is mainly expressed through their private and personal lives) where pathology is most evident. Let me sketch the nature and the extent of these malpractices.

The aim of the people in this group is to take the most out of life in every possible way and to use people to help them do it. Anyone who can be used is used and it does not matter if they are black, white, male or female, rich or poor, sick or well. They play on and prey on the fact that people in South Africa seldom complain or make a fuss. These were the only people I came across who knew, really knew, how things actually were – and they used what they knew, cynically and openly. I quote from an interview with the managing director of a large concern:

'Look, the Nationalists have this country sewn up by making people scared and confused. Look how each cabinet minister has vague and fuzzy powers so that he can hold more power than he should. If you want something you have to ask the Minister and most people are too scared to, too put off by all the red tape and so they just put up with it. I'm not. I've often spoken to the minister and it's all a game. And we do the same. We fix prices, we crook the customer, especially those who take things on hire purchase. They don't know we're not allowed to charge an extra one percent on the interest, they wouldn't dream of checking or questioning us – we're too big. And if some smart alec does, we apologise and say it was clerical error. You see, everything is fuzzy and blurred and we all use it.'

Cape Town is full of old-boy networks such as this man describes. Take, he said, any kind of business; it would use a firm of accountants and a firm of attorneys who could be relied upon to act in ways necessary to maximise profits for all concerned. Audits and court actions, and so on, were all well co-ordinated, illegally if necessary, with the attorney, accountant and directors of this group gaining financially at the expense of smaller concerns and less powerful people. Thus, as I was told by other professionals I treated, it was common practice for them to advise clients wrongly if they were in conflict with their relationships with other clients. Professionals often received income for this kind of service, not always in the form of direct payments, but in being referred key business, being offered partnerships, inside information about new developments, investments, contacts with government officials, and so on.

It could be argued that this kind of thing takes place in all communities and I am aware of that. What was astounding about Cape Town was that nearly every professional or business person of any standing I came into contact with or treated was involved in some major way with this kind of exploitation. I was frequently informed that you were *abnormal* if you did not participate and would soon be squeezed out of practice if you insisted on going against the system. One medical practitioner, for example, reported to me how he had wanted to reduce the cost of the medicines he used by buying directly from a wholesaler and had been prevented from doing so by other doctors. The price of bulk medicines had gone up and doctors had passed this increase along to patients. He had a poorish practice and was aware that some of his patients could not afford to pay the new price and he could not afford to cover it. So he investigated and found a way to cut costs, but his colleagues found out about it and threatened to ruin him. They did not want to reduce their incomes, and if he cut costs they knew they would lose patients to him.

Much of the working time of these groups of professionals was spent looking after their and their relatives' interests. So much so that Cape Town has an abundant supply of people 'in the know' who could get you off anything from a parking ticket to income tax to murder. At a price. After 1974, many of these people became involved with currency smuggling for themselves, their friends and their families as the South African government clamped down on the amount of foreign currency being allowed to leave the country. These practices were prolific and little attempt was made to hide them – in fact, they were used as a form of status: people, often strangers, would tell you proudly how they pulled off now this coup, now that. Occasionally some were caught and received prison sentences but this was rare precisely because, as I will explain in the next chapter, government officials at all levels were deeply involved in these activities and, in fact, encouraged them.

In professional and business practices, these people would set up little cliques with themselves and their friends at the top. Apart from cheating their customers, clients, students or patients, they behaved as overlords of feudal dynasties towards their staff. It was not unusual, for example, to find women employees being used to act as escorts for visiting professionals and businessmen and, again, being extensively abused in sexual matters. For example, several groups of friends, directors of companies, used apartments in blocks of flats which one of them owned, to which they took female staff during work hours and which friends were free to use for the same purpose. Members of staff were expected to co-operate or lose their jobs – not in a direct 'conform or be fired' way but, since they had refused, some fault would soon be found with their work and they would be asked to leave.

Officials would have an affair with secretaries in their company. When the affair was over, the woman would be fired – as a matter of principle – usually with an extra month's pay as compensation because the man concerned did not want her around – she embarrassed him. This practice happened very often and it was accepted by the women – because everyone did it; 'It's a small industry, a woman can earn a lot of money by being difficult,' one told me.

Some medical practitioners made routine use of their staff and their patients, They had, for example, special patients whom they saw at any time of the day or night. They would pay 'house calls' on these patients but not on others. These sexual liaisons went on for several months, every time a patient fell ill. Then the patient was replaced by another. Some doctors and dentists made a regular habit of attempting to seduce their patients or touch them sexually while they, the patients, were under the influence of anaesthetics or premedication – thus being able to deny anything if they were charged.

What was disturbing about all this was that in most cases the mal-practices and deceit were often well known to members of the same professions and sometimes to clients or patients as well. Yet in the six years I was in practice, few were ever stopped – nobody was pre-pared to act or to complain. People accepted these irregularities as part of the living pattern and, in the case of doctors, many women willingly engaged in them, even encouraging their friends to par-take. 'It helps to brighten up the week.' Amongst certain sections of Constantia and Sea Point womenfolk, for example, there is a 'hot list' of medical and legal specialists circulated amongst friends. Not everyone, however, complied with these irregularities; some staff members and patients were so incensed that they willingly provided me with accurate descriptions of these activities, often going to great lengths and taking brave risks to provide me with whatever documentation they could. Because of the widespread acceptance of this manipulative ethic, the perpetrators made no secret of it at all, so some of my patients, for example, who worked for com-panies, often let me see files and letters taken from work over lunchtime.

Some university departments were arranged on the same lines. I quote from the experiences of several student patients:

'On the first day of term, the Professor and his entourage waltzed in to look us over. It was like a slave auction; he quickly picked out the ones that were the most attractive and sure enough, within weeks, you would be told discreetly that the professor or this or that lecturer was having an affair with x or y; and sure enough, no matter how bad they were, they would be in every-thing, get all the best work to do, get the firsts. Then, suddenly, it would be all over and he or she would be "out" and someone else would be "in". Bang would go their world and that was that. The next year, the whole cycle would begin again.'

In some cases I was told that key appointments, research funds – especially those controlled by the heads of the departments – often went to ill-qualified people with whom the professor was having a liaison.

There were several abortion rackets in Cape Town run by medical doctors. I personally was frequently asked to help in arranging abortions and so was in a position to know about all of them. I disapproved of South Africa's stringent anti-abortion laws and so did several other professionals, many of whom took brave legal and professional risks to ensure that their and my patients' health were attended to. I do not refer to these practices as rackets; they were done as routine procedures in the best medical tradition and with no extra charge.

Abortion rackets, on the other hand, were just that – rackets. Again, I quote from the experience of several of my patients:

'You can't get a legal abortion unless you have a statement from a psychiatrist saying it is in the interests of your mental health to do so. Usually this means that you had to have a history of mental disturbance. So how it worked was you were sent to one of three psychiatrists who wrote you out a certificate and you gave him R100 in cash – no receipt. You took the certificate and then went to a gynaecologist he had told you to go to who gave you a real rough time, lecturing you on your morals, treating you like dirt. Then you paid him in cash and in advance and he did a D&C.'

These were some of the means whereby financial or material gains were made out of the suffering of people. Again the people who were used in these activities were those who were least power-ful in the South African situation: women, patients, students, non-whites, poorly educated people. And it was this principle of misuse that runs through all three groups; misuse of the inexperienced and each other in the first, misuse of the family and children in the second, misuse of everyone else in the third.

Exploitation is also engaged in by non-whites in a position to so do. A number of non-white traders make considerable sums of money by charging excessive prices for goods, knowing that their customers could not and would not complain; many established near-monopolies (and were encouraged to do so by the authorities) by setting up in or near locations; people *have* to buy from them because transport to shops in white suburbs is expensive. In certain parts of the country, where curfews operate, Africans are not allowed even to leave their locations and so the local trader does very well.

Other Coloured and African people use different ways of profit-ing from the situation. African Bantu Affairs officials often terro-rise Africans working in white suburbs by 'raiding' a house alone and, finding the maid working without a pass, threaten to turn her in unless she gives him favours. It is thus possible for these men to receive regular food, sex and money from a number of people for a long time and with complete immunity. Coloured policemen often operate on the same basis by extracting goods from shopkeepers.

Exploitation of a different type occurs amongst those white people who have the closest contact with non-white people in their lives – ordinary working people, traffic policemen, civil servants and the like. Their activities range from the frustrated adolescent who beats up Coloured people for pleasure, to the office secretary who makes up for her own feelings of inadequacy by tyrannizing her Coloured staff, from the mental patients who use Coloureds as playthings, to the housewife who pays her maid just R3 for a twelve-hour day.

Most people are familiar with this side of South Africa; everyone's stereotype about South Africa or the American South has the white lazing away while the black does all the labour. What I want to report on here are the little-known aspects of this kind of practice which are nevertheless widespread, everyday occurrences in Cape Town. I got a good insight into one side of this when two students of mine conducted a study under my supervision into male homosexuality and transvestism in Cape Town.[3] During the course of interviewing members of this community, I learnt of several well-established homosexual prostitution rings operating throughout the Peninsula.

Basically, there are several areas in which white men regularly pick up Coloured males and young boys. Since South Africa has very stringent laws about sex across the colour line, few white males risk engaging in picking up Coloured women (although this does happen). There is, however, a huge market in homosexual prostitution because this form of cross-racial contact is not regarded in the same way as heterosexual contact. Policemen and the authorities turn a blind eye to the practice and Cape Town has a reputation for being the most homosexually permissive city in Africa.

The lists of clients of these prostitutes include Afrikaner businessmen, clergymen and government officials as well as many well-known members of Cape Town's English-speaking society. Some customers set up their contact in flats in white areas where the Coloured contact is quite safe from official intervention; others hire them, put them on their staff and form stable long-term affairs.

Again the distressing side to all this is that it is engaged in by people who are, in normal life, hypocritically pretentious about white prostitution and actively furthering *apartheid*. It also takes gross advantage of a loophole in the system to exploit the underdog – in this case, Coloured males.

A similar kind of activity occurs amongst mental patients who are only able to relate to Coloured people because of their inferior status in the white community. Let me give some examples: the thirty-year old son of a wealthy white professional couple regularly picked up Coloured girls with whom he slept then beat up, then went to his family GP for an anti-VD prescription. When he was arrested he was got off by an attorney friend of his father. When I began working with him, this had been going on non-stop since he was fourteen.

A second example concerned the case of a businessman who had an affair with an African employee of his for several years. On the face of it, it was a compassionate, serious matter between two adults. But alas, this was not the case. The man was 'happily' married and both he and his wife were 'deeply religious' people. How he justified the affair was to say that because the woman was an African, she therefore did not count – meaning she did not have a place in his society. He was, in his mind therefore, having an affair with a non-person. This absolved him from having any conflict with his religious convictions because, as he said, he was not having an affair with a 'real' person. The matter came to a head when his mistress developed cancer. Once she had told him, he dropped her immediately, forced her to leave his employ and never spoke to her again. She had ceased to serve her function.

Other patients took on Coloured and African causes as part of their attempts to work out their own pathology. They identified with and took part in Coloured life, living as a Coloured person and with Coloured friends until such time as it became inconvenient. The status they obtained in these communities often provided a boost to their levels of confidence and helped them to function. Some people developed permanent liaisons in this way and 'survived' as people simply because of *apartheid*. They taught or led Coloured groups, had Coloured girl- or boyfriends; whilst filling their previously empty lives, they gained status as 'liberals' and 'philanthropists', always escaping back into the white world when the unpleasant realities of Coloured existence intervened.

Some professionals posed as liberals appearing to help black people. This gained them considerable prestige and status in liberal circles and helped them make a profit too. One group of medical practitioners, for example, runs a clinic in poor areas on a reduced-fee basis. According to one of them, this is an excellent way of making hard cash, tax free; they only treat if the patient pays cash in advance and this is collected and distributed amongst the five practitioners without being declared as income. This 'charitable' effort is regarded as easy money by those involved.

One can sit back and say, 'Look, this sort of thing happens every-where, it's no surprise that South Africa too has bad elements.' People visit South Africa every year and return saying they can find no difference between the people there and those at home. And this is where the evidence cited in this chapter is so crucial: South Africans do nothing different – there is no act or set of acts that South Africans do that is special – *they differ in the way they do familiar acts*. What I have described here is *widespread*. These are not isolated incidents confined to a few but are engaged in by the majority of people in the country.

Every white South African, for example, in one way or another fits into these categories and engages in or has engaged in these activities. And in many cases, the same people often partake in several different exploitations; the same professional who takes advantage of the system by practising errantly at work, probably gambles heavily at the gaming tables in Lesotho and Swaziland, views pornographic movies in Sea Point, engages in drug and sexual exploits at poolside parties in Constantia and considers himself liberal enough to fund-raise for the Progressive Reform Party, hoping all along that the system stays as it is just long enough for him to make his fortune *and* smuggle it overseas.

The point is that in South Africa the structure of the social system dictates the nature of the relationship between informal and formal institutions. In Western countries, the ethic of any particular system is dictated by the complex, balanced pull of the various power groups in a society so that an institution, to survive, *has* to blend its proper function with whatever personal structures exist within it. That is, its very legitimacy – its right to exist – is dependant on its serving its formal structure. Whatever personal contacts the judiciary may have with the government of the day in Britain or America, for example, it nevertheless *has* to do its job properly because if it does not, other interpersonal and power groups will take action against it. In the professional world, to take a second example, two counsellors or barristers may be personally the best of friends and share mutual material interests but, in court, they *must* do their job, even if it means attacking one another. There is, if you like, a separation between their personal contacts and their formal contact.

In South Africa, this process only, I think, applies, in a very narrow sense. I had a discussion about it with an attorney who felt that 'outside the political arena, South Africa's professionals are as good as any'. What he failed to appreciate was that there is very little in South Africa that is *not* political, hence the speciousness of his argument. In minor, politically safe ways, South Africa's institutions do apply the kind of ethic we are familiar with. But for the rest of the time, their ethics of practice are dominated by the personal contact, manipulative and corrupt modes I have described. What they are highly skilled at doing is bending the appearance of observing formal rules to suit the only reality that matters – personal gain and contact.

The best way I can explain how this system operates is to detail some of my own experiences and relate them to the other work reported in earlier chapters.

First, I was, like many of the students I studied, in need of both a career and finance. I soon learned that good marks and ability were not the most important criteria; it was who took a liking to you, who thought they could use you the most, that got you anywhere. Appointments, grants, government scholarships, anything, were given through a kind of personal contact system. Without false modesty, I, with a first class honours degree and academic publications, had to struggle for every penny I earned and every teaching post I got. Few others did; it all depended on their relationship with the person dishing out appointments or finance. I collected data about how several professionals misused funds; paid sums out to their 'disciples', used them to support their mistresses or lovers, and so on. Occasionally some were caught and made to quietly retire. In the face of this exigency, it was little wonder that the most radical and progressive students had eventually either to conform or to leave South Africa. You got bogged down in surviving for yourself let alone trying to change the system.

Then, once, when I was working at my lowest ebb, really short of funds and not sure whether I could afford to finish my degree, I was approached by a friend of a friend who suggested I contact a certain Doctor –, who he thought could help me. I did not contact him but a little later, the Doctor introduced himself to me at a function and, during the course of a little chat, mentioned two things; first, he was head of a psychological services section of a government department and secondly, if I liked, I could do a little work for them and in return, I would be given a grant to help me finish my degree. I declined the offer. Later I realised that this was an entrée into contact with the government and I wondered how many other struggling students were similarly approached.

Thirdly, once I had become established as a psychologist, I was approached personally and invited to join several of the most select encounter groups in Cape Town. People thought, no doubt, that since I was now OK, a professional, I would want to partake of the fruits of my status. I do not think they ever understood – or forgave – my refusal. Finally, just before I was going into private practice (on my own) I was approached by the senior partner in Cape Town's biggest practice and invited to join it. Later I found that this offer was made to stop me from breaking into their virtual monopoly of the market. At the same time, it was a very tempting offer; however, I declined it and paid the price: the senior partner promptly sent me patients whom he was trying to get rid of because they could no longer afford private treatment. I was also ostracised by his friends and many other practitioners for years – all at a time when I was completely vulnerable emotionally and financially.

There were other experiences, other offers which I will mention in the next chapter. What matters though, is that the ordinary qualities that give one access into any institution in modern society were, in Cape Town, of little importance. In fact, you got on better if you were prepared to *be* unintelligent, insensitive and to turn a blind eye on glaring irregularities.

The principle behind all this, of course, is the fact that agreeing to this kind of corruption is one of the conditions set by the Afrikaner for the participation of the non-Afrikaner in South African life. What the Afrikaners have done is to create a context in which the English are made to believe that they are in a crucial way inadequate and inferior. They are allowed to remain in South Africa on sufferance. This may seem strange because, on the surface, the English look down on the Afrikaners and ridicule them – 'country bumpkins, boers' – but the psychological structure behind this is simple and effective.

The fact of the matter is that the English *are* completely cut off from the political processes and from Afrikaner processes of power. The idea is subtly promulgated to them, though, that the only reason why this is so is because English whites are untrustworthy and inadequate. The only safe person in the country is the Afrikaner; to be admitted all you have to do is 'be like us', they say, and not unexpectedly this strengthens and focuses the direction of English fear and anxiety. English whites are first made anxious and apprehensive in general. Then a 'solution' is offered – behave like us Afrikaners and co-operate with us and your fear will disappear.

One of the Afrikaners' most powerful psychological weapons is that through his success and his social structure – he sees himself not only as perfect but he believes his actions show this – he approaches everyone else with a kind of an adolescent challenge: 'Show any weakness and I will sneer at you.' He is intensely competitive and strives at every level to prove that his perception is right. Because his psychology is fixed and his upbringing entirely devoted to protecting his self-image, he has to bend everything to this narrow schoolboy perception of the world. He has little outside contact and no experience of pluralism – that is, the idea that reality is complex and there are many explanations for reality, depending on point of view. Every new fact, every event that does not accord with his framework has to be bent and pushed and forced into shape.

Try arguing with a ten- or twelve-year-old. They talk the same language but they are worlds apart, completely unable to function in a world that demands an understanding of complexity, balance and compromise. The ten-year-old's world is black and white, heroes and villains. He has no understanding of good villains and bad heroes. This is authoritarianism. But in a ten-year-old, it is quite normal. Remember *Lord of the Flies*? A ten-year-old will make every single one of your behaviours into a sin if it differs in the slightest with how he sees reality. You do not like rugby? That makes you a cissy – and so on . . . In South Africa, the Afrikaner imposes this conception on a technologically sophisticated society.

I think that it is this clash between an essentially twentieth-century view of reality and an essentially nineteenth-century *status quo* that has always dominated contact between the Afrikaners and the English. The English, in fact, anybody with a complex, Westernized sense of political philosophy and social behaviour, are vulnerable to this incipiently unreal, unpragmatic – in truly democratic societies – reality. It was one that the Nazis forced on a weary, anxious and economically insecure Germany in the 1930s, and much the same pattern has been used by the Afrikaner Nationalists in South Africa. Just as the Nazis heightened and deepened the insecurity of the average German person by creating an enemy within (the Jews) and real street violence (their own), so too did the Afrikaner Nationalists. The Africans and communists in South Africa became the enemy within and served to justify the militarism and draconianly violent legislation the Nationalists used. The average person, seeing the public displays of government violence, presumes that they are in response to a massive threat. He is not to know – indeed has no means of knowing – whether it is justified or not. All he knows is that he then becomes grateful for any security he can get, no matter how simple or indeed, unrealistic. Let that same person *profit* from his security – share both in the wealth of exploitation and in keeping the *threat* under control – then you have a formula for political fascism. The Nazis bluffed their way into power by making ordinary Germans fear the Jewish 'threat'. The Afrikaners bluffed their way into staying in power by using the Africans. The English South Africans, the victims in this Goebellian drama, feel guilty. And grateful. Guilt because they are not good enough for the Afrikaners, guilt because they are English, guilt for being white. The Afrikaner will not allow the English out of this crucible in the same way and for the same reasons that he must maintain African living standards at a low level. Under this pressure, the English person takes the only possible way out – he conforms to what the Afrikaner expects of him just as the German people did in the 1930s. The Afrikaner has made the English person so anxious and so guilty that he is grateful for the simple, straightforward things in life: the English South African is so relieved he can carry on living that he willingly buries his head in the sand to be allowed to carry on. He is grateful for the very things we, elsewhere, take for granted. The *trekboer* concept of life with all its narrow insularity, its paranoia and its personal corruption has been very successfully transmitted to all white South Africans. It filled, indeed, the vacuum it was meant to.

The Afrikaners have been a good deal more sophisticated in their applications of these Machiavellian principles than the Nazis were.

They did not simply seek power, they wanted to maintain it. So the psychology behind this legitimization of the corrupt *boer* ethic had to be carefully and calculatingly applied; just the right amount of pressure, just the right balance of distance with personal contact, the correct degree of apparent movement, a truly efficient game of cat and mouse.

One last way I have of showing this subtlety is to conclude by describing two further examples of the corrupting processes. These, I think, aptly highlight the tactics employed by the Afrikaner. The first concerns the English press and the second, the judiciary.

The following is an extract from a discussion I had with a newspaperman who had just retired. His experiences spanned nearly thirty years of the English press in South Africa:

'The English press started off focusing on ordinary Western values. It was genuinely free. Then after the Nationalists came into power, we had to function under the continual threat that they would close us down at any moment. A couple of bannings of editions helped this along and were done deliberately just to warn us that they meant business. Now, in a quiet way, this worked very well for them. We didn't write what they wanted but we started censoring ourselves – keeping little things out, wary of offending them too much. Then they started banning individual journalists. OK if you're together, fine if a whole newspaper gets closed down, you're all in it – but an individual with a wife and family? Who wants to take that risk? So you're careful to be sure it's not going to be you.

'Then we began to get these rumours of pending strict government action against us. Panic. We *pressured* ourselves into being more and more censorial. Just when we were really nervous, the rumours stopped and suddenly they launched the *verligte-verkrampte* campaign. About 80% of English journalists really fell for this. Now I can see it clearly for what it was: firstly they soften us up then they threaten us; then, scared as hell, we see this crack in the wall – the *verligtes*. God, we thought they were our saviours. Enlightened Afrikaners *and* in power. So we rushed off to print to back them, to sell them to our readers. And suddenly the pressure stops. Suddenly the Afrikaner press becomes liberal, stops attacking us. Which ordinary human being under the circumstances wouldn't be grateful for the break, for the easing of tension? The freedom of the English press, I tell you, was lost when we took up the *Verligte*'s cause. And, do you know, we were so stupid. We never put two and two together. There we were, hanging on Piet Koornhof's [then Minister of Sport, now Minister of Plural Relations – in Verwoerd's old job] every word, like he was Martin Luther King and all the time, *we knew* he was secretary of the *Broederbond*; we just didn't put two and two together.'

There were other less subtle, more private ways in which journalists were coerced. Some were openly bought, others were turned into useful contacts by the simple process of being given privileged information. In many cases, the journalist involved seldom could (or wanted to) see what was really going on; in several cases, select journalists were taken into the confidence of ministers, state officials, police chiefs and the like – charmed, given scoops and so on – all in return for a loose informal friendship which had been clearly proscribed: to 'humanize' and 'legitimize' the cruel farce of *apartheid*. At the local level, this took on a more mundane form; a reporter on a daily paper, eager for success, gratefully accepts tit-bits not given to his competitors. He would be led to believe that it was because of his own personality and ability. Then he would be worked into a situation where he became dependent on the 'friendship':

'It was this major in the CID. We got really pally. "Phone me anytime," he said, "we'll chat." This went on for a year. My career really took off. I really thought he liked me and that's why he gave me the breaks. I never realized what he was doing. We'd chat about the blokes at work – he'd been a sport's photographer once or something and so knew a few people on the newspaper. We talked politics. He was a *verligte* of course. Wanted to see things change. Suddenly one day, he was gone. Wasn't at home, wasn't at the police station. Told he'd been transferred. About a week later, there were several arrests throughout the country, two in our newspaper. Only then did I twig. I checked on him. He'd been transferred *back* to the security police: he'd been on loan to the CID for just over a year.'[4]

The final crunch came for the English press in 1977; after years in which prohibitions on what the press was allowed to print increased through censorship, bannings, defence and prison and trial prohibitions, Vorster introduced the Newspaper Bill on 11 March to finally control English newspapers. After panic and uproar, the Bill was withdrawn when the English press agreed informally to control their activities.

The entire programme against the English press has been a long and slow battle of attrition. The above activities were all co-ordinated through the *Broederbond* committees charged with the task. From time to time, attempts were made to buy English newspapers through fronts. Other attempts were made to ruin newspapers, through cutting circulation to make profits marginal. The *Citizen*, for example, was timed to break in conjunction with the onset of television *and* an offer to buy South African Associated Newspapers.[5] The reasoning was that faced with a substantial profit loss, the companies would sell. Other means include establishing rival magazines to cut into the circulation of existing English journals and lastly, paying and encouraging prominent people both from South Africa and from overseas to set up magazines in South Africa.

This last experience, I think, accurately sums up the way the English system in South Africa functions in a way no text or research report can do. It depicts the ambiguities and discrepancies of non-Nationalist white South Africa in a clear and unpretentious manner so I will let the facts speak for themselves.

It concerns four murder trials that I had some contact with between 1973 and 1977 and how two of them were managed radically differently from the other two. In each case, the culprits were sent for psychiatric assessment prior to trial to establish their mental state. Two of those arrested were young males, one Coloured and one white; both were sent to Valkenburg where they were tested psychologically.

During my training, I had studied and done research on the Rorschach Ink Blot Test and its use in schizophrenic patients. I was, for a time, therefore one of the few people who knew how to interpret test protocols of psychotic patients with some degree of accuracy and was consulted in this regard by a number of professionals. In this way, I saw the test results of these two males. In both cases, I detected clear psychotic disturbances in their Rorschach protocols which was confirmed, in my mind, by both sets of case histories because each came from a highly disturbed background.

Now these facts were reported on, the cases went to court, the men found guilty and in due course hanged amidst little public notice and – to my knowledge – no outcry. Both had committed *impulsive* acts of murder *without premeditation*, both were unknown and without vast financial resources and both confessed their crimes.

The other two cases were managed in a very different fashion. In the one, a very wealthy and prominent businessman attacked and killed his wife. He was sent to trial amid great public interest; his defence was based on his denial of the crime and his attorneys advertised in newspapers for anyone who saw the mystery assailant whom he claimed was responsible for his wife's death to come forward. The businessman was found guilty and sentenced to a jail term; he did not serve his full term and is now a free man.

The fourth case, the 'Scissors Murder', as it was dubbed by the press, drew me in at an early stage when I was consulted by the defence team with a view to helping them plan their approach. I initially co-operated but later dropped out, bewildered by what was going on. Briefly, a young white Afrikaans girl had conspired to murder the wife of her middle-aged Afrikaans lover. She had carefully planned the event well in advance and hired a Coloured cripple man to do the actual stabbing, knowing full well, in my opinion, that if they were caught, she would not be held fully responsible partly because she did not do the actual murder and partly because she was white.

In the event, the murder was committed and both were charged. Great public interest was shown in the case because of the girl's youth and beauty (she was nineteen), the illicit love affair and the *apartheid* implications of her relationship with her non-white conspirator. The defence, which was *pro deo*, appeared to me to base their case on all these factors and they were helped in this by the obsession of South African society with race and sexual matters. They painted the case in a romantic light claiming that this young girl, in her desire to get married to her lover, had broken the racial barriers to befriend the Coloured cripple.

The case created great public interest and concern and many of the country's English-speaking academics and professionals offered their services to the defence and a number, in fact, appeared to give mitigating evidence in the defence of the two accused. They spoke of the background of the girl (Afrikaans and lower class) and the social and psychological pressures on her; and they did the same for the Coloured man, laying great emphasis on the peculiar South African context in which their liaison had taken place.

At the trial, they were found guilty and, on appeal against the death sentence, the girl was sentenced, as was the Coloured man, to long prison terms.

The marked contrast between the 'humane' justice administered in the latter cases (the psychiatric evidence in the 'Scissors Murder' showed the girl to be fully responsible for her acts) is self-evident. In the last case, a cold, brutal and premeditated murder in which this girl made use of *apartheid* was glossed over while South African whites aired their 'liberalism'. This fact indicated to me that even a relatively independent institution such as the judiciary, in the final analysis, was equally corrupted by the very nature of its work in administering justice in a grossly unjust society. In the rush to get involved in the case, everyone jumped on the liberal-humanist bandwagon; in the words of one professional: 'We won't get paid for this but it'll make our names.' It was Kafka at his best.

Chapter Six

Coercion and Terrorism

For some people, sharing in the profits of exploitation, material and psychological, is enough to keep them in line. In my practice, I was struck by the number of professional and business people who came for help to improve their ability to exploit. People seek treatment in most societies because they fail to cope with the demands made on them by their communities; they feel inadequate and unconfident because they cannot behave like everyone else does. In South Africa, with its inverted morality and its exploitative ethic, this desire to be 'normal' takes on a different meaning. Let me give some typical examples.

In one case, a professor at Stellenbosch University wanted help in getting rid of a troublesome member of staff who threatened his authority and personal security. Close examination of his case revealed that he was dangerously paranoid; he had ruined the careers of several young men in his department in the past, was in the habit of beating up his wife and children (it made him feel masculine) and was not above picking up an occasional prostitute (Coloured) when he felt like it. I was unable to convince this man that in any other society, his behaviour would be regarded as so abnormal as to warrant serious treatment, perhaps even hospitalization. He was supported by his friends and colleagues as well as his cultural milieu precisely because he was 'tough' and 'a fighter' who treated his subordinates and 'inferiors' in the right 'South African way'. After three months fruitless labour, he left, deeply suspicious of me because I refused to recognize, in his words, 'how we South Africans do things'.

In other cases I treated professionals who wanted more status. An attorney who was not satisfied that he was achieving enough ran, in addition to his law practice, a hire-purchase business, both concerns dealing mainly with black and Coloured people. He described several innovative and highly illegal ways he had developed to cheat his debtors and collect cash from them; he recounted stories about his homosexual exploits with Coloured boys working for him and detailed how he had tried to kill his first wife, unsuccessfully, when she refused to divorce him. This man was a well-respected member of Cape Town society and was often in the social pages with his wife and large extended family.

The interesting thing about this man and other men like him was that he wanted better status on what he called the 'insiders' circuit'. Like many of these cases, his profession was a front – legitimate cover – for a myriad of illicit and often illegal operations. Status, for these people in Cape Town, accrued not, as we would expect, from their legal skill or honesty but from their proven and creative ability to 'milk' the system. In certain circles these people and their pathologies were admired while the actions of honest men simply carrying out their jobs were denigrated. Like the African township profiteer, my patient's role and status in life was achieved through being a creative psychopath. In any other society, he would have been regarded as a middle-class criminal. He never forgave me for telling him so.

The psychological effect of these pressures works on the structure of a person's personality, not simply on his attitudes. I found the same *style* of thinking amongst people radically opposed to government policies. Many young people wanted help in coping with their various group experiences at university, for example. After listening to their 'complaints' about them and to their accounts of the pathological behaviour involved, detailed in the last chapter, I often – in my first years in practice – made a fool of myself by presuming that they were upset and disturbed by the behaviours they encountered. Far from it – they were distressed because they did not participate enough, because they were not as sought after socially and intellectually as other people, and because they had uncomfortable moral doubts they wanted to get rid of. Again, I must stress, these were not particularly disturbed people, not 'mental' cases – simply ordinary South Africans manifesting the kind of obsession to conform that I found in all corners of South African society.

For other South Africans, fear of failing to meet the basic criteria for membership of the *apartheid* society is a terrifying spectre which they will go to any lengths to avoid. Some people adopt split personalities, literally having one *persona* for South African society and another for overseas consumption, one for home and one for outside. Fear of being found wanting or weak in terms of the prevailing value system in South Africa leads to ruthless and pathological behaviour being turned on one's own family members. I give two examples of this.

The forty-year-old daughter of a prominent family was removed from my care because I discovered that the cause of her disorder was not in fact the 'hallucination' which, for twenty years, her family and her GP had pretended it was. At the age of nineteen, she witnessed her father in bed with one of the household's Coloured maids. This had been steadfastly denied and covered up to prevent any word of it leaking to the outside world – the woman's father was a prominent member of the provincial government. Now, while the woman was undoubtedly disturbed, in my opinion, she did not have schizophrenia. I detected an element of truth in her 'hallucination' and asked to see the father, whereupon I was warned off the case by the GP who told me under protest that it was not a hallucination after all, that whenever the woman brought it up, she was treated as having a breakdown, hospitalized and given shock treatment. Her previous psychiatrist, also fully in the picture, had actually recommended this course of treatment to the family because ECT tended to destroy memory and so would keep her quiet.

Another case concerned the son of a senior official in the government who was kept in the dark for several months about his son receiving treatment from me. The reasons for this secrecy were as follows: the father, who was politically a very powerful man, had asked a friend to recommend a psychiatrist to see his son who was having problems. The son was sent to an eminent psychiatrist who, after assessing the boy and his history, advised him to get away from his home environment as soon as he could as his home circumstances were very abnormal. Owing to the father's position of power, the psychiatrist was reluctant to make this recommendation in a formal report. With the son's full knowledge, he described the patient as having no signs of mental illness in his report to the boy's father. The boy moved away from home and came to see me. Over time, I prepared him for a confrontation with his father in which he told his father he was receiving treatment from me. Every attempt was made by this man to get me off the case. In a series of phone-calls, he told me: 'There is nothing wrong with my son. Why are you treating him? He has been seen by a top psychiatrist who couldn't find a damn thing wrong with him. Perhaps you'd like me to send you his report.' Then, 'I want you to discharge my son. There is nothing wrong with him – he was merely suffering from exam nerves. If you are not willing to stop treating him and pretending there is something wrong with him then you must consider the fact that I have frequent discussions with General Van den Berg [head of Bureau of State Security] and perhaps he will be able to convince you of the folly you are engaged in!' I never did hear from the General, at least not directly, but the threat was there. As it happened, the boy revealed no skeletons in the family cupboard. The boy's father panicked and applied his usual form of pressurizing people. He was not the only one to use this particular form of threat; two other powerful sets of parents did so to me as did a senior member of the Rhodesian government – all of whom *did* have skeletons in the cupboard.

I too experienced at first hand the pressures put on the individual. The moment I went into private practice, I became a full member of South African society: I had a function to perform and was therefore immediately expected to be useful, to take part in the corruptive practices demanded of someone performing that function.

I had been in practice for a few months when I began to receive phone calls from a variety of police, army and government officials. First it was a lieutenant in the drug squad who wanted to know about the activities of one of my patients. A week later it was an army Kommandant who demanded a full report on a patient of mine who was having difficulties in an army camp. There were student protests in Cape Town in June 1972, during which several of my patients were questioned or arrested. Shortly afterwards, I received a number of calls from security police officers who wanted information about patients I was treating. Sometimes they wanted to know about patients not under arrest or even charged with an offence. In each instance it was made quite clear to me that I was inviting trouble by refusing to give information, that it was an acceptable and routine request with which practically every clinician in Cape Town complied. The calls stopped once I made it clear that I was not going to co-operate and that I was going to protest to the Medical and Dental Council and to the Board of Professional Psychology.

I discussed these matters with several of my colleagues, two of whom told me quite clearly that they had often given information to the Special Branch when their patients were under arrest or being interrogated. Discreet inquiries established further that nearly all Afrikaans-speaking and some English-speaking clinicians in Cape Town co-operated when asked to. Others had taken the same line as I had. Further, several of the clinicians who helped the police actually treated radical and liberal patients. Quite unknown to the victims – students, lecturers and the like – the security police had easy and regular access to their personal files.

I began to formulate a protest about this and to try and expose matters within the professions so that some concerted action could be taken but I was advised by a senior psychiatrist whose opinion I respected, to drop the matter. Not only would it be rejected at a high level, he said, because of the pro-government loading on the various councils, but it would also mean trouble for me which I could ill-afford. Given my experience at Valkenberg, I took the hint and proceeded with caution.[1]

This kind of breach of privilege was an institutionalized practice in Cape Town, not limited to the security police. Everyone did it. I rapidly discovered that psychiatrists, doctors, social workers were regularly giving out information about their patients to people who had no right, in my opinion, to receive it even if they were concerned with the patient. Parents, for example, would phone demanding to know what I had discovered about their son or daughter – adult children, not minors – and would get angry when I refused to tell them. Irate, they would then phone their GP or a clinician they were acquainted with and get them to phone me to ask for the relevant details. At first, I provided the information – one is in fact obliged to render a preliminary report to a GP. But I found that the GPs told the parents, who then acted on their children; I was then faced with an angry and justly mistrusting patient. Eventually, I stopped giving reports to or discussing patients with GPs and with my colleagues.

These examples, I think, give some idea of the kind of pressures brought to bear on the individual. What, I wondered, did the Afrikaners do to those who took a third option; refusing to leave or to participate *and* refusing to rebel illegally? This is an important grey area in South Africa because one of the weaknesses of the system is that it cannot be openly what it is covertly. That is, if you are going to operate at this personal, nudge-nudge-wink-wink level, someone one day is going to call your bluff, take you at your word and defy you to show your iron fist. The Afrikaner government must keep up its pretences of semi-democracy because if it does not, it will attract the kind of determined opposition that it is ill-equipped to deal with. How did the authorities arrange things so that everyone fell conveniently into two types: the corrupted and the radical? What I was looking for was evidence of a level of intimidation that is seldom reported on in South Africa, something that fell between the acceptable, Western face of Afrikanerdom and the brutality. When, I wondered, did the coercion I had had a taste of, turn into terrorism? I got some idea of what went on very early on in my private practice and this led me into a new field of research.

1972 was the last year in which South African white English-speaking students as a body attracted major public attention in Cape Town. What began as a peaceful protest on the steps of the Anglican Cathedral in the centre of the city, turned into a major confrontation between the authorities and the students in which the police attacked the protesters *en masse* and brutally broke up the organized side of the protest. These events took place in June 1972 and were very tense ones for Cape Town citizens, many of whom worked in the centre and who flocked to see the demonstrators.

The full nature and extent of police activity and, more important, the reaction of the majority of the white non-student passers-by, was never made public knowledge. Through my students and patients, I learned of events which showed clearly and reliably that ordinary white citizens had expressed such shock and disgust at the way the police behaved that they had on several occasions turned on and attacked rampaging policemen. They had also actively gone out of their way to impede policemen. Several passers-by were beaten up in the process. The crowds of bystanders were provoked into attacking the police by the unwarranted and brutal beatings police dealt out to young students. In one instance, a young man, being beaten, fled into the crowd. His police assailant, flourishing his baton, attempted to rush after him, only to flee in turn as the crowd repelled him, outraged at the uncalled-for brutality. A small group of policemen who witnessed the incident charged at the crowd who turned their wrath on them so successfully that the police were routed.

Among those arrested or detained were patients of mine who told of the intimidatory and manipulative techniques used by the police. Still others provided evidence that volunteer army trainees – conscripts led by permanent force officers – had taken part in attacks on protesters. Another of my patients, who was in the army at the time, later recounted how he and other trainees were recruited and deployed in civilian clothing to appear as if they were groups of passers-by.

All this was fairly easy information to pick up. What was strange was the level of distortion of reality that everyone was prepared to live with – the students involved, the passers-by, the army trainees. How was this done? Did South Africans live at an even higher level of perception of intimidatory behaviour than I had previously thought?

The South African authorities, through their control over key aspects of social functioning, create the coercive impulse to join in the rewards of *apartheid*. But not everyone in South Africa is susceptible to these pressures. There are many South Africans who are well-informed and not confused in their thinking, who are prepared to take action against the government, who are not prepared to reap the gains to be made by co-operating; nor are they willing to lose themselves in the pursuit of normal South African values.

In order to deal with potentially troublesome people, the authorities needed an organization both to collect data and to act on it effectively. In this respect, the Nationalists had several advantages not ordinarily accorded to repressive regimes. To begin with, they had the advantage of gaining power with legitimacy and continuity; they did not seize power and then have to form an overtly repressive regime to keep it. They were accorded the rights and prestige which helped them to keep the allegiance of the most dangerous group, the English, for long enough to subvert them.

A second advantage was that the people who gained power were able to call on a nation of fellow-Afrikaners to assist them at all levels and in every way. Provided the new leaders of 1948 followed

Afrikaans dictates and morality, they were assured of the co-operation of virtually every Afrikaner man, woman and child to provide information, to shape and direct propaganda, to man the army and police forces, to organize business, the economy, and so on. Afrikaner Nationalists formed a state within a state and were able to produce a regime that was not circumvented by the physical and intellectual limitations of a single, narrow ruling clique. This is the third advantage: the Afrikaner state serves Afrikanerdom; not only through the *Broederbond* but through each Afrikaner's own desire to look after his interests.

These advantages meant that the Nationalists had a head start when they took over the security apparatus after the war. They inherited a well-established system that was deeply embedded into all levels of South African society, black and white. It was run by, and relied upon information supplied by, many people who had a broadly South African political and social view and who were, in the main, orientated towards the Western world and Smuts' notion of co-operation and slow change. The Nationalists could draw on this information, which they did, while slowly weeding out any potentially harmful members. Just as the Nationalists took over all the institutions of state slowly by replacing key personnel and power structures while retaining the familiar appearance of the organizations, so in the security services little was changed at first, and when in the late 1950s the system was overhauled and revamped (and thoroughly Nationalized) it was too late for non-Nationalists to do much about it. To this system has been added the information gathered by Afrikaners and their fellow-travellers in their daily lives.

Because of the historical situation in South Africa and the continuity between Smuts' government and the Nationalist government, prominent whites and non-whites in every sector have long-established relationships with each other and with key people in their sectors. Like most cities, South African cities are run by people who are familiar with one another, who know one another or are even related to one another. South Africa has numerous prominent families who are linked through their business, educational and interpersonal interactions and who, in turn, because white society is so small, are familiar with other important people.

The Afrikaner system that was developed in the Boer Republics works well here because this web of personal contacts founded in better times is today being used to provide information on which the security police act. The task of *Broeders* is to hear the words, fears and reports of fellow-Afrikaners and to refer it when necessary to the relevant *Broederbond* committees to deal with. The teachers in the staff-room, the foreman at lunch, all have information of one kind or another – gossip. And on this the security services feed. Every Afrikaner, if he or she is a Nationalist, is a potential informer 'for the good of the *volk*'.

While, after 1948, it was possible to get information and assitance from some English-speakers who were favourable to the Nationalists' cause, this was not sufficiently widespread to achieve the complete security required by the Nationalists. English-speakers had, as we have seen, a different sense of South Africa. Secondly, they had powerful institutions of their own and contact with overseas groups thus making them relatively impervious to the kinds of pressures that could be brought to bear on the Afrikaans community.

There was a third danger: The English had certain institutions like the universities and the press and businesses that were both dangerous and yet could not be overtly touched without alienating and polarizing English opinion away from the Nationalist cause. I gradually learned the full extent of how English institutions were manipulated; far more ruthlessly and efficiently than I had at first realized. Since 1948, English institutions have been squeezed gently in ever decreasing circles by a web of government interference and legislation; slowly, inch by inch, the government made the English institutions watch it and its movements. It passed laws, it created powers for itself that forced the institutions to deal with it in a way that suited the Nationalists and to which the institutions were vulnerable.

If the Nationalists had passed a law closing white universities to non-whites in 1949 there would have been an enraged outcry; similarly, if in 1957 the government had threatened to close the English press there would have been an uproar. Both of these instances would have stiffened English resistance. By 1959, though, the government had established a whole network of laws and institutions such that education was effectively separate for black and white. When in that year it introduced the Separate Universities Bill, it knew full well that the two soundest arguments it had going for it that would effectively stifle any English opposition were a) that separate facilities were a *fait accompli*, and b) that everything was legal. Thus to overturn the Separation of the Universities Bill did not mean *just* that – it meant overturning the whole concept of separate development. By putting pressure on slowly, never letting it up, by confusing the issues, the government ensured that reject-ing the University Act came to mean for the English community, rejecting the government's whole ideology – a psychologically unmanageable challenge that no university can or should ever face. The government's logic was remorseless: get them to accept little changes spread over time until it is too late; acceptance of the first step means, inevitably, acceptance of every step.

In 1949, the government, barely in power, had little or no control over the powerful English universities. It needed time to infiltrate them and to buy people where it could; it needed time to plant spies and to set up the pincer movement I have described above. Where other countries commission security services to infiltrate into enemy institutions, the Afrikaners did this to South Africa's English institutions. Only when it was sure that it had enough influence inside the universities to balance the genuinely horrified English elements did it act to bring universities in line with its pol-icies. It took ten years to achieve, made some English academics wealthy and gave a lot of others chairs for services rendered, but it succeeded.[2]

This kind of operation was conducted on every major English institution in the country; the car industry, for example, was con-trolled slowly and effectively by a long process of gradual legal encroachment. Border industries were encouraged by concessions that made good business sense to some firms thus ensuring for the government their tacit acceptance of the homelands policy. Each act of policy was, in some way, tied to an act of concession from English institutions that was rewarded materially and psychologi-cally by the government. Profits tied to the Border industries, aca-demic freedom to segregated universities and, eventually, press freedom in return for publishing what the government wanted to hear.

This intimidatory process alone did not provide the security required. It still left English institutions with far more room to move and form pockets of resistance than was the case with Afrikaans institutions. There had to be other ways of creating control and so, alongside all this, three other central forms of coercion were employed.

English and Afrikaans communities were, by Nationalist design, separate. Gradually, however, especially in the 1960s, this was relaxed and far greater contact between the two took place. But this was because inroads had already been made into the English community during the 1950s by selected Afrikaans and English people favourable to the authorities. As time went by and the web of laws increased, English firms had to have more and more dealings with the authorities. This meant that they needed people to help them who spoke Afrikaans or, better still, had contacts in the Afrikaner world: the 'Fixers'.

Companies rapidly learnt that they got concessions if they knew the right people so they began to cultivate and socialise with key Afrikaners. They also began to employ Afrikaans accountants, attorneys, secretaries, people who, since 1948, had become the elite. Many English South Africans, in fact, encouraged their children to train at Afrikaans universities because of this need.

These Afrikaners become the vanguard of contact between the two white groups and provided in the process a valuable means of setting up information sources as well as acting as Judas goats for the English sheep. Let me explain this. The English system of interacting with the government was essentially Anglo-Saxon; it had its own old-boy networks and its own morality. When the Nationalists took over, this fell away and a new system had to be imposed; the English had to be carefully introduced to the Afrikaner way. They had, in short, to be divided to be corrupted and, by and large, they have been. By making the English learn to deal with *persons* and with vague powers and by rewarding them for so behaving, the Nationalists set a pattern of behavorial expectancies: a person corrupted in business could be corrupted in other ways too.

By this method, English businesses were made to stand behind the political policies of the Nationalists. What the Afrikaner did was to say, in effect, 'Look, we are going to steal the country from the Africans. If you want to continue to function, to make profits, you'd better steal with us otherwise we'll take away your rights and your money. Furthermore, if you deal with us, we'll save your face by making it all sound altruistic and, moreover, we'll make it legal.' Thus you had an English company *knowing* it was doing wrong whilst *pretending* (legally) it was not. The fear of loss of profits was greater than its fear of doing wrong. What better way than to hide behind the legitimacy screen provided for just this purpose by the Nationalists?

Every time this happened, the Nationalists had yet another company one more step on the road to being firmly committed to its policy. In vital sectors, once all companies had taken the first step, the government created the threats and the rewards for a second step and so on, *ad infinitum*. The government deliberately blurred its future policies so that the companies or institutions never knew what was coming next. Let me give one example to illustrate how this works.

An industrial group was having trouble on several fronts; its factories had been built in the Western Cape in the 1950s and had originally relied on the low cost and reliability of African labour to make very substantial profits. Gradually, under pressure from the government, it had been forced into severe difficulties: it had its allocation of Africans slowly cut so that it had to use increasingly more Coloured staff who cost more and were far less reliable. Eventually, it was refused permission to employ Africans and had to use Coloureds at every level.

Then its profits were systematically eaten away by inflation in the late 1960s and by the government which imposed a sales tax on some of its products. The group began to have a cash-flow problem and at that time it received a discreet offer from the authorities: if they would close some of their Cape factories and re-open them on the Transkeian border instead, the government was prepared not only to give the normal concessions for this but to lift the sales tax on their affected products.

After some debate and after some change in directorial staff the group decided to accept this proposal and re-locate, which they did. However, the government did not lift the sales tax, it simply reduced it. The group was caught. It had re-located at considerable expense (which it would not have done under normal circumstances) and while its profit position improved marginally, it was not nearly enough and certainly not what the authorities had promised. However, there was also no way back. The group struggled on, its labour problems partly solved by now being allowed to employ reliable blacks from the homelands at even lower cost than previously.

However, again, there was a snag: local labour was inferior and unskilled so the factory had to train its staff again, all of which took more money than had been planned for. After a perilous year, the government closed the jaws of its trap around the group. In return for complete removal of sales tax, the company was to agree to let its factories in the homelands be used as a government front project to export South African products overseas.

What this involved was packaging some of its produce in labels and tins purporting to come from a non-South African country; the company would appear to be simply transporting goods through South Africa *en route* from the company's 'factory' sighted elsewhere in Africa. The government has a number of South African front companies set up in black African states, sometimes without the knowledge of the government concerned. Thus South Africa is able to export its own goods using these front companies to countries which do not allow entry to South African products. The group had no option but to co-operate and this closed a long and carefully constructed operation by the South African authorities whereby a company had been taken on a confusing route step by step, until it was irrevocably tied to the government and its policies.

It is a well established and complex procedure involving careful co-ordination by *Broederbond* committees. South African firms employ foreign nationals resident in South Africa to act as representatives and set up contracts for the front companies. Payment is then made to the company via the country in which it is registered. The country, in turn, trades with South Africa and the South African government re-imburses the original company for the deal from the money made from exporting other goods to the country. This balancing-of-accounts act can only be done if the *Broederbond* controls chains of related companies. Hence the construction of such chains in interrelated sectors of the economy similar to this and to the one I described earlier relating to African townships.[3]

This was an example of the system at work at one level. The offers to and from government companies were transmitted through the select band of Afrikaners. As time went by the system became more widespread and more effective and the need to keep it under tight control fell away as industrialised corruption became widely established in South Africa. At another level, however, control was greatly tightened and the process of corrupting and converting the English community intensified.

It seems strange to an outsider that an ostensibly moral, religious and upright community such as the Afrikaners', with its emphasis on convention and Christianity, can permit so many irreligious and immoral actions to exist in a country which it controls so thoroughly. The Afrikaner has demonstrated his ability to be ruthless and controlling where he chooses to be, why be so lax in policing the moral behaviour of whites as a whole? The answer is that this policy is entirely in keeping with the security requirements of the Afrikaans state and it has a comprehensive logic of its own.

As I have said, when individuals are under stress, they put pressure on their private lives; they engage in fads and fashions in an obsessive way; they have sexual liaisons, they drink, use drugs, or they engage in the kind of corrupt business and professional practices I have described. The Nationalists knew this and they knew that as they closed around the English, they would be driven into themselves and would commit private and personal – and eventually public – indiscretions. Provided that the authorities had good sources of information and the means to control these behaviours, they could be put to good use in the Nationalists' cause.

More important: a person who engages in activities that are tolerated by the authorities but which are in fact illicit or illegal is highly vulnerable. By encouraging such a person to continue with and delve further into this activity, and by allowing him to believe that he is free to do this, a need for it is created which can then be manipulated. The security authorities in South Africa have systematically allowed the English, non-whites and certain sections of the Afrikaans community to engage in corrupt and pathological behaviours so that these actions can be so used should the need arise.

I quote now from a report given to me by one of my patients whose uncle was a security police officer:

'. . . he (my uncle) said that the SB prefer for people to do things in groups rather than alone although that can also be used. They also don't like really freaky way-out things or one-off things. They like their target to engage routinely in smallish ways – take drugs: OK if a person is on grass, or even acid, but it must be something he does regularly and not too obviously otherwise the regular police would have to bust him. Then they keep the guy or the group nicely supplied; they watch over the whole thing like a mother hen; tap all the phones; they even protect the merchants, who are usually Coloured, just so their target continues to get their supply. He told me how often the SB have to rescue merchants and targets in ordinary police raids – like they have to send the regular police on wild goose chases, anything to keep the group happy and of course, to keep the group from finding out that they are being watched.

'They would never arrest anyone, just watch and tap and bug. They picked up huge amounts of info because the group, you know, on acid or grass just talked their head off. Even if they weren't politicos they often gave details out about others or stuff like affairs, sex things, etc . . .'

This particular pattern provided information. But there were others where targets became operatives for the authorities, often unwittingly, simply because a group turned inwards tends to have a reduced sense of its own direction and loses contact with ordinary demands of reality.

In small communities – such as sections of the English or Coloured community – normal human functions, especially those concerned with internal power-structures and attachments, have a status far greater than is normally the case. They tend to dominate the activity of institutions and groups precisely because they serve no *real* societal function. Individuals tend to get over-involved in group activity, leadership politics, coercing of individuals: status in the group replaces reality-orientated functions and, in a deeper sense, individuality is replaced by a group mentality and a group sense. These are the established results which follow when groupings of people become isolated from the processes of social functioning. They are well-known to Afrikaans psychologists and to the authorities, and great use is made of the psychology of such socially deprived groups to shape and direct the internal directions taken by the groups.

This control does not always take a definite formal shape. Often groups within an institution can be left to their own devices and spend years engrossed in nothing more important than trying to decide which leadership clique to support. In other situations, the direction can easily be shaped by making use of information collected in such a way as to let the group's conflicting power groups eliminate any potential threat. Let me give some examples of this.

Several groups exist in Cape Town amongst academics and professionals which could become significantly influential if allowed to. Because of the fear-anxiety factor that dominates white and English functioning, many of these groups limit their own activities to options within the law, thus permitting a safe compromise along the lines I have already laid down – conscience-easing actions which stop short of defiance. There are groups that go further, and I will give two examples of how they are controlled.

The first, comprising concerned academics and professionals from a wide range of disciplines, got going out of shared feelings expressed at certain T-groups which they attended. Since it included some of Cape Town's prominent and clear-thinking individuals from the English, Afrikaans and Coloured communities, it could have served to polarise opinion – to achieve, as a group, something its individuals could not do alone. Further, it was a completely legal organisation. Yet it got nowhere. After several meetings its members were split between the various proposals it had for the type of action it wanted to take. One pole wanted to challenge the government and to be provocative, the other to be more tacit and to make converts quickly amongst professionals. Its members began to take sides and the whole thing fizzled out with small groups splitting off; far more energy was expended, in fact, by each pole (organised around several dominating personalities) attacking each other and, inevitably, gossiping. Urgent meetings were held involving all-night sessions in which petty details of who did what or said what – in short, gossip – were pored over with great fervour; people engaged in forays against the 'enemy' – not the authorities, simply the other pole – to undermine them or convert them to their side. The organisation lasted several months; it created great excitement and everyone concerned expressed deep satisfaction that 'something had been done'; two people got divorced in this time through frictions exposed by the tension, and further disruption was caused by another member's suicide.

What happened, in short, in these white-dominated political groups was precisely what happened in English society as a whole: without proper contact with reality, they exposed their disturbing feelings and destroyed the group. I knew of no such group that survived these pressures and stayed effective and, in fact, I conclude that they are not possible in the present South African context; a far more realistic perspective is necessary – one which recognises *exactly* what is going on.

The above example needed no interference to destroy itself. Doubtless, it was carefully watched and allowed to die a natural death. In a second instance, though, the destruction was helped along by manipulating conflicting members to break up the group. This group was comprised of several Afrikaans-speaking people as well as English: white artists, musicians and intellectuals, who met loosely to discuss art and politics among other things. Among them was a patient of mine whose brother was a *Broederbond* member. Concerned, the latter asked his brother to keep an eye on things for him and to let him know if things got serious. As it turned out, though, the 'progressive' brother was a powerful organising factor in the group's life. Without telling his brother, he spoke about the contact at the next group meeting, denouncing this as the kind of thing the Afrikaans community was trying to stop. The group meetings continued, but several of the members privately were unhappy that it had happened and they made their views known to one another; these were amongst the members most committed to the endeavour and who had the most to lose in the Afrikaans community at large if their meetings became public knowledge.

Now, someone amongst this group was also a *Broeder*, or had contacts with one, and several subtle things happened, all related to the member who had condemned the *Broederbond*. He received a Christmas card from a deputy minister in the government, and this was noticed when the group met at his home. Then he was seen entering a government building, then he was invited to dinner at a dinner party given by a *Broederbond* professor at Stellenbosch University. All these things appeared to happen by chance and each appeared innocuous; he had no idea why the card was sent, he was asked to produce a document by a government official and he actually declined the dinner invitation. But he was convinced that all the events had been engineered because their effect was enough to make the sub-group suspicious of him and, slowly but surely, the group disintegrated as mutual hostility and suspicion began to take its effect. Thus a potentially useful group was rendered harmless with very little effort.

Because of the anxiety pervading South African society and because of the involvement of people in the pathological processes created by the situation, most movements are contained by the application of these legalistic or interpersonal measures. They are based on a simple but effective psychological model: corrupt a person or a group and then lead them on to greater rewards and greater corruption, be it in business or politics. A political group which wants to have a definite end or effect corrupts itself if it fails to achieve that end through failing to recognise the reality it is dealing with and involving itself in its own personal gain. The first group above, for example, was corrupt; it put pleasure, excitement and the self-fulfilment gained by its members for themselves above the need to do something, to organise properly.

The last level of coercion is used on those people and groups who slip through everything else. It involves more definite action from specialist security personnel and more interference in the lives of their targets. This group, young students – black and white – offered by far the greatest threat to the South African government through the 1960s and early 1970s because, apart from the motivation common to all, the whites among them had the opportunity to travel and study overseas; many had British passports which allowed them free access and travel to countries to which South African citizens could not go. Black people rarely had the funds to travel outside South Africa and were rarely allowed to do so by the authorities anyway.

A combination of these factors with determination and personality enabled a number of South Africans to perceive the situation accurately and to escape the effects of the fog that usually minimises these capabilities. It was these people who took the overt and covert leadership of radical groups and who managed, too, not to have too much to do with the corrupting patterns of normal South African life.[4]

To do this, though, demanded a certain type of personality: a resistance to indoctrination and a determination to resist the onslaughts made by the authorities and the South African cultural matrix on an individual's personality. Some people escaped the impact of post-1948 South Africa by having grown up before these privations; others born into the Afrikaner state were fortunate to have been brought up in families which had their own counter-indoctrinatory techniques, or who were able to provide especially supportive systems of their own.

One of the consequences of being born into South Africa after 1948 is that as time passes the range of psychologically healthy options and outlets for individuals has gradually narrowed. I have described this effect for English white communities and groups and it applies equally to individuals. There is no healthy solution except to leave completely – but this is purely an individual solution; it changes nothing socially. To conform to the South African situation creates psychological problems and, inevitably, to fight it *demands* psychological disturbance in those individuals prepared to resist the system. The same personality that creates resistance and determination also contains pathology, and it is this pathology manipulated by the authorities that causes the downfall of many South African radical groups inside the country.

Resistance demands that the individual must cease to function as an ordinary member of society; she or he thus becomes deprived of certain key interactions and supports simply because to accept them means to accept the situation. This is especially the case in South Africa. To resist *apartheid* means you have to cease living in an ordinary sense because *apartheid* dominates every aspect of human functioning. You cannot enjoy sport because it is segregated and it remains so despite window-dressing. You cannot enjoy any amenity such as the movies, theatre, swimming, etc., because they are segregated. Your life has thus to be lived largely through two modes: through intellect and through replacing normal outlets and supports with others.

The stress placed on individual relationships, family relationships and relationships with fellow-group-members is consequently enormous, especially if the person chooses not to adopt the usual practices of his or her peer group (like drugs, profiteering, adventuring, and so on). These people develop 'normal' personal problems and by and large, like the Coloured and black adolescents I discussed earlier, are amongst the few people in South Africa who tend to behave decently, responsibly and reasonably.

Unfortunately, though, in South Africa, this in turn leads to *pathology*; it constitutes a maladjustment to the demands of both day-to-day *apartheid* and ordinary human reality, and the consequence is that many of these people develop a borderline personality disorganisation and use two broad types of personality to survive. Some cope by joining up with other radicals and forming a tight, interlaced communal group, highly intellectual and highly schizoid. By this, I mean that they are united at two levels, both poles in terms of personality function: an intellectual ideological level and a deep emotional level. Their ideology prevents them from being foggy and is thus used as an obsessive defence against outside interference, with group members watching one another and helping one another remain doctrinaire, faithful and *committed*. The emotional needs are met by the complex feelings they have for one another and the form these take; men and women form intense (unrealistically intense in a normal sense) relationships with each other and with the same sex. These intense needs have to be contained within their circle because there is no other means of support.

The second type of solution is for a person to wander in and out of various groups of this kind according to the nature of his own pathology or personality needs. Usually such a person is of the follower type and he generally maintains his vacillations by using relationships with 'ingroup' members and outsiders, usually family, all of which are characterised by borderline pathology.

The first type tend to come from homes in which the son or daughter has formed a very close supportive relationship with a single parent, usually of the opposite sex. This special relationship seems to ground the growing child's security and to make him or her relatively independent of having to form relationships with other people beyond the levels of intellect and emotional need I have defined above. A person who feels especially close and loved by a parent needs a peer group only to share certain, mainly sexual experiences with; all other needs are met by the parent concerned who is, in turn, over-involved with his child's life. It is this peculiar support which permits the radical to be psychologically equipped to withstand the South African normalising processes, but it is also this support which makes the person vulnerable.

These people tend to develop private personal pathologies which arise out of their lack of development in the middle ground between intellect and normal emotional needs. They exhibit the kind of private sexual perversion that is to be found amongst people of this type in other societies who get over-involved in causes, or their career. Many of the people Shirley Jenner and I studied were homosexual (male and female), some of the males were transvestic and obsessively fetishistic; many had illicit affairs with prostitutes (male and female) and with strangers. Others collected pornography, and nearly all engaged in obsessive adolescent fantasy: masturbatory activities, aggressive power-play and sadistic and vicious interpersonal games. What must be clear here is that these problems arose at the individual level – they were not shared communal acts in the fashion of the non-Afrikaner groups described earlier; they were secret.

They remained excessively dependent on their parent figures long into adulthood and became consequently over-involved and indeed obsessed with these relationships as they struggled to act out the pathology this kind of intimate relationship with one's parent involves. They could not break free; they both resented this and yet were scared to break away and resolved it all by engaging in an infernal and interminable cycle of hostility, guilt, compassion, resolution and passive-aggression which dominated, in turn, their relationship with others who came close.

All this served to fill the lives of this first type and helped them to remain fixed not only in their personality development but in their political involvement and commitment. In short, these people made a career out of their political life-styles and their personality pathology.

The second type of person in this category was less well-integrated, less supported. Because of this they inevitably became more obviously disturbed, more often inclined to seek treatment and more vacillating in political involvement. These people had an inferior status with the first group because they felt less 'committed'. They inevitably came from families of two relating parents who had more than one sibling to concern themselves with and who were also politically aware. These people were borderline and showed related symptomology, being schizoid, sometimes psychotic. Their personal lives were in disarray and they lacked the ideological commitment or single-parent support that *type one* people had: their main aim was ideological and personal security and they changed groups according to where they felt they would best get it. Because of their 'inferior' follower status, they became, as it were, ideological 'groupies'.

The authorities need information about the activities of these people and they get it by following three avenues: spies directly recruited and infiltrated into key groups; information provided by professionals in the community either directly or indirectly; or information imparted by people being blackmailed by the authorities in one way or another.

The authorities need to use force only where necessary; they are so in control of the situation that they are able to take effective action without resorting to the too-overt use of extreme measures.

By far the bulk of the information passed to the security police comes not from spies – although there are known to be a number – but from professionals who willingly or unwillingly give information, and from information leaked by the activists themselves. In some cases the authorities have acted on suspects without even having confirming information, by simply operating on psychological and social group patterns. In serious cases, the police or authorities move quickly and efficiently, but then allow secondary groupings to remain in circulation for long periods. By controlling and watching these they are able to identify potentially dangerous situations early. Let me describe first how the authorities collect data and then how they act on it.

The first and basic principle followed by the South African authorities in dealing with its dissident groups is to concentrate on establishing psychological types independent of information received. Since the actual information they can get from spying and bugging is minimal (most groups employ quite elaborate security precautions) and sometimes confusing, they prefer to rely on advanced systems of analysis to work out what is going on.

This is highly sophisticated and difficult to detect for the psychologically unwary. First, extensive tape-recordings are made from surveillance devices such as phone taps taken from every possible source related to the target's group. This includes family members, friends, even hairdressers. Extensive filming is also used. The ubiquitous photographs every student knows are taken at protest meetings are not taken simply to identify people but also to help the police experts build up a psychological profile of their victims. These photos are supplemented by movie films made of individuals as well as long-range shots. Again, these are not used simply as 'evidence' but to help capture an individual's moods and the type of relationships he or she engages in. People taking their dogs for walks or petting their animals have been known to be photographed. The work is done, incidentally, from vans or trailers and sometimes, I was told, from GPO vans parked outside houses or institutes; a genuine repair team at work outside while a police photographer and recording expert are busy inside the van.

The purpose of all this is to establish personality type and rhythm. Voice analysis is done from recordings, and mood range and personal style are determined from these analyses. A person, for example, who speaks in code will not necessarily reveal *facts* but he or she will reveal – through *how* they talk, whether or not they are excited – that something different is happening. Careful analysis will often reveal what it is.[5]

Taping a conversation between two parents or two housewives may seem innocuous, but in the hands of a security officer and his staff of experts these tapes can be goldmines of information because they reveal the nature of the psychological relationship people in the group have with each other, with their parents or siblings.

A second level of analysis is done on this data. Information which can be collected from various orthodox sources near to the target group helps to shape and give meaning to the profiles developed in the first analysis. Several sources are used. Radicals themselves may not talk, but their parents and friends may; they can be pumped unknowingly. A parent of a patient of mine gave away his son's entire history of neurosis to a kindly middle-aged man to whom he got talking in a hospital waiting-room. They both apparently had sons of the same age and perhaps they had been at the same school? Lulled, my patient's father spoke quite openly. The boy heard about the incident and mentioned it to me. The father, fortunately, remembered the man's name; it was on a new hospital folder and it had been on a certain day in a certain department at Groote Schuur hospital. I checked and there was no such person: no folder had been made out that day and the staff had not had anyone in by that name for over six months.

Other information comes from army experiences the target may have had. The army keeps a psychological dossier on every conscript and this is one of the reaons why BOSS[6] was given control over access to army intelligence. Like most white males, radicals have to do army service at a young age and this gives the authorities plenty of opportunity to report on them. One can see clearly now why psychological services are being computerised in South Africa – it saves time, money and awkward questions being raised in parliament.

Without doubt, though, the most valuable information is given to the authorities by professionals involved with targets. Let me detail how this is done. Firstly, as I discovered early on, several clinicians in Cape Town are in the habit of willingly giving information on request. Others are coerced; one clinician was threatened with detention as a state witness unless he co-operated; another, whose private pathology was well-known to the security police, was blackmailed into opening his files to the police.[7]

But there were other instances where doctors refused to help but from whom information was still obtained. Many clinicians use their secretaries as confidential clerks, permitting them free access to their files. Sometimes security policewomen try to obtain employment in this capacity to get at the files. There are other ways too. In one instance, a psychiatrist's secretary was having a relationship with a man. After several dates, he began to question her extensively about the patients in her employer's practice. She became suspicious and promptly stopped talking. The relationship was terminated by the man three days later and he disappeared. If he had not been careless, she admitted that she would never have suspected what he was up to. In other cases, clinical information is obtained through clinician's wives who are not always as discreet as they should be and in whom their husbands confide.

There are other sources of information within the professional sphere. The Coloured University in Bellville near Cape Town is a government set up and controlled institution staffed by pro-government academics. I treated several students from the university and several white lecturers as well as white staff from Stellenbosch who were seconded there, and I was able to confirm what the students from the university had long suspected: many white Afrikaans lecturers at the University of the Western Cape receive two salaries – one for lecturing and one in the form of special bursaries and grants for serving as agents for the Bureau of State Security.

These people keep an eye not only on their Coloured students and those of their colleagues who are suspect but also on foreign white lecturers and professors who the government imports from time to time to add prestige and, hopefully, status to the university. The civil service operates a similar system of spying on its Coloured and black employees and on suspect whites but this will be discussed in the next chapter.

The information gathered by these various methods is examined not only by security officers but also by teams of various 'experts' that the security police call in. Quite apart from the police's own experts, some of whom make frequent and extensive trips overseas to train and to be briefed on the latest techniques, the authorities draw on the skills of many Afrikaans academics and research establishments.

I mentioned earlier the way psychology departments at Afrikaans universities receive extensive funds and up-to-date equipment; in time, I discovered that several other key departments at Afrikaans universities receive similar attention, in particular sound-acoustics laboratories and departments of pharmacology, neurology, and psychiatry in Afrikaans medical schools. In addition, individual researchers receive special funds to conduct research into matters of value to the security police, in particular the development of advanced eavesdropping and photographic equipment, psychological assessment devices and, more disturbing, advanced techniques for extracting information from, and controlling, individuals.

I learnt that some researchers were conducting research into the effects of prolonged use of drugs for use in the interrogation of subjects and in the breakdown of personality. Others were developing drugs for a wide range of uses by the security police including a variety of poisons for limited, direct effects – especially neurological effects. Still others were investigating personality disintegration patterns by using a combination of paralysing drugs with sensory and social deprivation. One psychiatrist told me of one study he had taken part in in which subjects were paralysed and left alone in isolation while various forms of sensory deprivation, blindfolds, ear muffs and white noise were experimented with. Their reactions were studied on monitoring equipment.

I was told that under these conditions, simple human functions, like urinating or breathing, take on obsessive and nightmarish proportions for the sufferers. A drunken Afrikaans psychiatrist described a form of torture that he was working on whereby the victim is left with a blocked urinal catheter; the pressure of being unable to urinate is so great apparently, that the technique is considered to be a highly effective and cheap means of extracting information.

Great emphasis in some departments of psychology and sociology is placed on how to disrupt and control small groups. Clearly, some of this 'research' finds its way into the interrogation programmes used on detainees, but equally clearly some of it is used against radicals and other potentially dangerous social groups. Some of the experiments for these studies are performed on people under state control. While it is known that some researchers use student volunteers on 'safe' parts of research programmes, long-term prisoners – especially non-whites – are often used as subjects in return for privilege awards and early release.

Medical experiments are also carried out on the same basis. I know of one study which investigated the limbic system – a central part of the brain – and its function on Coloured prisoners. The researcher was studying means of reducing aggressive behaviour in violent prisoners and was removing sections of the limbic system in brain surgery known to reduce such behaviours in animals. This study was done under the guise of therapeutic surgery but I have reason to believe that it had a more sinister use. Drug-effect studies are sometimes conducted on mental patients – white and non-white – 'hopeless' cases in back wards whose deaths, in case of accident or policy, go unnoticed. Sometimes, political prisoners with medical problems are deliberately neglected or treated with placebos so that the authorities can study the psychological effects of pain or discomfort on the patient; in other cases, of course, this neglect is used as a means of inflicting pain and suffering within the 'legal' boundaries of the system.

Armed with the information provided by these 'experts' and especially with the directives provided by state and academic psychologists and psychiatrists, the security authorities are able to direct their operations with uncanny accuracy and relatively little effort. One form these operations take to try to remove individuals from groups and to extract information is to compromise the individuals using their personal pathology. Hence the unusual tolerance shown by the authorities of the various illicit activities that occur. Permitting such things as drug abuse, cross-racial prostitution, etc., allows the authorities plenty of opportunity to collect data and set up suitable coercive situations. Over time the authorities lull their targets into a sense of security and they regularly engage in their pathology, blind to what is going on. There are literally hundreds of people in Cape Town who have blissfully engaged in illicit activities for years feeling quite secure, but who will be caught at any time should the authorities decide to do so.

One professor regularly picked up young Coloured men and spent the night with them in his beachfront flat. One morning, though, he was woken early by a white man at the door saying he was a security policeman; the professor's pick-up from the night before was a police decoy – he was going to be arrested. The professor was let off – in return for information – as a kind of special favour: 'We won't say anything to the ordinary police, no charge and so on, but. . .' Not wishing to compromise his friends, the professor simply withdrew from the radical group he was in. He had no wish to have his 'problem' exposed.

Other 'prostitutes' are employed to sleep with a target and then to remove articles, documents, papers, etc., in the target's flat and deliver them to the security police. By stealing other objects as well, these incidents appear to be thefts and are not too easily suspected. Reports of theft are seldom made by the victim anyway since to do so means possible exposure. Other pick-ups are used to plant drugs or banned literature in homes, leaving them to be 'discovered' by raiding police.

Great use is made of what I have called ideological 'groupies' since these are often the weak link in radical groups and not always so easily identified until it is too late. It is a relatively easy process to play on these people's fears and anxieties and their lability. Information leaked to one of these people, for example, is sure to be used as a means of creating conflict in groups. These people tend to watch group activity closely and are motivated by a need to belong in the group. Once *in*, they try to evict those in a less committed or doctrinaire position in order to ensure their own survival. Correctly managed by the security police, the psychology of these individuals can destroy a radical group more effectively than direct police intervention or the arrest of its ringleaders.

Rumour, spread by such people in these groups, is crippling and paranoia-making. Since the groups tend to cut themselves off from outside modes of thinking and information, they rely far more on one another for correct information about what is going on. By feeding in select information, the security police create great conflict. Releasing information obtained from psychiatrists or psychologists about leading members has a devastating impact since the groups tend to have extremely high levels of expectancy, equating high ideological principles with aesthetic personal morality: a good leader who is discovered to have a perversion becomes suspect and his 'true' motives for being committed are questioned. Groupies can be relied upon to do the rest and split the group. Spies leaking information like 'X is really a policeman' are widely used to cripple many organisations in their early phases. Sealed off, inexperienced and frightened, these radical groups sometimes need little attention to ensure that their activities are limited to safe options.

The authorities from time to time create their own underground organisations, especially in the Coloured and African communities. Using operatives, they plant 'radicals' in institutions and groups who collect around them like-minded people – especially 'groupies'. These groups are permitted to grow and develop and natural leaders are encouraged to emerge, enabling the authorities to be in a position to 'set a thief to catch a thief'. The controlled underground group composed of enough non-government members to render it respectable then makes contact with other underground groups. In this way, the authorities are able to learn of the extent of radical activity while at the same time, through their own group, passing along doctored information as the situation demands. Some 'underground' groups function for years and many have become permanent parts of their communities.

These groups, together with the police, make or break the status of key personalities in radical groups by such devices as leaving certain people free while arresting or intimidating others, by scaring off unwanted people, by passing along accurate and personally damaging information, and so on. Key people in an organisation are watched and identified so that they and their actions can act, in the words of one, as a 'pulse' for what is going on. The authorities gain far more from this than from arresting them or removing them from the scene.

The effect of these tactics on the first radical type is to sap their ability or willingness to go on. Faced with the frustrations and fears involved in conducting radical political action in South Africa, these people tend to adopt one of four courses: embittered and out of a sense of hurt personal pride and ego, they sometimes turn against their own colleagues and become a security risk as they attack those who they feel have let them down. One of the side effects of the psychological strengths and clarity of perception these people possess is that the experience of constant failure makes them fall back on to the special relationship the person has or had with the one parent for emotional security. Using these they turn against their colleagues, blaming them for their own failings.

Sometimes the person's own self-confidence collapses and he discovers gaps in his emotional life which in turn, causes the person to collapse emotionally, turning to the authorities for support and sympathy. Many security police officers are experts in managing this kind of collapse and often enter into deep and lasting one-way relationships with previously radical activists.

The second option is for the individual to get out of politics altogether. Some become, in fact, deeply religious or deeply involved in non-political causes, channelling the same intense concern previously put into politics into safer options. They stay, however, in South Africa. Others take the third alternative and leave South Africa.

The fourth option occurs for much the same reason as the first: angry, hurt and embittered, the individual feels that he has to prove himself not by turning against his ideology but by engaging in even more extreme actions. He or she feels that they have to justify the validity of their 'specialness' (tacit in their relationship with their parent) and faced with their apparent 'helplessness' against the condemnation or mistrust of their colleagues, they undertake actions that will make or break their belief – and their friends' belief – in themselves.

This option obviously poses the greatest threat to the authorities since extreme actions, guerrilla acts and the like, embarrass and threaten the government. However, through the control they exert over the psychological context of the country and the radical communities, the authorities have little *real* trouble from people who choose the fourth option. Few radicals, in fact, have the correct psychology to undertake effective action; they are untrained and, moreover, they frequently have the wrong support. When they take the fourth option, they frequently do so impulsively, take risks and expose themselves to unnecessary dangers because, once they choose this mode, they themselves become the 'groupies'. They set out to prove themselves instead of to improve the situation. They make careless and foolish mistakes and inevitably are caught.

Too many of South Africa's radicals – especially whites – seem to me to go out of their way to get caught and they appear to use this as a form of status. It serves to prove in their eyes, their 'genuineness' and their 'commitment'. If only they could see how this 'evidence' is used after their arrest: Cape Town, after each arrest, becomes inundated with people who make cocktail-and-dinner party small talk and vegetarian restaurant-status by claiming to have 'known' or 'worked with' or 'been friends' with the arrested person. Suddenly everyone is 'committed'.

There is no regard for careful, longterm planning and for slow steady progress being made, built on well-constructed support systems. Little wonder then that the only truly effective unrest in the country could come from teenagers and schoolchildren whose organisations and levels of realistic commitment meet these criteria.

I studied a third and final type of security operation that is applied to back up the operation described above. Between the radical group, whose activities sometimes involve acts of violence, and the moderate opposition groups, who seldom if ever break even South Africa's repressive laws, lie the people who could form a potential threat to the government. These people, ordinary, thoughtful and concerned about South Africa, need little more than clear and legitimate leadership to rouse themselves into overt action against the government. Dedicated to the old liberal ideal of an equalitarian, multiracial South Africa, these people do not ordinarily engage in acts of violence nor do they break the law. Yet what is done to them to nullify any threat ranges from psychological coercion to a ruthless and thorough form of psychological terrorism. From 1973 to 1977, I kept records of information I received about these methods and their effects and so was able to establish the means used.[8]

The aim here is to terrorise chosen individuals rather than groups in such a way as to isolate and alienate the person from his or her emotional supports. For these people, the anxiety and fear that I have described as existing in South Africa is subtly and systematically manipulated to make the person's functioning neurotic.

Psychological terrorism involves four basic components: accidents to target persons or to material belongings of targets; overt intervention with parental, university, army and other authorities and obstruction in the form of official delays in getting such simple things as mail and passports. People would find their valuable documents 'accidentally' lost in the post or stolen. Term papers, essays, books and files, for example, would disappear just before exams. Motorbikes and cars would be damaged; people would get 'unintentionally' involved in fights or 'mysteriously' beaten up. All these were done in such a way that the person was made fully aware that they were from the authorities or related to their radical activity.[9]

The nature and type of interference was clearly determined by the psychological type of the target and ranged from minor but psychologically significant 'events' for the person occurring occasionally, to extensive and open daily contact. The difference between this and the tactics descibed in the previous section is that by and large the effectiveness of the group manipulations lay in the fact that the targets were unaware of the authorities' hand in their experiences. Individuals in radical groups protected and defended themselves from what they thought were their colleagues' criticism. Condemnation by one's colleagues for a personal 'weakness' is a far more crippling blow to the ego than any intimidation.

In this final type of operation a clear threat is used basically because the targets are able to resist the impact of ordinary rumour and smear either by virtue of the fact that they possess little or no personal or secret pathology that could be used against them or they are impervious to group effects. In some cases, especially Coloured and African people, they are better supported by their families and communities than other targets. Hence the need to introduce terror which wears down and restricts a person's emotional activity and gradually cuts him off from his supports.

At the simplest level, some targets are 'warned' off or frightened away from activities that the authorities want to restrict:

'Shortly after I began working with *x* [a well-known activist] on certain community projects, I began to receive strange phone-calls everyday. The phone would ring and there would be no one there, just a kind of faint shouting on the other side. One after-noon, it rang four times like this. It completely unnerved me. *X* told me to expect that kind of thing; it happened to anyone she worked with. It unnerved me.'

In another case, an Afrikaans university student who was involved with a group of friends who were open in their criticism of the government, was intimidated by car lights flashing and illumin-ating his home in the early hours of the morning. On several occas-ions a car tried to force his car off the road. Deeply shaken, he went overseas for a year to get away from the strain.

Sometimes the authorities acted through direct intervention with significant people in their targets' lives:

'I was warned by the police on two occasions, quite openly that I would get into trouble. Then they phoned my parents, told them I was a communist and did they want to see their son in jail? Then the police phoned me and told me they'd arrest my parents if I didn't behave. About six months later, Estelle, my girlfriend, and I were in a protest meeting when some plainclothes police came along and started pushing her around. They didn't lay a finger on me. It was clear what they were up to: everyone saw this and wanted to know why I got "special" treatment. Estelle and I broke up quite soon after. She was scared to be with me – she's Afrikaans and didn't want to get too involved with me or politics.'

Other subjects I studied were deliberately beaten up, by policemen or army trainees, irrespective of the sex of the target: one young girl, a student activist, was beaten up in a phone booth and her nose broken by a policeman in uniform. When she tried to lay a charge at a police station, she was jeered at and prevented from complaining. Other people were attacked while going home by gangs of short-haired, young white Afrikaans men. Inevitably, if the victim complained to the police, nothing was done. Sometimes policemen refused to write out a charge sheet, other times they 'lost' the sheet and sometimes they tried to shape the statement taken to make the complainant seem vague and unsure. I have no record of any of the complaints made by my subjects being followed up.

Some people had small but crucial things happen just before examinations: one young white student had his motorbike stolen a week before his exams and his exam notes stolen while he was writing an exam. He later received them back through the post, charred and burnt but recognisably his.

Usually events such as these made the targets more wary of getting overinvolved; they did not stop the person's activities but they did contain them. Other tactics were employed on more resistant cases and psychological, as opposed to physical, terror became more routinely employed.

One woman in her early thirties had had an illegal abortion when she was younger about which nobody knew. She began to receive anonymous calls in which the caller threatened to tell her parents about it. She was extremely upset by these calls because her parents knew nothing of her political activity and her mother was dangerously asthmatic. She was never able to discover how the caller knew and soon the calls stopped.

She was fortunate. As matters become more serious, so the intensity of police activity increases; in a similar case, a professional man began to receive anonymous calls in the middle of the night and at work threatening to expose to his parents his history of homosexuality. The police had obtained his psychiatric file from a hospital in Cape Town. To get round the threat, he told his parents. Then he received another call threatening to tell his employer. All of this was made conditional on the subject giving up his political activity. This went on for six months; the man became depressed and occasionally suicidal, eventually deciding to tell his senior partner. The latter was more concerned that the man was being politically intimidated than about the homosexual history and wanted him to resign immediately so that neither he nor the firm would have any connection with him. Later, however, he relented and the matter was closed. This did not stop the caller(s) though, and soon it was his parents' turn to be woken up in the middle of the night.

At the extreme end of the scale, the tactics employed by the security police assume quite unbelievable and nightmarish psychological proportions. As I gathered more evidence, it became clear to me that the aim of these operations was not simply to restrict or prevent a person's activities but to destroy his or her personality. In some cases, the police obviously hoped to drive their victims to suicide. If you remember that these victims are innocent people who simply object to the practices of *apartheid*, then the behaviour of the authorities can be seen to reach a new high in psychological repression.

Pressure is put on the target's most vulnerable areas, thus increasing the traumatising capacity of the area. The individual, to avoid the trauma, isolates him- or herself even further; each such step making the target more vulnerable. Think for a moment of how easily this can be done: many people are afraid of the dark, of the night, and to get comfort, they cling to the things that they find familiar or comforting. Suppose that suddenly the reassuring thing becomes itself a nightmare.

One woman, a middle-aged spinster, lived alone. She was scared of the dark and of noise and never went out at night. Over time, this fear was intensified by sets of regular incidents – rowdy gangs would roar around her home on motorbikes, bottles would be smashed against her wall. Then for a two-week period, her doorbell was rung at three in the morning. All this completely unnerved her and to cope she began to use tranquillisers during the day and sleeping pills at night. Her main comfort was the telephone; when frightened, she would call friends to talk to and with this she somehow managed. Then her phone line went dead but only at night. She called the GPO who tested the line during the day and found nothing wrong with it.

Gradually, the net around her tightened and she was driven to near-hysteria by the loneliness, the terror and the dead phone. She asked a friend to stay in the house and, suddenly, there was no interference; no noise and no dead telephone. If she spent the night alone, all the terror came back. Her friends began to suspect she was making it up and were reluctant to stay with her. She began to get bitter and resentful and broke with some of her friends which I think was precisely the aim of the operation. She continued to live with the incidents which in time slackened but by then, it was too late – she had lost all interest in politics.

Many people in South Africa have in fact learnt to live with continual psychological terror such as this as a way of life. Anonymous and threatening phone calls are for some a daily occurrence as too are visits from police officers, mainly in the dead of night, always abusive and always intrusive. This is a technique used especially on Coloureds and Africans who have no recourse to channels of complaint and for whom this is preferable than actual arrest or torture:

'I had been very ill and I was lying in bed recovering from an operation, my baby was in another room and we were alone in the house. In walked this major and his pal. They locked the baby out. I was so ill . . . I could barely take the questioning and for two solid hours they hammered me . . . I felt my energy sapping and it was the most horrifying and terrifying feeling, being locked up in this room with those two policemen. Then they left. But this wasn't all. Later that afternoon, a white man with a gun climbed in through a window and we were terrified . . . This was part of a whole ruse to frighten me. Frighten me to death.'

During the uprisings of 1976 these occurrences assumed terrifying proportions: Coloured and African victims were brutally assaulted and beaten up, sometimes killed by riot policemen who, in some instances, I believe, had been given specific instructions about who to terrorise and who to leave alone. Recourse to the law was no guarantee that it would be stopped; the following statement was made after a young man and his family had been assaulted:

'We complained about the riot police to our Police station . . .
The riot squad depot was in Pinelands and two officers came to
fetch us and they took us there . . . several of us who had made
official complaints. They were all lined up in the courtyard, thirty
of them, all armed. And they were drinking beer when I walked
past them. One of them said to me in Afrikaans: "Next time I
won't baton you, I'll shoot you with a revolver." This really
scared me and another one said: "Why are you here, you black
shit? You should have been dead." And the commandant was
walking right behind me and he said nothing. They all laughed at
me and then one went suddenly for his side revolver to frighten
me. So I didn't look at any of them, I just walked right past, terrified. I couldn't say anything; I was too afraid and I couldn't get a
good enough look at them.'

No one was charged in this incident and shortly afterwards my
informant began to receive anonymous calls from some of these riot
policemen threatening to kill him. He was sixteen at the time.

The authorities go to any lengths to terrorise people, all of it psychologically precise. Some people I studied lost their pet animals;
dogs, for instance, would be mysteriously run over, stolen, strangled, poisoned and left lying around for their owners to find. In one
case, the young daughter of the sister of a target was threatened
because she was apparently the only vulnerable link the target had.
When he ignored the threats, she was given 'lifts' home from school
by strange men and the target's sister was phoned and told to 'have
a word with your brother, otherwise something really nasty will
happen to your daughter'.

In other instances, death notices appeared in the paper for important people in the target's life; funeral directors would phone up
about coffins being ordered, and so on. In another case, a woman
who was deeply attached to her mother and who had been receiving
threatening calls, received a call one night 'from a hospital casualty
department' saying that her mother had been killed in a car crash,
would she come and identify the body. The target, already near the
end of her tether, suspecting a trap, phoned her mother's home and
got no reply. Then she phoned the hospital and was told, yes, there
had been a car crash and an elderly woman had been killed. Terri-
bly distraught, she rushed to the hospital, then to the morgue in Salt

River where she saw the body of a dead woman and discovered that it had all been a hoax. The police had established when her mother went out during the week and had simply waited for a suitable hospital report to spring their 'trick'. The woman's mother had been out playing bridge and was quite safe. Following this, the target attempted suicide on two occasions and had a psychological breakdown.

These are a few examples from the seventy-two case reports I collected in this time. The practices were widespread and by and large, successful. In extreme cases, people would be terrorised and intimidated until they literally killed themselves. The only recourse of some of these people was to leave the country, and in many cases the government prevented this by refusing passports or exit permits thus committing the person to a life of psychological terror.

A disintegration of personality is hastened by two basic techniques: the continuation of intimidation long after the individual has ceased radical activity or after the person had ceased to pose any threat and through the invasion of a person's physical and psychological privacy. This latter is particularly terrifying because a person's ability to resist depends on their being able to feel that they have somewhere at least that they can regard as their own; some personal privacy.

So conditioned are most of us to having such basic securities that, in the most part, we do not realise how much we take them for granted. Only when they are removed do we realise how essential they are for the preservation of our day-to-day security. In South Africa, the security police are able to systematically reduce the range of a person's security. Imagine how you would feel if every time you came home your front door was wide open, no matter how often you complained to the police or changed the lock. Imagine too how you would feel if nothing was missing but you knew that anything in the house or flat could have been changed or rendered dangerous. This happened to several people:

'For several months, this went on. I'd come home to find the door open, someone had helped themselves to booze or tea, put their feet up on the table, spilt milk on the floor; all little things but awful, in my house. It was the police – they phoned every night to tell me I needed more milk or to change my brandy label, they didn't like the one I had. I complained to our police but they didn't even send someone round – they told me I must've forgotten to lock the door. Then one morning after they'd been, I got up to brush my teeth and my mouth burned – they'd put something on my toothbrush.'

Another time, she found a rusty nail embedded in a sanitary towel she was about to use.

In another case, a woman who suffered from claustrophobia reported several incidents in the space of a few weeks: she was locked in a cupboard, trapped in a lift, alone, twice in one week, and terrified by midnight calls which kept her awake. Then a rumour was spread at work that she was an alcoholic and a half-empty bottle was left in the office drawer.

Normal people would become paranoid and suspicious in the face of this sort of occurrence. In South Africa, subjects become terrified, can't sleep, are depressed, suicidal:

'You have nothing. They can do anything. They can walk in anytime they choose, steal anything, blow up my car, steal my baby, even kill me. And no one can do a thing about it. They won't let me leave the country, they want me to die; they've told me. And in the end, I will because I can't go on being like this. I trust nobody, I've lost all my friends; nobody dares befriend me in case "things" happen to them. The authorities are vindictive; to have dared to oppose them was like a crime in their eyes, to be punished for evermore. Some of the bastards have it in for me personally – or so they say – and this makes it even worse. The state, you think, would hold back from actively murdering you but not an individual, not a security policeman with all the opportunity in the world and everything behind him.'

I see clear links between these procedures committed on people who are not technically breaking the law in any way, who are not under arrest, who are not banned, and the suicides in detention that have been reported. While undoubtedly in some cases, these 'suicides' have been the work of policemen, many I feel are acts committed by the detainees themselves for whom arrest is the final step on the long road of psychological terrorism that the authorities have inflicted beforehand. Knowing the Afrikaans authorities' desire to make everything look legalistic and to maintain appearances, it is entirely likely that some of their victims are driven to their psychological limits long before anything physical is done to them. Suicide is made an attractive option to victims by the authorities, who implant the idea in the detainee's mind that it is his or her way of taking revenge against them.

Arrest and torture in fact can be counter-productive in a context like South Africa where the experience of physical pain and fear breaks down the fog surrounding the government's real intentions and gives the detainee something concrete and real to fight against. The psychological terrorism used by the South African security police takes full cognisance of this fact. Note the use of advanced psychological techniques to achieve the desired results: the individual is rendered ineffective by isolation so that personal preoccupations become the sole focus of his or her attention. Psychological survival becomes the dominating obsession of the victim thus leaving no room for other matters, particularly political matters. Isolation is essential. If a person feels that he or she is not alone, then his or her resistance to attack is greatly increased. It was quite clear that white persons were least able to withstand the stress of terrorism and that African and Coloured people were the most resistant. The reasons for this are straightforward.

Unlike the white victim, the Coloured or African victim belongs to a society that is clearly oppressed. This helps the non-white victim to survive in two ways. Firstly, radical members of the African and Coloured communities as a whole are united in their dislike and even hatred of the system. This applies irrespective of political opinion: the system of *apartheid* unifies this kind of opposition. Secondly, African and Coloured people *daily* experience concrete harassment in the form of where they may go, where they may eat, which trains they can and cannot travel on, while at the same time seeing the ease and movement and freedom of action of the white people. In many instances, these people have also had first-hand experience of police intimidation and official callousness and brutality. These experiences give the Coloured or African person a sense of clarity about the reality of South Africa which it is difficult for a white person to get. Thus, for the African and Coloured person who experiences psychological terrorism, he or she is able to see the hand of the authorities in apparently random events much earlier than a white person and is thus able to resist disintegration.

Chapter Seven

The Afrikaners

We arrive finally at the Afrikaners – the most active participants in the game of *apartheid*. I had half-expected them to turn out to be a community of ruthless and determined individuals, dedicated single-mindedly to their own survival. And yet when I began to study them, at least those I saw in my practice, this was far from the picture I got. The people I saw were sad, almost disillusioned apologists for the regime; strangely tense and awkward outside their communities, like fish out of water. As time went on, though, I found out why. The Afrikaners I saw – and those most English people came into contact with – were not the *ware*, the true Afrikaners. They were urbanites, almost progressive in their politics (where they were political) very different from the *plattelanders*, the Afrikaners who kept close to the traditional homelands defined by the old Boer Republics in the Free State and Transvaal. The real Afrikaners, the Machiavellian manipulators of the country, however, are not the ordinary people of urban or rural South Africa. They are the men of the *Broederbond* and the women behind them. The *plattelanders* are the professional soldiers of the Afrikaner state, the *Broeders*, the generals to whom the ordinary urban Afrikaner is a mixture of cannonfodder and refugee, unable to go forwards or backwards for fear of becoming either. What I want to do in this chapter is to describe the kind of life that the Afrikaner state has developed for its own community; the way they are brought up, indoctrinated and regimented. In the next chapter, we will turn finally to the *Broederbond* and its activities.

From birth to death the Afrikaner is exposed to a unique process of living totally devoted to furthering the values and ideas of the Afrikaner. This process is more than a philosophy, it is presented to the Afrikaner child as an organising perspective. Through the control the *Broederbond* has over the Afrikaner institutions, it has been possible for the Afrikaners to raise its children *as if its views on reality are in exact accordance with reality*.

The Afrikaner child, like children everywhere in their different communities, is brought up on Afrikaner values and perspectives of life. But, unlike other children, the Afrikaans child finds these same values expressed uniformly at every level of his society. Thus he is taught that he is superior, Godly, a descendant of brave men and women who fought for their beliefs and values, that the English tried to take his birthright away and that the African is simply waiting his chance to do the same. He is encouraged to be watchful, lest he be overwhelmed. At school he hears this from *all* his teachers, he reads it in all his school books. At home, his parents reinterate the same values – if there is any conflict between school and home it is usually over degree of adherence to the same values, not over different sets of values. As the child grows up, he hears the same ideas expressed at church, on the radio and on television, reads them in Afrikaans newspapers, magazines, comics and in Afrikaans novels, plays and at the cinema.[1]

There is no escape. Not for the normal, ordinary child who is happy and wants to please his parents and elders. The Afrikaans child has his or her own youth movements, replicas of Boy Scouts and Girl Guides, and their own First Aid organisations. Everything is duplicated. As he grows older he is involved in communal affairs and goes to an Afrikaans-medium high school run on Christian National directives from the government. There, his 'youth preparedness' lessons and cadets ensure that the indoctrination processes established in infancy continue to hold him to his course. The message is drummed home by the repeated appearances of military men on television and on the radio; cabinet ministers, religious authorities, all continually warn the community to be wary and to avoid contact with undermining trends such as non-Afrikaans newspapers, movies, magazines, books, music, even clothes – denim jeans and miniskirts were frowned upon at one stage.

The government operates remarkably strict censorship on everything coming into South Africa. The present arrangement is done through hundreds of local censorship boards all over the country but in the past, it was equally effectively done by a centralized publications control board.[2] So what the Afrikaans population sees, hears, and reads is carefully selected for them by their own authorities.[3]

When the Afrikaner child grows up, if he is a male, he goes into the army, which is completely Afrikaans-orientated, then on to an Afrikaans university, joins an Afrikaans professional group, practices in an Afrikaans suburb or town, joins Afrikaner charities and service organizations and can in fact find Afrikaans organisations to fulfil his every need. There is an Afrikaans Automobile Association Club to save him joining the AA, Afrikaans banks, building societies, insurance groups, everything. The Performing Arts Councils in each province have separate Afrikaans and English-speaking sections. Tucked away in the background, he can always aim to be a *Broeder* and, if the need arises, go into politics. If he joins an Afrikaans company or organisation, he will be surrounded by Afrikaners and, to get on in his career, will need to belong to the *Bond*.

For the bulk of the Afrikaans population, this is the pattern of life. There are no conflicting values because no others exist; what little contact there is with outside values in fact acts as a kind of seeable threat which encourages the individual to keep turning inwards. Let us examine what this means for the psychology of the individual.

In normal society, the normal pre-school child is exposed to a very similar conceptual process in which his experiences with various aspects of his environment have a nomothetic continuity and order; that is, his world appears to behave *as he is told it does*. This conceptual and ideological world corresponds closely with his actual experience because, through his inferior status and his parents' power, they are able to protect him from experiences that *might* jar or upset the harmony between the fact and ideology he is taught. The shocks, bruises and conflicts of hard reality stay more or less outside of his world and so too does the fear and anxiety that they bring with them.

As the child grows older, however, especially when he goes to school, his protective wall is gradually removed and he learns to deal with reality, albeit still highly controlled by the protection offered through school, his family and the cultural milieu in which he lives. However, through exposure to teachers, other children, television, radio and the like, the continuity between his various cognitive attitudes is gradually broken: the child becomes aware of other views which conflict with those of his family.

These contacts with reality are the essential forces that shape not only a person's perceptions of the world and reality but also his personality and his character. By creating conflict and anxiety, they create resistance, dilemmas and problems for the child; how he solves them determines the sort of person he will become. Intelligence and creativeness, for example, arise out of problem-solving and coping with anxiety. So too does neurosis. Many people in modern society have adjustment problems arising out of an exposure to reality that creates unnecessarily high levels of conflict and anxiety.

In adolescence, how the child has solved or coped with these dilemmas is given a more adult shape and the child develops maturer concepts of reality, of himself and his role in life and society. Existing institutions give this direction and in most societies the existence of pluralities or multipluralities of institutions based on alternative views or values is a necessary prerequisite for coping with the complex nature of reality. In this process, the individual develops an individual adjustment in which he forms a relatively unique set of perceptions, values, ideas, some of which are nomothetic and some idiographic. Such an adjustment is necessary to allow the individual to remain independent and relatively stable in the world, to retain freedom of thought and experience and, above all, a strong sense of individual right and obligation.

Little of this happens to the Afrikaner child. The same patterns of development I found in the psychological tests conducted on students and on nurses described earlier characterised the pattern of functioning of the Afrikaners I met or saw in my practice. When a community protects and insulates its members from reality, the levels of intellectual and emotional development of the majority of its members remains stuck at the level of pre-adolescent functioning described above.

You see, a child has no innate sense of right and wrong, or idealised form of behaviour other than that his needs must be met. A child develops a sense of being able to deal with reality through his experiences; he learns to question the values of his society only when his own experiences are at variance with what he has been taught. Thus it is possible to teach a child *any* system, no matter how cruel or illogical, inhuman or insane. The problems for the parent or the community come when the child faces reality outside the home, the school or the community; for it is here that the system taught may bring the child into conflict with reality. A child taught to kick every dog he sees will *never know* that it is *wrong* so long as he lives in a society in which this is encouraged and, moreover, punished if it is *not* done. Such a child will experience shock, anxiety and conflict if he is suddenly exposed to a culture in which dog-kicking is forbidden.

In essence, this is what happens in homes that produce character disturbance and psychotic states like schizophrenia and severe depression. The child is taught a system at home which is in conflict with the outside world; when the supports and securities of the home are removed as the child grows up, the shock of conflict can precipitate personality disintegration. Imagine how you would feel if after six or seven years of life, your whole world was turned permanently upside-down suddenly and black was white and – which is usually the case – you *had* to adjust. It is hard to imagine, but this is what happens to people who become disturbed or insane.

The Afrikaner child is taught the Afrikaner system and its values and is exposed to a reality which supports these values. It is like the dog-kicking child being exposed to a dog-kicking society. So, unlike the person in an ordinary society who would become disturbed or psychotic on exposure to reality, having been given an Afrikaner upbringing, the Afrikaans child is saved from discovering that his ideology and conceptual system is at fault or inhuman or in conflict with reality by the fact that his system is supported long after he has left home and grown up.

The child who becomes mentally disturbed in the UK or in Europe does do because firstly, he or she is taught a faulty conceptual system and secondly, he or she is exposed to the system's faults. If, however, the latter does not occur, the child continues to function in a faulty way and can live to a ripe old age without ever showing psychotic symptoms. Some people in fact do have this experience: through wealth or beauty or privilege or circumstances, they get through life on false systems – this is why some people become disturbed following the removal of his or her protective blanket. The beautiful woman whose personality disintegrates as her beauty fades, the sportsman who loses form, the aging intellectual who is replaced by a younger man; the man who gets divorced, the wife whose mother dies – any of these simple events can precipitate crisis if the individual had been reared on a false system and protected from facing it.

The Afrikaans child shows no symptoms or distress because he is protected until he dies from facing reality. Further, he develops very little sense of individuality and has virtually no conception of either individual rights or individual responsibility because there is no exposure to the need to do so. My clinical experience confirmed what I had learnt from the MMPI studies: Afrikaners experience little stress or conflict and their personality structures are disturbingly uniform with the smallest degree of variation between individuals I ever recorded. Whatever anxiety is present, is a culturally developed one and directed towards outward threats and the preservation of the cultural pattern. The absence of neurotic or psychotic symptoms confirms the thesis I presented earlier – the Afrikaners are reared in a society that makes no demands on their conceptual system above the level of the schoolroom. They function inadequately without ever discovering that this is the case.

This, then, is the structure of the Afrikaner's psychology. But what is the content of the system? What are the values and beliefs that he is taught? Moreover, how is the system maintained? Clearly, such a psychology would have to be very tightly protected and supported to prevent the community from facing disintegration, especially given the urbanisation of the Afrikaner since 1930 and the increased availability of information about the outside world.

The growing Afrikaner is given two directions; two goals around which his life is orientated: to maintain the *status quo* in the country according to the dictates of the Afrikaans *volk*, which means through the interpretations of the *Broederbond* expressed through its various agencies; and to enrich their community, including themselves. The personal contact, lost to some extent through the urbanisation process since 1910, has been countered by involving everyone in the process of achieving these goals and creating a sense of personal responsibility and involvement in both aspects. This is achieved because the institutions constructed by the community employ the same pattern of personalised reward and favour as did the Afrikaner communities in the Boer Republics.

Modern Western states operate on the basis that power balances are achieved by using relatively independent institutions to check one another's power. Within each institution hierarchies exist, but there is no formal hierarchy among the various institutions themselves. In the Afrikaner state, the formal character of each institution is completely subservient to the informal power held by the *Broederbond*. Every aspect of Afrikaner society is organised around the twin tasks set; and the hierarchy within the state is determined by the *Broederbond*. Thus the higher an individual goes in an institution is determined entirely by his status in the *Broederbond*, not by his status in the institution. The *Broederbond* is the hub of the Afrikaans institutions' wheels. The lower-middle and lower levels of institutions are not necessarily filled by *Broeders* but top levels are and so are many middle layers; people who are favourable to the *Broeders* are promoted and given power.

Broeders and those sympathetic to the *Bond* operate in the same way, though less formally, as communist party commissars do in the Soviet Union. One of my patients described to me the way this system functions in the civil service:

'Everyone in every department has a formal supervisor; each supervisor is in turn supervised and so on right to the top. Every month, the supervisor has to write a report on you, your work, your attitude and so on. This goes to his supervisor and a copy goes to head office. Theoretically, you are supposed to see this report and sign it but this isn't always done. What you never see, though, is the report that the *Broeder* men or their protégés prepare on you. The head of every department is usually a *Broeder* and he has chains of *Broeders* or favourites beneath him. These men become his personal friends and they report to him. So let's say there are two supervisors of the same status and you work for both of them. Both will write reports on you but the one who is a *Broeder* or special friend of the head of the department will keep a separate record of your behaviour and that of the other supervisors. So let's say you get friendly with a non-*Broeder* supervisor, you chat, you get on. It will be noted and watched without you knowing it. One *Broeder* in the department, probably someone from head office, will be alerted to watch. At the routine meetings of *Broeder* cells, it will be brought up and anyone who knows you, your family, your private behaviour will pass on whatever information they may have. Because the *Broeder* interest is paramount, this information will be passed on irrespectively; because the *Broeders* are everywhere, powerful and hold prominent positions, the information will be thorough and far more than just gossip. A true Afrikaner will bank with an Afrikaans bank – if he doesn't, it will be noted against him; if he does; the status of his accounts, his borrowing, his purchases will be passed on by the bank manager, who is almost certain to be a *Broeder*. The same goes for the doctor, the insurance company, anyone who is important; if your kid goes to Stellenbosch University, the chances are his professor will report on his behaviour. All this is done to *place* you, to type you. Let's say your kid is having it off with an English girl and your wife goes to an English gynaecologist, it's all out of line, see, and they don't come to you – oh, sometimes they might – but what happens is that you will *never* get on in the department unless you conform. Never be powerful.'

This system is the logical extension of the personal contact system that obtained in the Afrikaner Republics. Like the former, the modern system is also corrupt. And just as the *Broederbond* has turned the personal system into a sophisticated means of controlling the behaviour of the Afrikaner, so it has turned corruption into a major obsession and industry.

A system like the *Broederbond*, indeed like the Afrikaans state, could not survive without a means of rewarding the various members who operate it. As I have said before, South Africa is a society that has been taken over by the Afrikaners; every Afrikaner shares both in the process of control and domination and every Afrikaner shares in the spoils. Apart from the high standard of living and security enjoyed by the Afrikaans community as a whole, there are several ways in which top Afrikaners are rewarded. I will mention a few.

Because the government has such total control over what laws it passes, which industries it favours, and so on, information about impending legislation is at a premium and select *Broeder* committees decide how people who have helped them can best be rewarded. It is not the policy of the Afrikaner to make overt and obvious rewards such as cash payments for services rendered; everything has to be ordered and accounted for through personal contacts for reasons that I will shortly come to. So, specific people are permitted to engage in legitimate business based on confidential information. An example: certain sections of Cape Town's non-white areas were to be re-scheduled as white areas. The occupants of the areas were Coloured and Malay and property values were thus low. Before the areas were declared white, however, as a reward for services rendered, several prominent citizens of the Cape were informed of the impending declaration and encouraged to form companies to exploit the situation. These companies then bought up whatever land they could, cheaply, then on declaration of the area, sold or built houses for the white market at enormous profit. This pattern is repeated in many other areas and, of course, whenever a desirable Coloured or Black sector gets rezoned for whites.

This operation was small-time, though, compared with others; the television industry, for example, is dominated by companies formed by *Broeder* activists; South Africa delayed introducing television until 1976 – ostensibly because it disapproved of it – in reality though, according to one of my informants, until it had set up the infrastructure to be able to control it and the industry it created, completely. It needed time to develop the necessary technology to set up the system, to select programmes and to master the medium so that it could be of use to government propagandists and, more important, to set up and train its own companies to produce television sets, programmes and advertising and so on. It restricted the number of companies permitted to make sets so narrowing the span of profits to ensure that *its* companies and select others would maximise the benefits.

This is the Afrikaner pattern. Whereas some governments may exploit the economic sector through selling rights, say, to produce television sets, to complete buildings, to mine, to explore or to fish and so allow unscrupulous ministers or officials to profit through favouritism, the Afrikaner state goes several steps further to ensure that every inch of profit is gained for itself. It not only allocates rights but it does so to its own companies and where possible, tries to exploit entire areas from start to finish; it creates companies to explore areas, to mine or to develop regions, and forms others to transport the produce and eventually to set up its own marketing outlets.

This exploitation is done mainly through the use of holding and front companies controlled by the *Broederbond*. The activities of these companies are hidden through complex patterns of registration of ownership with sometimes, for example, wives, children and relatives registered as the ostensible holders. By far the most effective method has been to buy into established English-owned companies and groups of stores so that the links with Afrikaner groups are not obvious. One example is the Dairy industry. The government controls the prices; Afrikaner companies truck the produce to market and, in recent years, the last link in the chain has been completed – Afrikaner front companies have systematically bought into and taken over all the different companies that market dairy produce. There are still different dairies, for example, but this is in name only to obscure the monopoly. Where possible, the *Broederbond* tries to ensure that the reward pattern is synchronised with the need to protect the Afrikaner state. The dairy produce chain is one such example. Apart from giving rewards to a large number of Afrikaners, it also serves as one of the pillars with which the African living standard is subverted as I described in an earlier chapter. There are other chains which serve similar functions in other key sectors of the economy.

The success of this practice lies in its closed shop of personal contacts; strictly speaking, nothing I have detailed is illegal in South Africa; it is all governed by law and the *Broederbond* works within this framework. But it works in such a way as to exploit the ordinary process of law and the institutions involved. That is, they *pervert* the morality behind the institutions and break the psychological understanding that normally attends the functioning of government. So assume a government contract is offered; it will be advertised in accordance with the law and various companies will tender for it, one of which will be a *Bond* company or a front company – the contract will go to the latter. There is no recourse to law, apart from the fact that collusion would be hard to prove and that the National Party Caucus is itself the highest court in the land.[4] What goes 'wrong' is that the normal gentleman's agreement to award contacts on merit is only occasionally kept. The fact that it is not broken all the time helps to cloud the issue and this with the various fronts used by the *Bond*, helps to camouflage the selective process at work. The fact that there is no one else to check on this, no alert Afrikaans press, for example, of course also helps the process.

The interesting thing is, though, that from time to time, certain officials in government or in Afrikaans institutions try to set up their own corrupt practices outside the framework set for these operations by the *Broederbond*. They engage, in other words, in the kind of small-scale (compared with the scale of the Broeders' ventures) operations that attend bureaucracy everywhere – company directors make 'gifts' or 'payments' to government officials in return for favours of contracts or 'special concessions'. These things are private and are kept from the law *and* from the *Broederbond*. But every now and again, they are discovered and the way they are treated shows up the workings of the whole system. Nearly all the information I got about *Bond* affairs came to me from people such as this and who got caught.

Firstly, what action the *Broeders* take depends on the size of the corruption and what is involved. If it is not too serious, little is done; the officials are chastised, the money or gifts channelled in the 'right' direction and the *Bond* takes over the operation, depending on how useful it is to itself or, as has become more the case since 1974, to the security services. In one case, I was familiar with, for example, the corrupt practice was allowed to continue – supervised by the Bureau of State Security – because it involved a non-South African company which was of use to the country. The company official was encouraged to provide services in return for continuing the system and for no legal action being taken. There are hundreds if not thousands of such arrangements which never see the light of day in South Africa.

However, if too much is involved or, as is most often the case, the *Broeders* are affronted, then the matter is blown up, it becomes public and legal action is taken. The government makes much capital out of it: on the one hand, it uses it as a threat to others – the small racketeers it does not know about and those *Broeders* who may be tempted – and on the other, it uses these incidents to present itself as a clean and honest organisation that is capable of putting its own house in order if need be.

But what happens to the perpetrators? For a start, very, very little. Prison sentences and dismissal, on the surface severe and punitive, are purely for show; few, if any, offenders serve anything like minimum time – parole is quickly and quietly arranged. Secondly, none of the perpetrators suffer little more than a drop in prestige through having had the matter exposed; most are quietly re-employed and even re-imbursed in other government or *Broeder* organisations. It is clear – and I was often told this – that the offenders are punished for *not* doing things the *Broeder* way, *not* for corruption in the first place. These Afrikaners are chastised and then *used again* because often they are much more useful after they have lost face than before. This is the Afrikaner way of doing things.

The *Broeders'* plans are executed in a careful fashion to blend in with the various institutions that exist in the country which are not corrupt to the same extent and which the *Bond* needs to help it maintain a respectable image for the country. Let me give an example to show how, through careful manipulation, this is achieved and how the *Bond* operates.

An act of corruption in a private company was discovered. The police conducted an investigation which indicted those responsible, one of whom the *Bond* wanted to manipulate. Through *Bond* higher police officers, the nature and the extent of the inquiry was carefully controlled to obscure the *Bond*'s own activities in the same area in which the misdemeanours had been uncovered. Also concealed in the police investigation was the full extent of the activity of the private company involved.[5] The whole inquiry in fact stopped at exactly the point the *Broeders* required. Now, this report was sent to the Attorney-General of the Cape and he instituted proceedings on the basis of the facts recorded. The process of the law then took over and a completely respectable and orthodox judicial procedure was conducted, the men found guilty and sentenced. Once the culprits were in prison, the judicial function completed, *Bond* activity resumed. The company official was given special treatment through the offices of high-up *Bond* prison officers and through a *Bond* prison psychiatrist, personal information about the prisoner obtained.

A deal was then proposed to the prisoner through the same psychiatrist: early release – he would have to serve some time, of course, to make it legally acceptable – in return for the prisoner's company, a company with international connections, doing certain favours for which, of course, it would be well paid. The prisoner agreed. The prison staff, psychiatrist, social workers then began to prepare a false set of favourable reports on the prisoner, showing he had deeply repented, was being rehabilitated, that his family was suffering in his absence. These were used to obtain his early release. The prisoner went back to his company where he remains today – a wealthy man who spends some of his time engaging in corrupt practices for *Broederbond* fronts with complete immunity from the law. The judiciary, in turn, thinks it did an excellent and compassionate job, which – on paper – it did.

The Afrikaans community then is geared to an authoritarian acquiescence to the dictates of the *Broederbond*. *Broederbond* agencies specify the ideology, the dogma, ensure the sharing out of rewards to the community and, centrally, ensure that all Afrikaner institutions serve the same end. This leads to contradictions which outsiders find perplexing but which are quite logical, given the internal value system of the Afrikaner state.

One contradiction, for example, concerns the Afrikaners' concern with religion and morality. God is such a part and parcel of every official occasion from the opening of a dam to the opening of a party political speech that one is tempted to think He is Afrikaans. Afrikaners today go to church more than most people and their behaviours are characterised inside and outside South Africa as Calvinistic, aescetic and deeply religious. How is this to be reconciled with the same people's ability to commit brutal and inhumanly callous acts and engage in institutional corruption so at variance with its Christian ethics?

The answer is simple: it has never been made to reconcile these conflicts. It does not *know* that its behaviour is more aptly characterised as Christian corruption than Christian charity because no one has ever told it so. Its structure prevents it from *knowing* that its system is corrupt and sociopathic. The very people who could question the contradiction in Afrikaner ethics are themselves at the forefront of the reward queue: ministers of religion, academics, and intellectuals are among the elite of the community; not only do ministers of religion have a directing role and status (many *dominees* are *Broeders*) but they receive gifts and services as rewards which make their existences very, very comfortable indeed. The brother of one of my patients said:

'I became a *dominee* because, as a child, I saw that they never suffered. They lived in the best houses, ate the best food, drove around in fantastic cars. Everyone in the village buys them presents, money, wine, books. They get their houses fixed, cars fixed – all for nothing. Nobody likes to offend the *dominee*. When I became one, I found out how wealthy and powerful the church is in reality. Top ministers, especially *Broeders*, have huge private fortunes, massive business investments, houses, flats, everything. They really have things sewn up.'

Clearly, no one benefiting in this way is going to raise objections of logic to the very system which supports such a lucrative life-style.

The Afrikaner value system preaches that you may take your reward where you can. It encourages the exploitation of those less fortunate in its hierarchy, in particular non-whites and the English, but it also encourages exploitation of those lower in its own hierarchy – women, for example.

Quite apart from the fact that South Africa and its laws restrict the status of women relative to men, the civil service, for example, regards married women as temporary employees and discriminates between single and married women in terms of salary and promotion, women are used in many ways that would enrage the average Western woman. Women, in the old trekker sense, came somewhere between the *trekboer* and his non-white labourer. The function of women was to provide for the family, rear and tend to the children and to keep house. While times and circumstances have changed, the role and position of Afrikaner women remains in essence the same, particularly in the more traditional communities in the *platteland*.

In urban communities this role has been redefined so that the services women offer are more in line both with the demands of urban conditions and with the need to provide modern rewards. The women in these circumstances are the reward:

'I joined this Afrikaans bank because it seemed a bright place – you know, jet-settish, pay was good, everything. There was an introductory period in which they tried to find out as much about you as possible – not like through interviews but gossip, chats – this manager would take you out to lunch and pump you about the others – and discussions. When they were sure you were suitable, then everything starts. First you had to look sexy – dolly-style – all the time; they gave you time off to have your hair done, paid you to do it and paid you a clothes allowance. This, I thought, was to attract the customers but I found no one ever checked on this and most of the female staff seemed to me to be very rude and abrupt to the customers. What we really did all the dressing up for was the entertaining the bank did. It was as if we were a pool of available females for virtually every activity the bank and its directors were involved in – we were constantly required to attend cocktail parties or dinner parties where we'd find groups of young Afrikaans men – businessmen, managers, politicians, government people, party officials, even – at one I went to – a professor from Potchefstroom University. We had to entertain them and this could be literally anything from letting them feel you to just dancing with them. Some of the girls went to special things right at the top where things were really wild, but it was pretty voluntary; you didn't have to if you didn't want to. Most of the girls were quite happy with it and saw nothing wrong in it and there were liaisons going on all over the place.

'Eventually I found out quite a lot. This bank had several other things that functioned in the same way, like gyms, massage and sauna houses, all of them run by it and designed to operate as normal businesses but available for the bank and its top customers at any time. One of the bank's top managers once boasted to me that you could get every kind of vice, courtesy of the bank and he wasn't joking. It was like all the pretty women had a double function – to do whatever routine job they had and then to be at the bank's beck and call.'

Other organisations did not have such elaborate set-ups but women employees often, informally, were expected to provide similar services. The bank in this case did not actually *own* the other services in law – they were usually run by friends or associates of the directors who acted as fronts; bank loans for example, would be transferred for legitimate activities and used to finance 'bank services'.

The process of reward-corruption continues to function right down to the level of city and town councils and beyond. Becoming town clerk or mayor in an Afrikaans town usually means becoming rich in precisely the same way that a Cabinet minister enriches himself.

At the bottom, as in the English sector, there are the poor people and the ordinary non-white people who act as rewards for the officials in the lower levels of Afrikaans society. For these people, power tends to replace material reward but the structure is the same. Two examples:

'I had to wait in this corridor with the baby. It was a typical government building, cold and harsh, grey and foreboding. Strange how you never realise how awful these places are until you have to go to them for something. After an age, I was ushered into this horrid little man's room. Honestly, in the street, you'd have walked right past him. He looked at me with a sneer and began talking to me in Afrikaans. He wanted to know everything. About me, the birth, the baby, about David, the father – everything. He wrote it all down. He already had my birth certificate but the problem was that David wouldn't come in to see him. He was relentless like a policeman crossquestioning you. He treated me like a criminal – worse. I'd never been treated like this in my life. He wanted to know about David in particular. What his parents did, where they came from, what they look like, what he looks like – I had to describe them in detail. It all seemed so crazy. Then this pig grilled me about when it all happened. "Are you sure," he says, "that David is the father? I mean," he sits back with a leer, "given your behaviour, it could be anyone." I had to tell him who else I'd been out with and how far we went. Then he wanted to know about the time when David and I had intercourse, whether he had ejaculated or not. Had I? he asked as if it was the least he expected. He wanted to know where it was, whether it was in the middle of my period or not. I could tell he was getting a real kick out of this. Really power-tripping. Him with his pictures of his wife and four children on the desk next to him. Then he asks me to stand up and looks at me hard, carnally. Looks especially at my face and my skin colour and my hair colour and texture. Then he asks me about David and his colour. Last he looks at the baby and examines its face, hair and finger-nails. He takes out a book with pictures of babies in it, head sizes, figures, profiles and compares the baby's with it. Then he let me go.'

This report is from a young unmarried Afrikaner girl who had fallen pregnant and wanted the baby adopted. The sole job of the government official questioning her was to establish that the child was in fact conceived by the girl and 'David' and not by someone else, such as a Coloured man or a man who may not have been 'pure' white. His questions were routine and are set down in the relevant civil service manual; by law, he has to ask them, just as he has to look at the baby and the parents and try and see whether the child looks white or not. Often this is the only criteria he has to go on and if he suspects that the father looks 'impure', the child can go down as Coloured.[6]

The important thing here is that this power is the official's reward for doing a job that just would not exist anywhere else. The enlargement of the civil service since 1948 has occurred partly because of the need to have Afrikaners in key positions but also because of the need to reward Afrikaners and to save them from taking Africans' jobs or becoming unemployed. The *Broederbond* knows it must look after *all* the Afrikaners or its control could be broken by the grouses of a large, poor and unemployed labouring class. So it has eliminated this risk by creating this kind of job.

Here is the second example:

'The riot police are a breed apart but among the rest of us, it's probably regarded as the most exciting part of police work – especially for the young blokes. To them, it's all a huge game, like cops and robbers, there's no danger – you have all the guns, all the batons, squad cars, Landrovers, everything. You know how, in the bioscope, it's so exciting when you see the baddies being beaten up by the hero? Well, the idea of beating up *Kaffirs* or *hotnots*[7] is the same for a lot of young Afrikaners and in the police and in the riot squad, you get a lot of chances to do this. And if you go out of your way, you can spend all day being a hero. The officers keep an eye on it, of course. They will tell the blokes to lay off if it looks as though they'll kill someone and if the *kaffir* is educated and liable to get stroppy. 'Course, there's always the tough *hotnot* who is like a special challenge and then two of the *ous* will get stuck into him. The captains of each police station keep a look out for blokes for the riot squad. Anyone who is really rough or really into beating gets sent along and sometimes if the Captain doesn't like a bloke, he sends him down. Now, these blokes are something else – they turn it into a real profession; they keep records like wartime fighter pilots. They are killing-mad: they spend their time chatting about how to hurt best, how to maim, the lot. Then they go out off-duty together in gangs and fuck up anyone they like. They are real terrors, they train in all the big-deal stuff like kung-fu, hand-to-hand combat – it's like a religion.'

This was a policewoman recounting with excitement and obvious pleasure the career opportunities in the riot police. For her, as for many young Afrikaners, there was nothing wrong in this because it was a culturally tolerated value, a reward for being a good Afrikaner. From the window of my consulting rooms in the centre of Cape Town in September 1976, I and several of my patients saw the way these 'heroic' riot policemen handled a lone, drunken Coloured man who heckled a traffic policeman. Six truck-loads of fully armed riot police in camouflaged combat gear drew up in answer to the policeman's radio call. There was no crowd but it was rush hour and the road was full of homeward-bound traffic. The riot police grabbed the drunk, ripped his shirt off, dragged him across the tarmac on his bare back, beating and kicking him. At one stage, he struggled up and was promptly thrown onto the bonnet of one of the cars in the traffic jam and beaten over the head with a baton. Six policemen finally picked him up and threw him into the back of a truck amidst grins all round and shouts of encouragement from car-owners stuck in the traffic jam. I interpret this behaviour as the psychopathic acts of individuals engaged in sociopathic functions. The Afrikaners, because they have no place in their thinking for non-whites or indeed non-*herrenvolk*, for people outside the use they can make of them, actually see these acts as completely acceptable. Fun. To be enjoyed, like the movies. Because there is no internal sense of individuality in the community, they think it does not exist outside it. Afrikaners do not have the conceptual structures to recognise other possible styles of thinking.

Behaviours like this are culturally tolerated and approved of. The Afrikaans community looks to its young men to protect it from outside interference of any kind and they are duly rewarded. John Vorster, for example, praised the policemen who, I described earlier, attacked a student demonstration in Cape Town and followed fleeing students into St George's Cathedral beating some of them before the altar. The key to understanding how these 'irreligious' acts can be approved of by an ostensibly religious community lies in the fact that every aspect of Afrikaner life is subordinated to the demands of the state and the *Broederbond*. What I wrote in Chapter One about the kind of immoral boer society then, still persists today. Religion, values and the like are changed and used today according to the demands of the state, just as they were by the frontier boers in the nineteenth century. Institutions of Afrikaner society, such as the church, have no independent existence apart from their role as supportive moralisers for the state. Thus, for example, the *Nederduitse Gereformeerde Kerk*, the largest Afrikaner church in the land – approved of and supported a lottery for the Defence Force when the army mounted a campaign to encourage people to invest in Defence Bonds. Vorster's brother, Koot, who among other things, has been the Moderator of the Church, appeared on television to give the campaign the church's blessing. All this after three decades in which the church had steadfastly preached against lotteries, had condemned them in fact as immoral and communist-inspired.

The secret of the system's success lies in the fact that it is learnt from childhood and in an all-encompassing way. Every action committed is then seen in terms of the 'wholes' provided by the system; a policeman kicking an African bystander is an unfortunate incident but it is acceptable because the policeman was doing a 'good' thing by defending the '*volk*'. The African should not have been there in the first place, he should have been at work – the lesser cause for us becomes the major cause for the Afrikaner; the system's axioms remain unquestioned and everything else is explained around it. There are no areas in which the system fails so badly that its axioms must be checked, and so no internal psychological conflict.

The propaganda generated by the government and by *Bond* agencies in the last thirty years has ensured that Afrikaner (and now English) people see a continuity between their institutions, acts, behaviours and those that are considered normal in other Western countries. The West's hostility to South Africa and its criticism of *apartheid* are cunningly used to cement the myth of continuity: the West is being misled by the communists – only the Afrikaner can see clearly what is going on.

The Afrikaner state in fact needs communism and it needs criticism. Just as it needs English institutions, just as it needs religion. Each is used to stress the *sameness* that exists between Afrikaner society and the main streams of Western development. Close analysis of Afrikaner institutions reveals, as I have shown, major differences both currently and historically: universities look and sound like those in Holland but they are not and never have been. Three religious denominations all stem from Dutch religious movements, they even use the same name – the Dutch Reformed Church (the largest) for example, but they are not the same. Afrikaner institutions in South Africa have always been changed to suit the community's self-interest.

The Afrikaner's warped perspective has survived unchanged and intact since the 1830s, he has withstood every onslaught, he has defied the British Empire and now is one of the most powerful nations in Africa. Because of all these 'facts', the Afrikaner not only thinks he is right, he thinks he is better than anyone else. Who else has such an impressive track record? Nearly two hundred years of successful psychopathy.

I pointed out earlier that the *trekboers* were essentially a simple and frightened community who used their *fears* as rationales for what in the circumstances was an unnecessarily stubborn and foolish act. Frightened people tend to act rashly and to strike out at any point that threatens them: it is a kind of survival-at-all-costs principle – 'us or them' fashion. We tolerate such behaviour when stress makes it a necessary and understandable human act. But we do not tolerate it outside of a dangerous, extreme and, hopefully, rare set of circumstances. If we do, we expose society to animal and inhuman acts which disrupt and harm normal social activity. We tolerate a soldier killing an enemy who is about to kill him in wartime; the same action in civilian life is called murder. If the soldier cannot see this difference, or if he *believes* the other to be an enemy in his own private fantasy, we call him unbalanced, psychopathic and, in extreme cases, psychotic.

I have so far discussed the structure of Afrikaans upbringing and shown how the twin pillars of the community – corruption and hierarchical authoritarianism – are imposed on the growing Afrikaner through the institutions of education and religion and the reward system. I have, I hope, in the process, explained why Afrikaners do not experience anxiety or guilt or show personal mental dysfunction – one of the puzzling findings of my earlier research. The average Afrikaner is not mentally disturbed; his culture is. He functions well in his community without being aware of the overall dysfunction.

What happens to the Afrikaner who rebels, who tries to reject the system? What, indeed, is there to keep the Afrikaner in place? To a certain extent, obviously, a large proportion of the Afrikaner population will never question their value system; but some will. Some people, through travel, through outside contact, must surely present a danger to the state? No matter how rewarding an authoritarian system is, no matter how totalitarian its internal organisation may be, it still requires repressive measures to keep its elite and its intelligentsia in check. How is this done in the Afrikaner state? In my opinion, one of the most effective means of control is the army.

The social role of armies has changed considerably over the years; some modern states have professional armies while others have systems of conscription. The purpose of these systems is to train personnel in the eventuality of that country being attacked. This is one of the roles of the army in South Africa but it is by no means the most important. The primary tasks, in the past thirty years, of South Africa's army have been, I think, to brutalise white, mainly Afrikaner, youths, to provide the physical reality, the power, that will descend on them if they rebel; to deprive Afrikaners of any sense of personal privacy and any will to go against Afrikaner doctrine and thirdly, to imbue English and non-doctrinaire Afrikaner whites with a similar indoctrination. Not as is the case with Afrikaans conscripts – by providing a logical and coherent extension to a familiar ideology – but by sheer force of intimidation. Permanent Force officers are issued with instructions in special manuals and by means of training administered by secret psychological section lectures in procedure to be followed in dealing with these matters and in particular, with English-speaking conscripts. In them, they are instructed to follow precise rules for inducing fear and terror in conscripts. Among these rules are the following:

'Never speak to an English white in English. Always use Afrikaans *except* when the trainee behaves in accordance with approved behaviour. Then *be friendly and speak in English*. Encourage discrimination against English trainees on any grounds whatsoever. It is acceptable to use religion, appearance or habits in any way to create a feeling of not-belonging. Put where possible, two people of the same denomination together with a barrack of Afrikaans-speaking trainees and then show preference for one of the pair.

'Behave at all times in the presence of English trainees as loud, aggressive and brutal as possible towards him, the task and everyone else around. Relent systematically *only when* the target behaves in the same brutal way towards others (that is, trainees, not staff) or to the task.

'Always listen to complaints, no matter how irritating. Give the appearance of sympathy, encourage the trainee to talk to you, to confide in you. Tell him you will try and do something for him. Do nothing. Train him to accept his lot by letting him talk while changing nothing. If you do not let him talk, he will resent it. The English trainees expect to talk – it satisfies them.

'Use whatever sympathy you have obtained to encourage him to talk more. Carefully move the discussions to others. Encourage him to inform on his friends and their ideas. He will not suspect you if you do not act on the information.

'Build up stress situations for likely targets who are weakening and be there when they crack. If necessary, encourage Afrikaans troopies to gang up or beat up English.'[8]

These directives show the influence of sophisticated behaviour modification techniques; reward patterns and hierarchies as well as the interpersonal structure employed come straight out of advanced research reports and text books. The army has a large psychiatric and psychological section devoted entirely to doing research in the development of means to indoctrinate and control army trainees.

It was clear to me both from what I was told by army personnel and by the results of this process on some of my patients that this provided an effective real fear in English trainees to back up the psychological fear that I had earlier found to exist in my student samples. Since all male whites have to do army training it is clear that the intention of the army is to make all white trainees fear the power and might, the determination and ruthlessness of the Afrikaner state in the most psychologically effective way: if I point a gun at you and tell you I will kill you if you do not behave, the chances are you will run away or get a gun and come after me. For sure, you are not going to stand around after I take the gun off you. The Afrikaner does not do that. He points the gun at the 'enemy' (always African – army targets are *always* black) and shows you how good he is with it. Then he looks at you to see what you are going to do.

The imperative is clear – you are either for him or against him. If you are against him, you become the enemy. Few trainees have the insight and psychological strength of character to withstand this kind of 'free' choice. This is a crucial element in Afrikaner coercion at all levels. It creates what you think is free choice – it does not coerce you directly. It establishes two options and leaves you to choose. You never get a chance to choose *the context* and you know you have to choose one or the other, so you choose the easiest. The point is that the choices are often set in such a way as to leave you, deliberately, with the illusion of freedom. Let me give an example.

Blacks can choose to work in the homelands or they can be contract labourers. If they choose to be the latter, they have to abide by the government rules – they are not allowed to bring their wives or families, they live in dormitory squalor and return home at the end of the contract. All this creates immense social and psychological problems, not the least of which is disruption of family life. But, the Afrikaner points out, the African is '*free*' not to take a contract. He can stay in the homelands. Therefore it is not the government's fault: these people willingly enter the system. What is tacit to the problem and which we know removes the element of choice is that staying in the homelands means poverty, unemployment and death. The Afrikaner will only grant freedom on his terms and in this kind of context.

And so it is in the army. You are free to choose to conform totally or to be brutalised. Few trainees realise this. So concerned did I become at what was being done in the army that eventually I readily got anyone off their service if I could and if they wanted.[9] Often, though, in order to do this I had to train my patients in symptom structures and patterns – not only to resist the psychological testing they would be put through but to withstand the psychological intimidation and terrorism they were exposed to, to conform. The information I had about the army's methods was however only a fraction of what actually obtains. I was told by an army major who telephoned me one day to warn me that they were aware of what I was doing with my patients and that 1) it was ineffective because the army had far better techniques than I had counter-techniques, and 2) if I did not stop, I would face a charge of subverting trainees.

The army, for the Afrikaans community, while ostensibly teaching its sons the skills and motivations necessary to carry out the acts deemed essential for the Afrikaans state's survival, in reality provides the iron hand that coerces Afrikaans males into accepting Afrikaner ideology. The army programme does not stop when conscription is over. It retains a yearly hold over its trainees for up to twenty years afterwards in the form of camps and 'special contact' missions. Every Kommandant in charge of citizen-force soldiers makes it his job to have at least some contact with a soldier's family or place of employment. The whole Afrikaans family is drawn into the military process; the army knows that it will cut off effective opposition at its simplest level if every Afrikaner mother can pick up the phone and get through straight away to her son's commanding officer with her fears and complaints. And so it is; it is in fact an important priority for permanent senior army staff and effectively catches the trainee in an inescapable doublebind between the army coercion and family coercion.

Few Afrikaners slip through this process and those that do suffer a peculiar fate that arises not so much out of the actions of the authorities but out of the psychological effects of being cut off from Afrikanerdom. I regard Afrikaners who have left their community and who stay in South Africa as being analogous to large animals once free, who have now to spend the rest of their lives in captivity – both die a long slow agonising death out of loneliness and isolation. Afrikaners who do not conform are psychologically savaged; they are cut off from the process of being Afrikaans and as such, they show the true weakness of the Afrikaans system – without it, people are not capable of leading normal full lives.

Afrikaners are reared to fit into the system: they are developed in such a way that they are completely dependent on the system for survival. Once removed they never recover. I treated over sixty such Afrikaners between 1971 and 1976 and *not one* recovered from the break. All developed major pathology, nearly always alcoholism, and all had the same obsessional ideology – they behaved as if their parents had rejected them and their lives revolved around the possibility of being taken back into the community. Let me detail some of these cases.

Several of my patients worked for Afrikaans newspapers, magazine groups or for the Broadcasting service. Their dissent always revolved around a particular point:

'I suppose the blame really goes to my mother; she was a strong person who protected me so when I went out to work, I was a bit naïve and stubborn. Anyhow, I studied well and eventually got a good job with an Afrikaans newspaper. Through this, I got in with a liberal party crowd of Afrikaners and I began to see that the newspaper I worked for was dishonest. Basically, Afrikaans newpapers act as propaganda tryouts for the government, editors and top staff are always *Broeders*. Anyhow, what happens is that if the government wants to feel out a response to a new direction it wants to take, it gets an editor to put in a sample opinion and then see what the reaction is. Anyway, I was asked to write one of those things; they put it in and it was all wrong so the government withdrew the idea. I was very upset. I got called up to the editor for being upset. He reprimanded me and I suppose I lost my head. I took it higher, urged on by my liberal friends. It got nowhere but quite soon I was hauled in again and told to find another job. Not fired or asked to resign – just kind of "Look, you have no career here." So I left, got a job somewhere else and my life really went wrong. My wife's father, a *Broeder*, called to see us and talked to her without me. Then she began to put pressure on me too. To cut a long story short, I was interested in another girl so this was the end: my job and now my wife. She never did approve of my friends anyway. She was from a Free State farm so what can you expect?'

This journalist drifted for many years and ended up with a drinking problem which is now chronic. He was cut off from his community ruthlessly and at every level. He entered a mental hospital after the death of his only support – his mother. Despite the fact that he had had a good job and had been healthy physically and mentally, he could not stand the strain of being rejected by the Afrikaner community. He knew his isolation was helped along by *Broeder* activity.

Some Afrikaners, in their hurt and anger at being kept out of Afrikaner life, turn radical and revolutionary to try to get their own back but rarely succeed at this because the motivation behind their actions is not revolution because of oppression, but revolution because of omission. Under pressure they collapse. The security services boast that they *never* have trouble with Afrikaner dissidents or revolutionaries because 'they all respond like Pavlov's dogs to authority'. When caught, 'they're like children, they break down and cry and ask forgiveness. Then they tell us everything we want to know.' Further, they behave as if they want to get caught. Like naughty children, they plan and organise their 'revolts' with childlike simplicity expecting their Afrikaans 'parents' to smack them, laugh and then send them out to play again. Because of their completely unrealistic upbringing, they have no real appreciation of what the Afrikaner state can do to its enemies and conceptualise their role and that of their interrogators in a heroic adolescent fantasy. Here is one of them:

'I want to come home leading a revolution. I want to show the Afrikaners the right way. I want to show them how corrupt and brutal they are. I want to be the one who leads the Afrikaners out of the dark into the light. I want to have a place in Afrikaner history.'

Some creative and intelligent Afrikaner authors and academics cannot afford to leave the very system they abhor. They are tied to it and some of them openly admit this fact:

'Look, the Afrikaans community brought me up. It's the only way I know. Without them I am lost. Sure, I'd like them to love me, to let me in. Somehow I've survived outside but not without their help. You see, I am big stuff now *outside* their community. People come to me as a brave man – an Afrikaner who has seen the light. Every word I write or say is taken down. I really am the darling of the white liberal set and I owe it all to the Afrikaans community. I have never been so adored or admired. God, man, I take any woman I want. Any. They're only too pleased to lie with me, to tell their friends they've slept with the *grootse*. You should have seen me years ago – a nothing, back home in the Transvaal. Nobody gave a fuck for me then – just like an ordinary *boetie*. I'll tell you one thing. My life comes to an end the day the *kaffirs* take over. What would I do without the Afrikaner. They're my life, *ou*. I wouldn't know what to do with myself.'

Tragically, one of the reasons they cannot survive is because they have no means of replacing the corruption they are taught as an integral part of their upbringing. Determined to eliminate their Afrikanerness – the bad, ugly parts they rapidly learn the outside world condemns – they are continually at war with themselves because they only know about *using* relationships. Above all, they cannot cope with women or with honesty. They inevitably get caught out for the most simple and childish acts of dishonesty in interpersonal relationships because they have no notion of personal responsibility and individuality. In short, they corrupt their personalities and their relationships outside the community. Only an Afrikaner reared in the same tradition can cope with them.

Chapter Eight

Feudalism, Machiavellianism and the Broederbond

I started off my explorations into South Africa by positing an obvious and, in some quarters, popular thesis that the Afrikaner is essentially authoritarian, even Nazi-like, in his attitudes and behaviour. As I think the preceding chapters have made clear, this concept became so much a part of my thinking about South Africa that it became almost redundant. Eventually, though, I had to shift my understanding to a different axiom because the concept and meaning of the Authoritarian Personality was not enough; Adorno and his team who had researched fascism had concerned themselves with individual psychology and not with social systems as uniquely sociopathic as the Afrikaners'.

 As I got closer to the centre of affairs in South Africa, I had to accept that what the Afrikaners were trying to enforce in South Africa was not in essence a fascist order but rather a feudal one. In a deep sense, the whole structure of the *apartheid* state is controlled by the secret activities of the power groups within the *Broederbond*. Like a feudal monarchy, the *Broederbond* holds the Afrikaner state together. It is the elite of the elite and directs and coerces life inside the psychological prison that is the Afrikaans community. It was not possible for me to get anywhere near direct access to the activities of this secret society, but it was possible to piece together from the various reports I received some of the major phases that have occurred in it since 1948.

In a crucial sense, I think these phases provide the missing political backdrop to my own studies and help, in part, to explain some of the significance of the more recent events in South African public life.

By far the most important fact I unearthed about the *Broederbond* is that its main focus of activity is the Afrikaans community. Like most outsiders, I had presumed that the *Broederbond*'s main effort would be devoted to controlling South Africa as a whole, but as I gathered more information about its internal activities it became clear that I had made assumptions about the *Bond* that simply were not true. I had assumed a tightly closed society united in its aim of controlling South Africa. Far from it: the Afrikaans *Broederbond* is a closed and secret society, correct – but it is not united nor does it in practice act as a collective. The Afrikaans *Broederbond* is essentially a battle-ground in which various groups of Afrikaners fight out battles for power and control of the Afrikaans community. It is in fact so obsessed with these battles that the task of running South Africa has often been given to people of little significance. Let me explain.

The Afrikaner Nationalist Party's victory in the 1948 elections had been preceded by the rise in the *Broederbond* of hard core Nazi-influenced Afrikaners determined to eliminate deviationists such as Smuts and Hertzog who, they felt, were losing sight of their commitment to the Afrikaans community. Smuts and Hertzog are familiar examples of the tendency that the Nationalists acted to halt, but there were many other Afrikaners who had strayed – Brahm Fischer, for example. An ordinary Afrikaner, born on a farm in the Orange Free State, he grew up with an intimate knowledge of Afrikaans traditions and an admiration for some of its early leaders such as Paul Kruger. He went to boarding school, and through his abilities eventually won a scholarship to Oxford. While there, his interest in Marxism crystallized and he went on to become one of South Africa's best-known communist activists.[1]

There were many such Afrikaners, and in between existed less polarized groups who would have followed any political dictum. South Africa in 1948 was, despite its traditions, ripe for liberalism and progressive change. Malan's Nationalists, therefore, once in power, had to take control of the Afrikaans community before they did anything else. They had to control the *Broederbond* and through it the rest of the community. Once the Afrikaans community was safely in their hands, they could turn to the rest of South Africa.

Each era in the *Bond* since 1948 has been marked in fact by differences in approach to this central problem rather than to any other problem.

As I understand it, there have been three basic phases through which the Nationalists have passed since 1948. Each has had its own form of ideology set, as things always have been for the Afrikaner, by the personalities who predominated in the *Bond* at the time. The basic type of ideology follows the conservative traditional Afrikaner view of how the state should run. That is, within the axiom that the Afrikaner should dominate South Africa and its affairs, its proponents follow the lines I have described in the last chapter. *Broeders* who hold this view believe that the *Bond* should operate slowly and systematically within the framework of established Afrikaner values and exploit South Africa for the benefits of all sections of the Afrikaans community. I would describe this as orthodox Afrikaner ideology.

The second type I term ultra-orthodox. These are people who are doctrinaire Afrikaners and who believe in the ideals and myths created by the community. They believe, for example, that they are charged with a holy duty, a responsibility to God, to preserve white civilization; they believe that Africans are inferior and have to be helped, they believe in the Immorality Act – that cross-racial mixing is immoral, unChristian and against the scriptures.

The third type follows a different morality and it arises out of the kind of society that the Afrikaner has created for himself. Its ideology is best described as self-seeking and, in the context of South Africa, can be described as successful and creative psychopathy.

In a society such as I have described, the only outlet for creativity, intelligence and rebelliousness is through the structure set up by the *Broederbond*. Thus any individual who masters this hierarchy and rises to the top in any sphere is then in a position to apply his intelligence and creativity to his own ends or to the ends of his immediate group of friends and acquaintances. Depending on how tightly he is controlled and directed, his efforts to act for the Afrikaner – to the outside observer – will be either sociopathic, that is, for the good of the Afrikaner but not for the good of South Africa; or psychopathic, that is, for the good of the individual, not either for South Africa's good nor for the good of the Afrikaner community. This is a crucial distinction because the line between the two is very fine and under the circumstances obtaining in South Africa, very important, as I will show.

A community organized in such a way as the Afrikaners' continues to function as a closed, tight community only so long as it is
tightly controlled, its internal hierarchy functions for the good of
the community and it has an outside environment that permits it to
remain as it is. The same split political forces that unify and preserve it can also destroy it if left to their own devices; in the absence
of a strong central control at the top, its various sectors will use the
same processes that generate tight control and organized corruption to further the aims of whoever controls them. In the absence of
a sense of personal rights and responsiblity, the individuals who
make up such a pre-adolescent and unrealistic community will, left
to their own devices (as would be the case under a loose leader),
simply further their own interests. Personal obligation, duty,
responsibility are the attributes of a free society in which its individuals, in the face of reality, co-operate for the greater good. These
attributes do not exist in the Afrikaans state.

Given the feudal structure of the Afrikaans state, the leader does
not have to operate between limits imposed on him by institutions
or by the populace. He is not bound by general elections nor by fear
of offending the press or even public opinion. He leads from above
and his community looks to him to interpret its morality. The whole
system is geared in fact to directives from the *Broederbond* elite; all
the leader has to take cognisance of is the power hierarchy within
this elite. All else is subservient to it. Since 1948, the *Broederbond*
has been dominated in turn by four people: Malan and Strydom,
who followed the orthodox ideology; Verwoerd, who was ultra-
orthodox; and Vorster and his associates, psychopathic products of
their sociopathic society.

South Africa under Malan and Strydom – leaders who maintained their positions through tight and ruthless personal control –
was relatively free from internal conflict partly because of external
circumstances and also because they were tough political fighters
with strong survival instincts learned from the years in opposition to
Smuts. I cannot comment in detail on this era – I started research
only after Verwoerd's death – but I have sufficient evidence to indicate that its form was essentially that of the orthodox Afrikaner
ideology. What is important, though, and what dominated the
decade of my research was the impact of Verwoerd's personality on
the *Broederbond* and how he adopted and changed the orthodox

ideology and power structure developed by Strydom and Malan.

Verwoerd and, later, Vorster, as we will see, more than anyone understood the feudal and Machiavellian nature of Afrikaner society. Before taking power, Verwoerd used his understanding of Afrikaner psychology to build his empire in African Affairs. Verwoerd was regarded with bemusement by his fellow-Afrikaners in government because he concerned himself with something they were not interested in: the African problem. They were grateful to him for 'solving' the problem simply because no one else could be bothered with it; he tidied up a loose end for them while they got on with the important thing – Afrikaner politics.

Malan and Strydom took control of the Afrikaans leadership at a time when the Nationalists were fragmented and split. They welded a cohesive political force out of relatively little through the weight of their own personalities. When the time came, though, to replace Malan first, then Strydom, the effect of the feudal system they had rationalized became noticeable. It is part of the inherent structure of the authoritarian and totalitarian *Broederbond* that there is no institution or process for changing the leadership. This is a crucial point and Verwoerd saw it, I think, because he was an outsider while his fellows, too, accepting of the system, did not. In Western societies, we are so used to the ordinary stable process of political change within power groups that we take for granted the complex balance of institutionalized power necessary for peaceful change to occur. Beneath the fabric of democratic society there is the normal psychological process I described earlier whereby a growing child experiences conflict as he tests his theories of reality with reality. He develops and grows an ability to manage reality properly provided he is able to make flexible use of alternative theories to fill the gaps between his parents' ideas and his own experiences. Democratic principles are based on this. Most of us accept that reality is so complex that no one single human or group of humans can explain or deal with it all; political democracy arises when a community makes it a rule to let the other side try their hand if one side fails. This is institutionalized and defines flexible, stable and open societies. The right to think otherwise, to have a point of view, is so much a part of Western life that trouble arises if we feel we are not being listened to or given our right in law. All this is meaningless to the Afrikaner. There is no place in the individual Afrikaner nor in his society for notions of changing systems to fit reality. Just as the

Afrikaner individual would not think of questioning or changing his system of values, so the Afrikaner state has no institution for changing the system of leadership and its direction. This is the major flaw of personal leadership systems everywhere and it means simply that no formal means exists to remove peaceably a person judged to be incompetent. Stalin, Mao Tse Tung, Hitler, Mussolini and Franco were people who came to power in the same way as Afrikaans leaders do and who were replaced only when they were killed or if they died. There is no proper room in these systems for either conflict or personality clashes. One eliminates one's opposition or is oneself eliminated. Each such system has its own meaning for the term 'elimination' and the *Broederbond* is no different.

In place of normal procedures of election or removal of leaders, the Afrikaans community has institutionalized a devious, secret process. Every Nationalist Prime Minister since 1948, with the exception of Strydom who died on the job, has been removed in strange circumstances which, within the framework I have described here, can be seen as a manifestation of the secret processes at work.

In the Afrikaans *Broederbond*, one eliminates one's opponent by smearing his name rather than by killing him or taking other such drastic action. Survival in such a community revolves around identifying with one or other dominant personality or clique – a process that the Afrikaner has engaged in since the 1830s. The dominant personality wins by blackening the name of his opponent, by discovering corruption or perversion outside the approved *Broederbond* framework; by recruiting enough people in the individual's cause or, if this fails, by spreading gossip and rumour.

Malan, the first prime minister of the Nationalists, resigned in November 1954 in the middle of apparently complex and demanding parliamentary manipulations over the Coloured right to vote. No one on the outside knows why and the most often-cited reason is that he was wearied by the stresses of putting *apartheid* legislation through parliament. Yet, as I have shown, prejudice and *apartheid* legislation are minor concerns to the Afrikaner compared with their own power manipulations. Strydom outmanoeuvered Malan and 'eliminated' him.

After Strydom died, Verwoerd was then in a position to become premier because he was regarded as a 'safe' option by the elite of the *Bond* – someone who would do their bidding as efficiently and ruthlessly as he had run African affairs. Too late did the various *Broeders* realize his true nature and power. Verwoerd was an obsessively ambitious and fanatical man, prepared to work very hard and to go to incredible lengths to be accepted as a hard-working neutral in the *Broederbond*. Once inside the organization, he set about learning the psychological processes that dominated it and then manipulated them to achieve his own supremacy. He meticulously prepared his ground, building up contacts and confidence over nearly two decades. As an outsider, that is, a non-Afrikaner (he was Dutch-born), he knew that he would have to do three things to take power of the *Broederbond*: make himself seem neutral, make his abilities indispensable and keep himself clean. He took on tasks outside the main arena of power – in particular in Bantu Affairs – to this end. Here he built up a formidable reputation and solved a problem for the *Bond* while at the same time did not appear a threat. Finally, knowing well the power of rumour and gossip, he obsessively kept his own life spotless, thus ensuring that he both appeared safe and protected himself.

When Strydom died, Verwoerd was elected for one reason only: the various factions in the *Bond* thought that he would be easily controlled and manipulated; a better choice in fact than either of the two existing and warring factions. Interestingly enough, Verwoerd used the same device on the *Broeders* as they used on outsiders: he appeared to be one thing (reasonable, open to discussion and concession) while in reality doing another (behaving with ruthless self-interest). Verwoerd was intelligent and articulate, capable, well-informed and efficient – he made others, in the words of one of my patients:

'feel completely inferior. You were so busy trying to keep up, be as good as he was, there was no time to question him. He ran his affairs brilliantly, he argued brilliantly and anyone who met him always had the same impression – he made you feel guilty. He had this stern gaze that made you wilt.'

The joke, if it can be called that, was that the *Bond* had elected more than the super-efficient party man they thought they had. Verwoerd was totally imbued with the spirit of Afrikanerdom. He identified with it and saw himself as a messiah come to lead his people to their highest pinnacle. Once in power, not only did he dominate the political division of the *Broederbond* but he controlled the hierarchy as well.

One of the few things that awes the average Afrikaner is one of their own who actually believes their myths. Verwoerd knew this and had built himself around it and so the Afrikaners experienced under him something they had not before – the logical results of their beliefs. Verwoerd applied the doctrines of orthodox Afrikanerdom fully and he ensured that everyone else did the same. Like a stern and hard schoolmaster, he ran the Afrikaners strictly and like the psychological schoolboys his colleagues were, they remained obedient and doctrinaire, scared that he would punish them. Far from being manipulated, Verwoerd ended up pulling the strings.

The difficulty for the Afrikaners was that Verwoerd made of Afrikaner philosophy something that it had never intended to be. Historically, Afrikaner values arose essentially as a means of justifying the insular and retrogressive behaviour of the *trekboers* and the Boer Republics. To turn power-grabbing into a philosophy was something that many Afrikaners could not identify with and did not want. Fine if Verwoerd had limited his vision to the lecture halls of Stellenbosch University – but he did not. Once in power, Verwoerd set about turning the fantasies of Afrikanerdom into reality with every intention of turning South Africa into what Afrikaans philosophy said it was: racial *apartheid*, separate but *equal*. I quote from an Afrikaans businessman who suffered as a result of Verwoerd's policies:

'I'll admit that we all thought Verwoerd was fantastic at first. Clever, clear, he was like our answer to the world, our secret academic weapon. He put the guts back into South Africa because he could take on anyone and win. He could talk and argue. But we should have known. He wasn't a real Afrikaner like the rest of us – he tried too hard to *be* an Afrikaner and really, despite all his brains, he got it wrong. Let's face it, would you, being honest, believe in *apartheid* and all that bullshit he came up with? No-one does. We all know that the whites here are really in it for the money, for what they can get out of it. *No* Afrikaner, deep down, believes the crap that we put out; it's all cover. We know sooner or later we'll be stopped, we've just been very lucky to get away with it for so long. But there are certain freaks in the *Bond* who are really insane. Verwoerd was one; they believe the hogwash and they want to be Afrikaner heroes. Verwoerd nearly screwed the whole thing up with his insane philosophy. We *trusted* him, man, thinking he was just like us. But he wasn't. Like Hitler, maybe, like all those wartime Afrikaners. Racial philosophy; my goodness. Thank God somebody stopped him before it was too late.'

Verwoerd's programmes from 1958 to 1966 were radical and revolutionary compared with the orthodox ideology that had dominated Malan's and Strydom's rule. His Bantustan policy is one of the best-known of these programmes but there were others made less public. Verwoerd had ideas about everything and he interfered with the running of every department. He demanded, for example, a balanced budget, restrictions on government spending; he channelled massive funds into African Affairs and he demanded absolute allegiance from everyone. He double-checked on every one's work and he made *all* the decisions in *all* the areas.

By 1962, the *Broederbonders* were beginning to feel the full effects of his actions. For one thing, playing Afrikaner morality to the hilt, he was bent on separate and equal Bantustans; for the first time in Nationalist political history, Verwoerd had made white government departments wait for funds or cut back on their spending while his African policy went ahead. The crunch came when he began to insist that his fellows in the ruling elite behave as he did; in other words, adopt his aescetic and ultra-orthodox life-style. To back this up he began to put a stop to some of the profiteering and the corrupt life-styles and this, of all things, was the straw that broke the camel's back. In this case, the *Broederbond's*.

Once it was clear that Verwoerd was committing the Afrikaners to a 'pure' ideology, there was panic in certain quarters of the *Broederbond*. Slowly, they discovered that they had more than just cause for panic. Not only was Verwoerd bent on a programme that many prominent Afrianers regarded as insane and suicidal, he was almost impossible to get rid of. He had foreseen every eventuality. Not only was he in a powerful and unassailable political position but he had ensured that his private life was beyond reproach. Like the Machiavellian he was, he had covered every possible exit. Worse, as many *Broeders* came to realize, he had systematically created a state within a state to protect himself and ensure that his hierarchy prevailed. One of the first things Verwoerd had done when he took power was to appoint John Vorster to his cabinet in 1958. Ostensibly Vorster's promotion was for his capacity to work hard and he was given the ministership of Education and Social Welfare and Pensions. Verwoerd, however, was motivated by other reasons to appoint this unconnected and uninfluential outsider.[2] Using him as he himself had been used by Strydom, Verwoerd brought in the neutral Vorster to keep a close watch on anyone who posed a threat to his authority and power. He knew of Vorster's reputation for ruthlessness and efficiency and his ability to carry out orders. More important, Vorster had contact with many members of the security forces who had not been part of Malan's or Strydom's hierarchy. Vorster and his friends from the *Ossewabrandwag*[3] were in an ideal position to serve Verwoerd. Hard-core, ambitious and bitter about having to eat humble pie after the war in order to gain an entry into Malan's National party, they were sufficiently widespread throughout the community to keep Verwoerd informed about any possible threat.

Verwoerd well knew that gossip and rumour are the life-blood of the *Broeder* elite and that he who controls the gossip, controls the community. Verwoerd wanted Vorster to provide him with the kind of information that would keep his competitors in check and to provide an active means of ensuring Verwoerd's will be done, even in areas where he could not himself reach. So successfully did Vorster do his informal job that Verwoerd appointed him Minister of Justice in 1961, giving him more formal means of achieving the control Verwoerd wanted. By 1961, Verwoerd was more sure of himself and more in control of the Afrikaner state than he had been earlier and he was on the point of embarking on several actions that he knew would shake the Afrikaans establishment. He knew too that there would be a lot of opposition to his intentions and he needed to make sure that his protective screen was firmly established, formalized and budgeted for in the difficult years ahead. Vorster as Minister of Justice could achieve all this.

By late 1963, the opposition to Verwoerd in the *Broederbond* was fragmented and being spied upon by Vorster and his men. It was powerless to move and many gave up hope of ever getting rid of Verwoerd. Doubtless if Verwoerd had been more thorough he would have continued but he made one fatal mistake; he misjudged the calibre of the men he had hired to protect him. Vorster created a secret service based on himself and his close ally, Hendrik Van den Bergh, and several ex-internees who rose to high positions in their organization. In doing so, a different ideology was introduced into the equation of *Broederbond* power-play.

Vorster and Van den Bergh were not in the same class as Malan, Strydom or Verwoerd; they were ordinary Afrikaners with nothing to lose and a proven ability to be ruthless and fanatical. Their entry into *Bond* politics ushered in a shift in emphasis and introduced the psychological climate that permitted the three types of ideology to come into conflict for the first time since 1948, and for the third, creative and self-seeking psychopathy, to emerge triumphant.

Verwoerd changed the *status quo* of the *Broederbond* and in so doing sowed the seed of his own destruction. In disrupting normal *Broederbond* procedures, Verwoerd ensured that the system in order to cope with him had to draw on resources which previously had remained untapped. In using Vorster, Verwoerd introduced a dangerous aspect of Afrikaner ideology that had in the past always been kept away from the centre of power and under control. This structure of the act of deposement is important because, as we shall see in Chapter Nine, Vorster was deposed by a similar 'drawing on untapped resources' procedure.

Orthodox ideology, before Verwoerd had mastered it and led it into areas that were disastrous for the elite community, was, despite its failings for Afrikanerdom as a whole, a relatively stable and broadly based method of dealing with Afrikaner needs. Certainly Malan and Strydom and their *Broederbond* cohorts had acted to preserve and improve the Afrikaner community as a whole. Vorster and Van den Bergh and their friends were not of the same ilk nor were they from the same backgrounds as either orthodox or ultra-orthodox ideologues.

Vorster, as a young man, was an ideological zealot whose pro-Nazi activities in the *Ossewabrandwag* were regarded by the orthodox Afrikaners as verging on the lunatic. He was never regarded as either an intellectual or as a particularly intelligent political in-fighter; he was a good NCO in the army of the Afrikaner faithful and was never expected to rise very far. Van den Bergh was also regarded as a political nonentity before Vorster called upon him. He had a feared reputation in the police force which arose out of his borderline activities:

'The fact that Van den Bergh became a policeman and not a master crook was pure luck. He'd been an opportunist all his life and as a young man tried his hand at a lot of things, not all of them legal. He was very rough and wild in a quiet and menacing way. He was guiltless, cruel, no feelings – while all the time pretending to be social and charming. He became a policeman because he made more money than being a crook. Also it gave him the power he needed. He had hundreds of contacts with every kind of hoodlum there is in South Africa and he had a way with them – he played both worlds off against each other, letting his friends in the underworld *donner* people he wanted hurt and then letting the crooks off. I think he made a bit of a pile on the quiet too.'

These are the comments of a policeman who worked in the same area as Van den Bergh had. Van den Bergh was known to be unstable and for the pleasure he took in inflicting pain on people. His superiors were very wary of him and of promoting him because while he got results, his methods were unscrupulous.

But Vorster and Van den Bergh had two things in common: they were opportunists and Verwoerd despised them; he made no secret of the fact that he regarded them as inferiors and as intellectual dullards. Verwoerd thought that they would be satisfied with the power and the status he gave them and that they would never pose a threat to him. He failed to realise that just as he had taken advantage of the Afrikaner feudal system, so too could others. He also reckoned without the longstanding underlying tolerance Afrikaans society has for brutality and harshness from within its own ranks.

Vorster, through Van den Bergh and his agents, learnt of the growing dissatisfaction with Verwoerd and served, I am told, as the unifying pivot for anti-Verwoerd sentiments. Because of his role in Verwoerd's hierarchy and because in time, through his ruthless enforcement of the law and through his obvious ability, Verwoerd came to trust him, Vorster was, for several years prior to Verwoerd's death, the only available avenue for the safe expression of rebellion and resentment against Verwoerd's growing curtailment of *Broederbond* activities. When, because of Verwoerd's progress, the anti-Verwoerd faction in the *Broederbond* put themselves in Vorster's and Van den Bergh's hands, they were committing themselves to a dependency on people who did not share their ideology and who, because of their opportunism and personal rather than communal self-seeking, would not, once in power, willingly return to a state where they had very much to play second fiddle to the intellectual elite of the *Broederbond*.

The important thing to bear in mind for what follows is that the kind of people Vorster and Van den Bergh collected around themselves were not the kind of men that had previously dominated Afrikaner affairs. Whatever the old Nationalists' grievances with Verwoerd, they were bound, psychologically, to adhere to his line and to content themselves with petty grumbling. The people that joined Vorster were, I believe, in the main like himself – a kind of middle- to-lower-order group in the *Bond* hierarchy, without ideals and with no clear ideology (as Malan and Verwoerd had had). The main unifying factor was, as far as I can see, a proven ability to intrigue and to take whatever action was necessary to achieve their ends. I conclude from what my various informants told me about the personalities of those involved with Vorster that these were the kind of people who embodied something of the hard immorally self-seeking core of the Afrikaans community, similar in many ways to the worst of the old *trekboers* I described in Chapter One.

You see, I had no direct access to recent Afrikaner political history, as I had had to the trekker communities. Once the *Broederbond* went underground in 1924, the kind of personal-feel data that was freely available about boer life and life in the Afrikaner Republics ceased altogether. I had fragments only and in putting them together, like a jigsaw puzzle, I knew that there were gaps. I was looking for continuities, historical and psychological, between the early history of the Afrikaner, which I knew well, and the tit-bits of rare information I was getting from my patients and their friends. The early history was dominated by bitter enmity and clashes between personalities right up to and including the Boer War. I knew, theoretically, that this principle must have persisted in the *Bond*, but in secret. As far as I could judge, therefore, it seemed to me that Vorster did embody the kind of opportunistic *trekker* spirit albeit within a more tightly controlled hierarchy.

What I have no doubt about, though, is the role this group played before and after Verwoerd's death in 1966. Whatever variance there is in my informants' reporting about Vorster's role in Verwoerd's timely death, the one thing they all agreed upon – it is, in fact, common knowledge amongst thinking Afrikaners – is that

Vorster and his men were much more deeply involved in the matter than the outside world is aware of. The debate in Afrikaans circles is where and when did their involvement begin?'

The events leading up to and surrounding Verwoerd's death are, on the surface, fairly clear and straightforward. Dmitri Tsafendas, a parliamentary messenger, stabbed Verwoerd to death in the House of Assembly on 6 September 1966; he was apprehended, tried, found insane and committed to be detained at the State President's pleasure. There was apparently no plot and Tsafendas was described as a hopelessly paranoid schizophrenic.

The debate, for Afrikaners, went as follows: on the one hand, many people I spoke to believed that Vorster and his men were highly organized, simply waiting for an – any – opportunity to seize power from Verwoerd. My informants believe that Van den Bergh let Tsafendas continue in his job in parliament, well aware of his demented plans, not in the firm hope that he would act but as one of several loose and vague possibilities and fantasies that Van den Bergh entertained:

> 'Remember, Van den Bergh was Vorster's right-hand man. It was his job to keep Vorster *totally* informed about anything that could have been of use to them. I can't see someone as *thoroughly* ruthless as Van den Bergh making a slip-up. He was in charge of security – always remember that. The perfect man in the perfect position just waiting to do whatever he was told – or paid to do. And remember, he is crazy enough to do anything. Anything.'[4]

On the other hand, there are people who believe that the whole thing was arranged from beginning to end by Vorster and Van den Bergh. They cite several 'facts' to back this up. First, the judge who conducted the commission of inquiry into the assassination presented before Parliament in 1967 was unable to answer one question – how it had been possible for such a man as Tsafendas, the assassin, who had a long history of mental disturbance, to get through the security screen protecting those employed in the House of Assembly. This still baffles a lot of Afrikaners brought up to believe in the efficiency of the security services. Secondly, during Tsafendas' attack, Vorster, who was to present the first question on the order paper, was going over his papers wearing P.W. Botha's glasses, having apparently mislaid his own. He conveniently did not see

anything until he heard a scuffle by which time it was all over. Thirdly, Vorster's wife was that day with Mrs Verwoerd in the House and
looked after her 'instinctively', she is reported as saying, before she
knew what was happening. The many Afrikaners I spoke to do not
place much emphasis on 'instinct' – they think Mrs Vorster knew.
Fourthly, the police had, for some unaccountable reason, delayed
deporting Tsafendas after being so instructed by the Department of
the Interior before the assassination. Fifthly, Tsafendas' trial was a
farce and no one seemed interested in probing deeply into any
aspect of the case. Sixth, Vorster was the man with the overall
responsibility for both police and security affairs, both services
indicted in the commission's report. Seventh and last, Vorster
charged one man with the urgent task of establishing whether or not
there had been a conspiracy to kill Verwoerd. This man was his
friend, Van den Bergh and, not unexpectedly, he reported in the
negative within forty-eight hours to Vorster.

In short, they (my informants) felt that Van den Bergh or somebody close to him had either contracted Tsafendas and commiss-
ioned him or befriended him and deliberately fed him deluded
ideas, false promises and the like, so, in effect, priming and directing a human bomb, which Tsafendas was undoubtedly capable of
being.

A handful of people believe that the assassination was entirely
fortuitous, that Vorster and Van den Bergh were simply better-
organized and in the best position – in Verwoerd's hierarchy – to
take advantage of the situation. But this was a minority opinion.
Obviously I am in no position to be definitive about this matter; I
can only report the debate as it was told to me. But I can throw a
little light onto what happened to the assassin after the event. Since
there is a very real chance that we will never unearth the truth about
this particular episode in South African history, I think it is important that I digress slightly here to detail what I know.

What happened afterwards to Tsafendas is certainly very
strange. I never had a chance to interview Tsafendas although by
chance, I did once catch sight of him at Caledon Square police
station late in 1966. My information comes, rather, from those psychologists and psychiatrists who did.

Tsafendas was examined and tested by psychologists and psychiatrists, some of whom I later worked with. One, R. Van Zyl, was
one of my supervisors at Groote Schuur Hospital and one of the

psychiatrists, Harold Cooper, I came to know later as a colleague in private practice. Both spoke to me quite openly and at some length about the matter. Several features of the case were puzzling. From the start, all involved appeared to have been given a clear directive that they were to find him insane – this was informally transmitted in Dr Cooper's case as a general consensus of opinion. Secondly, the professionals were discouraged from probing too far into his state of mind or into his activities immediately prior to the assassination – this, they were told, was a job for the police. Thirdly, they were all, in my opinion, over-influenced by his long history of mental disturbance to the extent they closed off avenues of exploration and ignored inconsistencies in their findings.

The court's finding was that Tsafendas was 'hopelessly' insane. Van Zyl said to me that he was 'quite, quite mad'. The evidence on which they based these findings however, tells a more complex and disturbing story.

Tsafendas was certainly some of the time, very disturbed but he appeared to have areas of functioning which were quite lucid and in those times was a capable and efficient person. From what I was told, I think Tsafendas was not 'hopelessly' mad nor was he 'hebephrenic', as he was termed. These, along with the term 'paraphrenia' used at his trial, help to give the picture of a bumbling, babbling idiot who, in a moment of deep disturbance, killed Verwoerd. But the psychological test results do not show this.

He had an IQ of over 120, well above average, an unusual score for someone supposedly so disturbed. This was glossed over and his sub-test scatter was used instead in the court proceedings to attempt to build up a picture of gross disturbance. The psychologists argued that his intelligence was scattered and irregular throughout the various sub-tests on the IQ test. Not so – at least not to the extent that they implied.[5]

The examiners also gave him the Rorschach Ink Blot Test and the Thematic Apperception Test, yet few of the people who tested him using these tests were formally trained in the procedures – Van Zyl, for example, who was appointed by the *pro deo* defence, could not formally score an Ink Blot protocol, his grasp of psychotic signs was superficial, and he was unfamiliar with the research literature pertaining to Rorschach scores and schizophrenia, then, as now, still in its infancy. Examination of Tsafendas' responses and the interpretations given in court clearly showed that the testers were inexperienced.[6]

By far the most significant anomaly occurred in attempts to explain how the insane Tsafendas could hold a job in Parliament without his disturbance being noticed and how he could conceive of and execute the deed while in a deranged state. Tsafendas appeared, after the event, a very different kettle of fish from that beforehand. While beforehand he had coped relatively well with the day-to-day demands of his existence, his examiners found him withdrawn, demented and helpless – a strange contradiction that someone should have looked into. It suggests that far more was happening inside Tsafendas than those doing the investigation were aware of.

The examiners should have examined his character structure to see what his *real* personality was, as opposed to the symptoms he was showing. There was ample evidence from the psychological data available to show that he was a very *dangerous* man – wilful, intelligent, devious, manipulating – moreover, he was a man infinitely acquainted with the workings of psychiatrists and mental illness. He was quite capable of manufacturing whatever symptoms the doctors wanted to see. These facts alone cried out for careful reconstruction of his psychological activities before the event and a comparison of his psychological actions afterwards. Harold Cooper, in discussion with me, said that they were not encouraged to do this since everyone seemed to think that the whole thing was so straightforward.[7] In the event, such an analysis was not done.

These factors alone were puzzling but there were others. I was at Valkenberg in 1970, some three years after Tsafendas' trial, and there were people there who had dealt with him or knew him. A clear and often-expressed opinion amongst both patients and staff who had had contact with him was that Tsafendas was shamming, that he was able to appear insane any time he felt like it but otherwise functioned well. There were various 'explanations' as to why he was shamming, most of them nonsensical but there was common agreement that he was shamming.[8]

In 1976, Dorrian McLaren, who later worked for me, attempted to get background information for the play *Tsafendas* by Bill Tanner which she directed for the Space Theatre in Cape Town:

'In wanting to get a clear picture of Tsafendas' personality, physical characteristics and mannerisms, I and my cast searched for people in Cape Town who had known Tsafendas before the assassination of Dr Verwoerd. One of the people we came up with was his landlady with whom he'd rented a room for a while up till the time of the assassination; others were a family who owned a warehouse where Tsafendas had been employed. There were others who had met or knew him but none whose recollections interested me as much as the two sources I mentioned.

'We went to see the landlady first. Apart from describing Tsafendas' eating habits [she said he had an enormous appetite and shovelled his food], the fact that he appeared to be religious in a "hearty" way and that he was always dapperly dressed in a suit, panama shoes and a broad-brimmed hat and that he was always courteous to her, she seemed unwilling to discuss her infamous lodger any further. When I pressed her, she asked us to leave. When we saw how frightened and adamant she was, we thanked her and left, puzzled.

'At the factory where he had worked, the two gentlemen who had had the most to do with him found him competent at his job but overly talkative and sociable (he was employed as a clothes rep.). Although the older man said that he would have fired Tsafendas in the long run because, overall, he was not selling enough, when Tsafendas did leave, it was because he said he had "better things to do". He left the job on good terms with the people there.

'I got on with rehearsing the play and about ten days later a youngish woman appeared at the Space. She introduced herself as the daughter of the landlady and wanted to explain about Tsafendas and her mother. Since our visit to her mother, she had apparently been upset and very anxious. The daughter explained that at the time of the assassination, the house had been besieged with reporters, sightseers and the like, which in itself had been a strain. But her mother had also been threatened, said the daughter. I asked by whom. The young woman looked away for a while and then said, "My mother doesn't talk about it to me. But she is very frightened, she doesn't want you to mention her name."

[I had said that I would credit anyone who helped me in my inquiries, in the programme.]

'The various people I spoke to who knew Tsafendas in any way told me that they wouldn't have said he was "mad" or that different from other people. A number of people said he was a "character" on account of his clothes, social etiquette, his habit of reading the bible and telling religious stories.'

One last word; having been found 'completely insane', Tsafendas is to this day imprisoned in Pretoria Central Prison and not in a mental institution as is normally the case when a person who has committed a crime is so judged.

It is very difficult to say more. All I can be sure of is that in South Africa, given the structure I have described in this book, there would have been no need for conspirators at the top to organize a massive cover-up. In the feudal authoritarian framework I have described, one word from the top would have been enough to settle any issue, smother any doubt. And all the state's institutions – formal and informal – would close around the 'truth' as given from above.

What happened after Verwoerd's death? On Verwoerd's death, Vorster, the outsider, became Premier because after Verwoerd he was the most powerful man in South Africa for two reasons. Firstly, with Van den Bergh, he had co-ordinated and focused anti-Verwoerd feelings in the *Broederbond*, and secondly, as head of the security services, he had done his job well and possessed information on every important member of the Afrikaans elite. He drew on the former in the internal election to enter the running and on the latter to eliminate and outmanoeuvre the opposition.

Once in power, Van den Bergh embarked on a programme that he apparently had spent years setting up and working out. Vorster may have won power but the *Broederbond* was full of people who regarded him as an intermediary. There were also many, like Jaap Marais and Albert Hertzog, who had been entirely happy under Verwoerd and who wanted to continue the traditions and morality laid down by him. Deep inside the Afrikaner establishment, the orthodox core harboured its suspicions about Vorster and Van den Bergh but were prepared to let things ride until a clear direction emerged which they could control. No one was entirely clear about what to do and the assassination had severely shaken the community.[9]

Van den Bergh had been fascinated by Nazism and communism and he spent a long time absorbing the latter's revolutionary strategy, in particular how it advocated using key portfolios in semidemocratic governments to serve as footholds for gaining power. In fact, Van den Bergh often boasts of his knowledge of communism and how familiar he is with its mode of operation. What may come as a surprise to many South Africans – and to some Afrikaners and *Broeders* – is that Van den Bergh used communist strategy to ensure that Vorster's control over the Afrikaans state was made secure in those early years.

Vorster lacked a broad-based support in the *Broederbond*. He owed his position and power simply to the role he had been given by Verwoerd. Without Verwoerd he was nothing, and he knew it. In time, he could easily be removed and so could Van den Bergh; only their 'special knowledge' protected them if the *status quo* was Verwoerdian. To cope with this, Vorster and Van den Bergh first ensured that they controlled the key portfolios in the government. Following communist strategy, Vorster appointed trusted friend, Piet Pelser, to his old job as Minister of Justice and recruited P. W. Botha to his cause as Minister of Defence. In 1967, Van den Bergh began setting up the Bureau of State Security (established by law in 1969) and set about using it to undermine the rest of the ministries and the threats to their power base that remained.

Van den Bergh knew that once in control of the police, the army and the security services, nobody could effectively usurp Vorster. Foreign Affairs remained the elusive fourth Ministry that is usually seen as a key target for Communist revolutionary operations, and this too was slowly gained although in a roundabout way.

The two men had to move slowly in order to maintain the structure of the *Broederbond*. Whatever they did had to be seen to be 'legitimate' in the eyes of the Afrikaner elite. The English were undermined by the same kind of programme which is the Afrikaner way of doing things. Sacred institutions had to be carefully filled with Vorster's men or their function changed without too much notice being taken in order to keep things moving freely. Van den Bergh's BOSS was the instrument for doing this; in time, he removed many of the functions necessary for his and Vorster's survival from established Afrikaans institutions to his own. The army lost their intelligence service as too did the police and, funny though it sounds, the Ministry of Foreign Affairs lost its Foreign Affairs portfolio. Vorster and Van den Bergh set up the Department of Information under Connie Mulder, and this took over many of the functions of Dr Hilgaard Muller's Foreign Ministry.

Vorster and Van den Bergh's take-over needed a lot of planning to cover up the real nature of the change and to sell Vorster to the Nationalists. In the process, Vorster introduced a new ideological direction – the third – to the movement of Afrikaner Nationalism. Although Vorster and Van den Bergh had been interned during the war, they had taken little part in the orthodox Afrikaner Nationalist struggle and lacked a commitment to the kind of ideology Malan, Strydom and Verwoerd had strived for. Many in the *Bond* hierarchy inherited by Vorster, even if they disliked Verwoerd's ideas, were nevertheless imbued with the spirit of the Nationalist movement in the 1930s and 1940s. Vorster, out of a need to survive, therefore attracted to himself younger Afrikaners or Afrikaners who had never expected to get close to the centre of power. He needed creative people, technocrats, efficient fixers and manipulators, image-makers, ruthless people imbued with the kind of ambitious self-seeking drive that he and Van den Bergh possessed. And he got them.

The order and cohesion at all levels that had characterized Verwoerd's rule gave way under Vorster and Van den Bergh to a looser and far less doctrinaire Afrikaans hierarchy. The new doctrine of self-interest was by and large acceptable to many Afrikaners who had resented Verwoerd's intrusion into what they considered to be their own domains and in the first years of Vorster's premiership, all the old corrupt practices that Verwoerd had restricted were re-established and extended. Van den Bergh greatly extended his own empire and quickly built up a vast internal security network.

In place of the *Broederbond* controlling and directing the exploitation of South Africa for the common Afrikaner good, the *Broederbond* – still powerless after Verwoerd's then Vorster's and Van den Bergh's stranglehold – became the instrument for the new elite's programmes.

One of the first jobs after securing the various ministries was to remove those in the hierarchy who remained faithful to Verwoerd's ideology. This was a complex task because virtually every *Broederbond* member had to be checked and watched. Thousands of Afrikaners in powerful positions had been firmly committed to Verwoerd and these had to be slowly prised from their positions without disrupting the hierarchy.[10] The process took nearly three years and involved a very delicate and carefully constructed operation in which the more prominent Verwoerdians were systematically cut off from their support. In a master stroke of Machiavellian strategy, Vorster confronted his 'right wing' once he had been informed by Van den Bergh that he had succeeded in threatening, persuading or bribing their *Broeder* support away from them. Albert Hertzog and his close supporters, confident of their following, broke with Vorster and formed the *Herstigte Nasionale Party*, expecting to find a massive upheaval within the Afrikaner ranks willing to throw the *interlopers* out. None came. Van den Bergh had succeeded in his job so well that the support of the *Broeders*, the essential link between Hertzog's group and the people, never materialized. It was as if white ants had been at work in an antique table. While the top and the base of the legs were sound, the insides had been eaten away so that the table collapsed when anything was put on it.

My information is that a majority of ordinary Afrikaners would have supported the HNP without Van den Bergh's activities. HNP candidates' offices were flooded initially with people concerned and upset about what was going on. Gradually, however, the *Broeder* network got to work and helped by the covert operations of the security services, *Broeders* eventually became very frightened of voting for the HNP or of holding Verwoerdian ideas. Van den Bergh sent teams of his own men into country areas to form local vigilante committees whose aim was to wreck HNP followers' reputations and meetings and if necessary, to physically harm them. Off-duty policemen were used to attack HNP meetings and an unprecedented wave of hooliganism swept through South Africa in the months preceding the general election of 1970.[11]

My informants kept constantly reiterating that Vorster's ascension to power changed the direction and impetus of the *Broederbond*. It was as if all the energy that had initially been channelled into securing power and then into Verwoerd's grand programme was suddenly switched into climbing onto Vorster's bandwagon. This swing is predictable, given the authoritarian-feudal nature of Afrikaans psychology; the whole focus and interest of the society, its productive efforts and its creativity centres on the controllers of the *Broederbond*. Change the leader and you change the direction. In a society that is personally uncritical and has no institutions to serve a critical function, the community is in the hands of the leader.

Van den Bergh and Vorster knew that once their leadership had been legitimized and accepted by the *Bond*, everything else would follow. Hence the steady but slow changes made in the first few years. Caution was their watchword. Van den Bergh's elaborate security apparatus was constructed to watch the effects of each of these manoeuvres carefully and to isolate and neutralize every person who formed a potential danger to the change. Van den Bergh was not satisfied that a person *said* he supported the new ideology – he well knew how rudderless the Afrikaans elite was – he needed some hold over that person to *ensure* his support. This was done by using precisely those techniques I described earlier, used for conducting assessments of non-Afrikaner radicals, on their own colleagues. They established background data and psychological profiles of their targets and so worked out the best means of coercing them. Sometimes this was as simple as promoting a person of little merit and keeping him in his position by coercion – such a person would then lose everything if he turned against Vorster. Other times and in other institutions, blackmail was used, people were set up in embarrassing situations and thus controlled.[12]

What is important to understand is that the men who ran South Africa between 1966 and 1978 were not simply Afrikaners nor were they simply *Broederbonders* as Malan and Strydom and Verwoerd had been. They were also ardent and fanatical members of the *Ossewabrandwag*. In fact Vorster was a *general* in this paramilitary organization, responsible for the Port Elizabeth district.[13] The men who succeeded Verwoerd had in their youth worshipped heroes such as Hitler, Franco and Mussolini. Moreover, they came from the same kind of background as Hitler and Mussolini had. Impoverished, inadequate and frustrated, they rose to power through the back door because the situation arose which demanded a specific type of psychopathic ruthlessness and fanaticism. Vorster and Van den Bergh were anyone's men – if the price and the rewards were right. Afrikaner power maintenance under Malan and Strydom and Verwoerd had been sociopathic – under Vorster it became psychopathic, modelled on the ideology that he and his friends shared and on which basis their personalities were constructed. Let me detail what I know about the processes that arose out of the shift in emphasis and where they have led.

Verwoerd used the *Broederbond* to further his own vision of what was good for the Afrikaner community. Strydom and Malan had used it in the same way but for more practical ends. Vorster and Van den Bergh used it to hold onto power, increasing its size to swamp the older, more reactionary members and to bring in their own men. Once the change-over was safely achieved, the *Broederbond*'s structure was changed, and instead of serving the Afrikaans community it was used to serve the needs of Vorster and his colleagues. The *Bond* became a means of involving select people favourable to the new cause in the process of profiteering and power-building that Vorster and his colleagues rapidly started engaging in. This function was achieved through channels directed and controlled by Van den Bergh. In this way, key figures in the existing hierarchy were enlisted and united as well as some top military and police leaders brought in by Botha and Van den Bergh. But this was not all. Van den Bergh also recruited businessmen, top criminals, newspaper men – Afrikaans and English and some overseas correspondents of foreign press agencies – African businessmen and, most surprising of all, several members of the now defunct United Party.

Not all of these people were involved in the central decision processes of the new axis but, through Van den Bergh, they contributed to or were used to further the ends of the new leadership. Van den Bergh had also to prise away old existing contacts and replace them. People like Jan Haak, for example, a former minister of Economic Affairs and who did for Verwoerd what Mulder and Rhoodie did for Vorster, had to be removed to make way for the new men.

Some of the bright young men recruited to the cause devised a brilliant psychological strategy to cover up this realigning and profiteering. They needed a suitable ideological blanket so that *Broederbond* members would be caught in the same trap and by the same device as English whites were: they had to be made to think one way and have their attention diverted by a set of false issues while Vorster and his colleagues in reality were doing something else. The device used was the red herring we now know as the *Verligte-Verkrampte* struggle.

Using Van den Bergh's psychological services, they analysed the sympathies and personalities of leading *Broeders* and using moderates and liberals against the conservatives, they created false issues within the structure of the *Bond* so that the natural inclinations of the various people involved were used to ferment internal dissent. Vorster and company ensured that they were on the *Verligte* end of things and drew a number of uninvolved Afrikaners into the fray as their supporters. Many *Broeders*, through this, ended up inadvertently supporting a regime that they had not the first idea about.

The *Verligte* strategy gave Vorster and Van den Bergh excellent cover. Under it, they appeared to be acting in the Afrikaans interest while actually ensuring their own safety and survival. Further, it provided a useful means of explaining the very un-Afrikaans activities which Vorster and company were engaged in. Verwoerd, Malan and Strydom were motivated to enrich the Afrikaans community and they kept non-Afrikaners out of the process. Vorster's motive was self-profit, and the process of enrichment united many non-Afrikaners with the new ideology. South Africans of all races were involved in the Vorster Cause and thus one of the surprising by-products of this essentially low-grade ideology was to broaden the base of South Africans who were allowed to participate in the exploitation of the country.

As Vorster and his colleagues grew more confident and their operations blossomed, this broad-based corruptive agency began to take on the forms of an institution. As more and more contacts were formed, Van den Bergh's role as co-ordinator of contacts had to be extended and rationalized. In the process, the new institution began to demand more and more time and attention from its key figures. In time, it began to replace the *Broederbond* and government processes which had traditionally been the channels through which the ideological goals were achieved.

I have been told that Cabinet meetings and *Broeder* executive meetings became, after 1971, purely ritualistic. The real core of state action lay in the meetings of people like Vorster, Van den Bergh, Mulder, Kruger and their contacts which took precedence in both energy and importance. *Broeders* were being ignored and many had to wait until they read the papers to find out what was going on.

By 1972, things had settled so much that the members of the new elite began to think in terms of establishing strategies to ensure their long-term survival outside and inside South Africa. Obviously some of these interests coincided with the interests of the Afrikaner which helped appearances. But close analysis of these strategies reveals their true psychopathic and self-seeking nature.

Under cover of setting up pro-South African activities overseas, Vorster and Van den Bergh ensured that substantial funds were transferred overseas to provide for the leadership clique if things reached an impasse or if their system was undermined and disbanded. Some of the money used or lost through buying into newspapers, companies and so on, found its way into the private accounts of members of this clique. Vorster and his entourage travelled overseas not only to meet foreign leaders and to set up pro-South African contacts but also to further their own ends. They had, for example, to open personal accounts. Escape routes were also prepared using various pro-South African countries, one of which was, until the collapse of the regime in 1974, Portugal. Paraguay is another. Many of Vorster's close operatives apparently have funds and property there.

Van den Bergh's favourite occupation, the accumulation of power and position, once established in South Africa, spread beyond its borders. He apparently liked to see himself as the mastermind behind South African affairs and shared with P. W. Botha a toy soldier mentality towards this game. So, under cover of looking after South Africa's affairs, he set up numerous activities and contacts that sounded as if they had come out of a James Bond novel.

On his travels, he made contact with underground groups in Africa and Europe. He expanded his contacts with criminal organizations in Europe as well as with various forms of espionage services groups – people who sell secret information, armaments, technology and so on to whoever will pay for them. He also established contacts with ODESSA – the ex-Nazi organization still in existence – and through them was put in touch with German industrialists and agencies prepared to deal with South Africa or some intermediary. He also has contacts with mercenary recruiters and private army specialists (which, I was told, BOSS and the Defence Force have occasionally used). More relevant for affairs in South Africa, during his travels to African states and using his contacts as above he maintained contact with Black African guerrillas and radical groups. While Vorster and Mulder were engaged in diplomacy, Van den Bergh was liaising with various groups that could be of use to him. Through providing finance, weaponry and, on occasion, South African army support units, he encouraged them to engage in guerrilla activity in a ring of African states around South Africa. These include Zaire, Angola, Mozambique, Rhodesia and Zambia. Army sources told me that Van den Bergh or his agents, in dealing with these groups, made use of their knowledge of Western security services – codes, operating procedures, names – to pose as operatives for Western countries such as the US, Germany or France.[14]

Thus, over the years, the new ideological movement took shape and drew in many people – outside as well as inside South Africa – not normally associated with *Broederbond* or Afrikaner activity. On the surface, things appeared to have changed for the better. In place of the rigid Afrikaner exclusivity practised by Malan and Strydom and the suicidal fantasies of Verwoerd, Vorster's new approach seemed outward, realistic and, above all, it seemed to break once and for all the cultural exclusivity of Afrikanerdom. Vorster's new ideology embraced English and Afrikaans whites and explored the possibility of closer contact with the country's non-whites. It could be argued in fact that Vorster moved in the right direction for the wrong reasons: he and his own group's self-interest, desire for power and need to revenge their years in the wilderness turned them outwards away from the hard-core of the *Broeders* who had kept them in place during the 1940s and 1950s.

The people who kept me informed of events inside the Afrikaner state were by and large happy with things even if they did not like the new order or were apprehensive about how it came into power. South Africa prospered, they prospered; the Afrikaners were securely and firmly in control of South Africa and the Southern tip of Africa was protected by powerful white-led countries. Vorster appeared to be easing matters slowly; foreign investment was flowing in; the immediate future looked very comfortable.

The only people who were not happy were the few orthodox Afrikaners I came across: they missed the aescetic old days of Afrikaner unity and they all had dreadful forebodings that things now would go radically wrong. They mistrusted the new order and were bitter and angry at the way things had turned out. I could see, though, that they were to some extent mollified by the general wealth and stability that many of them had been able to accrue. Once again, I thought, Afrikaners' consciences had been silenced by their over-effective reward system.

Chapter Nine

Conclusion

We have come the full circle now, historically and psychologically. The psychology of *apartheid* is not simply the psychology of the Afrikaner – it is the psychology of all the races in South Africa who contribute to maintaining the *apartheid* state. I hope I have shown that each group I studied – white, Coloured and black – plays a significant part in permitting the sociopathic Afrikaner community to dominate the country. So many people share in the profits of *apartheid* in one way or another, either through direct involvement in exploitation or in taking psychological profit out of opposing the Afrikaners, that there is no real incentive to change things. It is a feudal, authoritarian system and like those in the middle ages, it holds each person fixed in his position and role in society.

It is hard to put a figure on the *apartheid* – support equation. People tend to see it in terms of four million whites against eighteen million non-whites and wonder how this domination is possible. But this is to miss the point. I estimate that, psychologically, roughly ten million South Africans of all races are comfortable with *apartheid*. Of the rest, the most – mainly rural blacks and poor Coloureds – do not like it but have not the energy or the psychological motivation to do anything about it – being neither too rich or too poor, neither too free nor too repressed. About two million (some white, mostly young black and Coloured) people, I think, are motivated and dedicated enough to act against the system and it is against these that the Afrikaner state acts the hardest.

These are overwhelming odds – ten million for and two million against – if one tries to see a solution in some form of revolutionary or military activity. But they are misleading. *Apartheid* is essentially a psychological phenomenon and South Africa as it is today is a mentally deranged society. Whatever its military and material situation, South Africa is psychologically fragile; its structure has not developed and matured beyond the adolescent structure it possessed in the nineteenth century. Its institutions are façades, its psychological power-base miniscule; South Africa has survived – as I have repeatedly indicated – through fortuitous circumstances. In the face of real stress and real confrontation, the powerful façade will be revealed for what it is; the efforts of a small, insular, ingrown opportunistic minority to delay the inevitable for as long as possible. The system survives at the moment because its inhabitants – exposed to only one hierarchy, one way of living, seeing and thinking for nearly seventy years – know no other. They believe what they are told even in the face of glaring and obviously inconsistent facts because no other interpretations matter, neither to them nor to the Afrikaans state.

This very fragility is both the strength and weakness of the Afrikaner state. On the one hand, given the right external circumstances, given pressure and determination on the part of the outside world, it is very possible that the Afrikaner would take whatever safe and face-saving solution was offered or insisted upon. Like an old lag caught robbing a safe, he is likely to go quietly – provided he is confronted with reality properly. On the other hand, if he is slowly cornered, allowed to get away with things until internal resistance escalates and forces the Afrikaner to defend himself, his behaviour will be very different. People in a fog, confused and frightened, resort to dangerous ends to preserve their safety and in the process, cause untold destruction and misery.

This is why it is so important to understand the psychology of the Afrikaner and the psychology of *apartheid*. The behaviour of the outside world, favourable and unfavourable, is based, I believe, on falacious assumptions about the state of South Africa. Most importantly, the Afrikaner's psychology has been overrated: people talk as if they 'understand' and even sympathise with the experiences of the Afrikaner because they appear to bear a historical resemblance to other oppressed people who hold on to power. The Afrikaners have never been proper 'victims' – they suffered few real hardships and most of these were self-imposed. He who chooses to beat his head against the wall must suffer the pain.

It is crucial to understand that the Afrikaner state today is in no different a condition from that of the Boer Republics in the nineteenth century. Nothing inside the Afrikaans community has changed; it simply has been extended in the same form until today it applies to the whole of South Africa. And this completes the full circle that I mentioned earlier. The Boer Republics could not manage their own internal affairs and would have collapsed financially if they had not been saved by the discovery of raw materials. And so it is, I believe that the present crisis in government in South Africa is occurring because, under pressure from the outside world, the structure of the Afrikaans state is again crumbling. Once again, it is possible to see, with careful analysis, the same patterns of disorganisation and confusion that marked the Boer Republics' last years, re-enacted in the drama over the downfall of Vorster and his men.

South Africa has often been the subject of debate and controversy over the past thirty years but it has never been in the limelight quite as it has since September 1977. Initially, it was the killing in detention of black leader Steve Biko, and almost immediately afterwards the general election, which virtually wiped out white opposition to John Vorster's government. But far more important and lasting, in terms of newspaper headlines, has been the subsequent exposure and fall from grace of most of South Africa's prominent and powerful Afrikaner politicians. Prime Minister John Vorster, Cabinet Minister Connie Mulder and their associates have followed each other slowly and systematically, rooted from office, along with Van den Bergh, into the Afrikaans political wilderness. For once, since 1977, the focus of attention has not been on the repressive actions of the South African government but on the government itself.

The story has been one of scandal, corruption, embezzlement – even murder. It is widely believed that Robert Schmidt, for example, a Nationalist parliamentary candidate, and his wife were murdered to stop them revealing too much of the illegal activities of South Africa's political elite. Eschel Rhoodie's flight, his threatened disclosure of intrigues and subsequent arrest, the claims and counter-claims of cabinet ministers over the Department of Information's newspaper – the *Citizen* – and the irregular and eccentric series of reports emanating from the various Commissions of Inquiry have all been star turns in a drama that has fascinated and intrigued a world used to the calm, steadfast solidity of the Afrikaner Nationalist governments.

The real story, though, started in April 1974. In that month, the Portuguese dictatorship fell and the circle of white states around South Africa shrank. Suddenly, the game turned sour and, for Vorster and his men, disturbingly real. They now had to actually take the roles they had previously only played with.

Everything had gone well for Vorster until 1974. He and his friends had indulged in their power-seeking and profit-making games, secure from the realities of both running a modern state and the specific circumstances of South Africa. It must be understood that South Africa's government institutions are only that in name: they provide a means for institutionalising the needs of the ruling elite. Institutions like the Treasury, for example, are there simply to try and tie all the ends together and make everything look respectable. When Vorster and Van den Bergh introduced their ideology, the finances of the state had to be geared to pay the costs. In the process, chaos, I believe, sometimes reigned. For one thing, the cost to South Africa for Van den Bergh's 'white-anting' the HNP's *Broeder* support was very high. Rewards and bribes for over three thousand influential Afrikaners were, I was told, one of the contributing reasons behind the Johannesburg stock market collapse of 1969–70 and the almost uncontrolled growth in inflation since 1970. Moreover, once this new reward hierarchy was introduced, it set the pattern for what followed. While it attracted people eager to climb on the bandwagon and, in the process, to back Vorster, it introduced a new demand; pay-off after pay-off to keep the support. The good of the Afrikaans community became secondary to keeping his supporters profitably happy. In the ensuing rush to join in, the amount of money and profits available became sorely stretched and has remained so ever since.

All this would have been exposed if it were not for the old standbys – gold and all the other valuable raw materials. The collapse of the Portuguese hold on its African policy was, like the Boer War, a shock to Vorster's system. It introduced an element into South African politics that Vorster's ideology was unable to cope with. Gone were the iron men of orthodox and ultra-orthodox Afrikaner history who had led the Nationalists to power. In their place was a company of ill-equipped fortune-seekers, quite unable to face the new balance of power. From April 1974, it was only a matter of time before the bubble burst and Vorster's ideological incapacity revealed itself to the *Broederbond* for what it was.

There were problems, however. Van den Bergh's grip on the *Bond* was formidable and his control of BOSS and its intelligence agencies all powerful, far tighter, I believe, than even Verwoerd's was. The task facing those who wanted to depose the two was indeed monumental. However, in time, it is clear that they managed it. And now one scandal, now another rocked the Afrikaans establishment.

I am not referring to the 'Muldergate' affair. This took place shortly after I left South Africa and about which I knew very little. Instead, I refer to far more serious events. More serious than either the setting up of the *Citizen* newspaper – in the light of my revelations in this book, hardly an unusual Afrikaner act – or Rhoodie's 'embezzlement' of R88,000 – a sum far below that allocated yearly to each cabinet minister for house improvements. No, the most important events that precipitated Vorster's downfall concerned the South African army's débâcle in Angola in 1975–76 and Soweto and other disturbances in 1976–77. These more than anything else unsettled Vorster's opponents and served to unify their concern and determination to remove him.

As far as I am aware, the Angolan episode was undertaken by P. W. Botha against the advice of his army staff and was based on Van den Bergh's fanciful estimation of the realities of the situation, one of which was his assumption that the Americans would be coerced into helping South Africa out, militarily, if the need arose. This, incidentally, is an example of the kind of unrealistic self-glorification that Van den Bergh indulged in. *He* could deliver the Americans, he boasted, if *he* wanted to. Well, he did not – and when Soweto followed shortly after the Angolan disaster Van den Bergh's real incapacity to provide adequate and accurate intelligence data was revealed for all to see. Especially to those in the army and police force who had to face the brunt of his miscalculations. Van den Bergh could rough up a few white students and harmless radicals if he had to, but when it came to the real job of providing security for the state, which his Bureau was supposed to do, he failed miserably. It was on this crack in his and Vorster's previously invincible wall that his opponents seized.[1]

This, unfortunately, is as far as I got. I was not able to continue receiving information after April–May 1977, and so am largely in the dark about what action his opponents actually took. What is clear, though, from the newspaper reports I have read, is that his opponents – organised, I think, around Andries Treurnicht – had to stoop to taking steps that had previously never been used in Afrikaner society; they went public. The Muldergate scandal is the result.

As far as I can gather, the only way that Vorster could be got out was to make use of the only remaining arena – the 'free' press in South Africa and the fact that there are many South Africans who believe in the myths of free institutions in South Africa. Accusing Vorster and his followers of 'illegal' dealings that had to be answered in public, ensured that Vorster and his colleagues would be drawn out into the open. I do not think this was an organised 'plot'; more a question of making the various segments of Afrikanerdom aware of the state of affairs in order that the fragmented and terrorised opposition could be united. Again, desperate acts of desperate men – a last gamble against Van den Bergh's stranglehold. As of now, September 1979, it is not clear whether the overthrow of Vorster's ideology by orthodox Afrikaners has succeeded. In fact, I believe the fight is still going on.

I want to close by making a number of points about the current and future state of South Africa. First, although I did not know much about the details of the Muldergate scandal (as late as the time of my flight, in February 1978, I did not believe that Vorster could be removed), nothing could have helped prove my arguments more. It was and is a highly effective paradigm case; proof, I think, that what I have set down in this book is the real state of affairs in South Africa. Without Muldergate, I doubt whether people would have believed me to the extent that they now, I think, will. Without being falsely modest, I do believe that this book goes a long way towards explaining the last decade in South African history.

Now, to the future. For those who hope that the end of Vorster and Van den Bergh will herald a new era of enlightenment or peace in South Africa, let me say that I discovered nothing in my research to indicate that the Afrikaner state is capable now or in the future of behaving in any way as we would want. As far as the prospects of peace and the possible moderation of the Afrikaner hold on South

Africa go, I see only a continuation of the Afrikaners' sociopathic behaviour in the years ahead. For one thing, the military aim of the Afrikaans establishment remains fixed and shows a psychopathic disregard for the peace and stability of Southern Africa and the well-being of South Africans. As I understand it, the plan is to create a belt of states around South Africa who are neutralised and crippled by the presence of disruptive civil disturbances in their midst. Zaire, Angola, Mozambique, Rhodesia and Zambia all apparently have internal groups supported in some way by South Africa and all are unable to stabilise because of this. The aim is to ensure that civil war in one form or another will occupy Southern African states around South Africa, Angola and Rhodesia being the most obvious examples. But Namibia, it is planned, will meet the same fate.

South Africa will give up Namibia but only after it is sure that it has established a powerful black opposition to Swapo. If Swapo takes over the country, it will be faced with a debilitating civil war in which South African trained guerrillas, working with mercenaries and South African army units, will maintain a constant pressure, directed and controlled from Pretoria. After the Rhodesian white regime falls, there has, I am informed, been a long-standing plan to encourage civil war between the rival African guerrilla armies. If these plans succeed, the argument goes, South Africa will not face serious incursions on its own soil for a number of years.

The last point is this. The pace and development in Afrikaner society has always been dictated by the personality of its leader. What of the new man, Andries Treurnicht, that many South Africa watchers expect to emerge triumphant from the present power struggle? Let me, in concluding this study of South Africa, allow two of my patients to give a brief vignette of this man – to show something of his character and personality. He does, I believe, truly manifest what South Africa and the Afrikaner is all about:

'One evening, the two of us were at home when a guy who lived in the same block of flats called to tell me that someone had bashed into my car. In fact, he had been on the point of simply driving off but Tony had gone after him on his motorcycle and called him back. We went down and the man told us he was Andries Treurnicht. He was driving a huge Cadillac. He mentioned something about having to get to a late-night Parliament session; I said that I thought it was pretty shit that he was simply going to drive off without informing me of the damage. He just stood there and looked at me. I called the police to inform them of the accident in order to cover for me – for insurance. He didn't actively resist it – he just stood around, never once offered to say, "Yes, let's get the thing done." I phoned them from our flat and went back downstairs.

'By this time, he had been speaking to Tony. He was really underplaying himself but slipping in the odd thing about the government – Parliament – oh yes, he might even have actually said something about him not being such a big deal. The police didn't come. I phoned them twice. He came upstairs and sat down uncomfortably. Then he started asking politely what we did – oh, students were we? – oh, we were at the University of Cape Town? His face was completely cold and unemotional – he was asking us questions, interested questions and telling us about himself – he was a grandfather, all his children had been students too, like himself. They had studied at Stellenbosch – his daughter was going to a women's army camp in George. Oh, he had been a minister he said, of the Dutch Reformed Church – done theology, he said rather piously. But he was watching us. Then he somehow introduced into the conversation the fact that he had to give a speech in an up-country town in the Transvaal. A big Afrikaans community. Mary asked him if he didn't get scared speaking in front of large crowds; he smiled paternally – oh you get used to it "with God's help".

'Then he went on to tell us more things about his family – I remember one of us saying that he looked young to be a grandfather and he smiled. There were also odd bits flung in about Stellenbosch not being exactly the same as UCT. He did make that clear – in a kind of a "the *Engelse* go to UCT and *die Afrikaners* go to Stellenbosch" way – you could feel he was one of the Afrikaner flock – the English were a different species.

'We tried to ask him about his job but he was very vague about what he did – just that he was deputy minister for Bantu Affairs – you got the impression that he was doing all he could for the Africans – he was their friend. Efficient. Somehow the Second World War was referred to and I asked him how come the Afrikaners, the *Ossewabrandwag* people, were interned during the war for their pro-Nazi sympathies. He said how terrible the war had been. He spoke of blackouts and said that he had Jewish friends. What was especially frightening about him was his blandness and his coldness. It was as if he was playing a game and was quite at home doing it. His behaviour was a very clever pretence – he had a front and other things were going on inside – he would carefully plan his answers to us, not letting things slip. He was tough, hard. Maybe it was the glib way he started speaking – it unnerved me – about Hitler, about the war years – he wrote to Germany and they sent him a photograph of Hitler. He told us this in a "well, why shouldn't it have happened?" way. Anyway, he kept it in his room at Stellenbosch. This was his "rebellious" thing. By this time, we had been waiting for the police for nearly an hour.

'He eventually went to the phone and spoke quite calmly and softly in Afrikaans – they were there in a couple of minutes. I got his telephone number – and the police noted it down and off he went. He asked me to get a quote on the damage and he would submit it to the government garage for me. That was the note on which he left. What he didn't tell me was that the Parliamentary session was nearly over and that he was going back to Pretoria within the next two days. I phoned back – he was rather brusque and wanted to know whether the quote wasn't excessive.

'When I called him back later, he had left – I managed to get his forwarding address. I had told him I was going ahead with the repairs and I sent the account to his Pretoria address. Then there followed a six month wait, letters from the government office – the panel-beating shop panicked because they had done a repair job on a car which a government vehicle had gone into – the minister responsible had refused to pay the bill of nearly R300 and just left it – the panel-beating guy was vehement about the shit way the officials just left bills because they were in the government, expecting the man-in-the-street to be intimidated and not to pursue it. Eventually, I got a cheque for R80 from them.'

Treurnicht is not an ordinary man, nor an ordinary MP. He was one of the men responsible, with M. C. Botha, the Minister of Bantu Affairs, for creating the conditions in African education that were the direct cause of Soweto and the student uprisings in the Cape. His frightening disregard for Africans contained in his official pronouncements and public statements at the time indicated his approach and attitude towards non-whites and their well-being. He is therefore a prime example of the average Afrikaner statesman's attitude towards South Africa as a whole. At the time my patients had contact with him, Treurnicht was on the *Broederbond* executive and Deputy Minister of Bantu Affairs. He is now the National Party's Transvaal leader in place of Connie Mulder and, after the prime minister, P.W. Botha, is the second most powerful man in South Africa. A true Afrikaner, he was also, before he entered politics, a minister of religion. Need I say more?

Source Notes

CHAPTER ONE

1 This modicum of understanding is extended even by South Africa's enemies. See, for example, a publication of the South African Liberation Support Committee (*Towards an understanding of the role of whites in the South African Struggle*, London, 1977). The boers' behaviour was itself, it is argued, precipitated by the acts of colonists, imperialists and the like (see p. 14). Other examples of this 'understanding' can be found in Bunting (1969), Zubaida (1970) and in the work of the Soviet historian, Viatkina (1976).

2 A good example of this is contained in a critical report of a committee of the American Psychiatric Association who visited South Africa's mental institutions in 1978. They were impressed by the graciousness and hospitality of their hosts and stated that many of the government officials and psychiatrists that they met were quite aware of the problems of *apartheid* (Pinderhughes, *et al.*, 1979, p.3).

3 South Africa, because of its racial structure, is considered to be a plural society. For examples of the way academics approach these societies, see Barth and Noel (1972), Hines (1971) and Smith (1969). Studies specific to South Africa can be found in Allport (1954), Kuper (1971) and Tiryakian (1967).

4 South African social scientists tend to employ models and theories fashionable in Britain and American professional communities rather than develop their own based on empirical investigation. This can be seen clearly in the race cycle theory of Park (1950) taught in South African universities (see Van der Walt, *et al.*, 1967); in the way Parsons (1966) is used extensively (see Cilliers and Joubert, 1966); and in the use of plural society theory referred to in footnote 3 (see for example Rex, 1971, and Van den Berghe, 1975). The only other models used are those derived from Max

Weber and Karl Marx (see Loubser, 1968 and Kuper, 1971).

5 Two examples: Van der Spuy (1974) talks of the basic 'National insecurity' of the Afrikaner arising out of his precarious position as a dominant minority. This gives rise to a pervasive 'national anxiety' which acts in turn as the source of an obsessive 'national character'. Archibald (1969) argued similarly that the Afrikaners' long history as a discriminated against minority resulted, once they took power, in their present hostility towards other groups. A similar argument advanced by a group of Durban scientists, suggests that while this may have been the case initially, the Afrikaner minority, once in power, became concerned with the domination of the whole of South African society (Close, *et al.*, 1971).

6 See, for example, Viatkina (1976) and Simons & Simons (1969).

7 See, for example, the studies of Morse & Orpen (1975), Macrone (1965) and Van den Berghe (1962; 1970; 1971).

8 The best known of these studies is a series by the American researcher Pettigrew (1959; 1960) who compared South African white students with samples he took in both Southern and Northern American states. The studies in Cape Town were conducted by Orpen (1970, 1971, 1973).

9 See, for example, Metrovich (1967) and Van Jaarsveld (1975).

10 Examples: Cilliers (1963), Robbertse (1967), Rhoodie (1972), Scheepers Strydom (1967) Theron (1950), Van Rooy (1977), Viljoen and Grobler (1972).

11 *Christian National* is the term used to describe the Afrikaans approach to religion and education. It combines Calvinistic dogma with National political ideology.

12 Studies critical of the bias found in South African academic work can be found in Abdi (1975), Cryns (1962) and Evans (1970).

13 These studies are described in Colman and Lambley (1970), Lambley (1968; 1973a; 1976) and Pokroy (1971). The advances in scale construction are described in Colman (1971) and in Lambley and Gilbert (1970). The major technical flaws in previous studies were that white subjects selected were predominantly English-speaking and at the universities of Natal, Durban, and the Witwatersrand in Johannesburg. The tests used did not incorporate advances made in techniques designed to prevent the subjects giving a false impression when filling in questionnaires. In the original F. Scale, it was relatively easy for people to give a certain impression on the test which did not necessarily correspond with what they actually felt. I also improved on the measures of prejudice used. Andrew Colman had earlier developed a Gutman-type Ethnocentrism scale which I used throughout my studies. The other scale I used was to measure social distance which is the degree of closeness a person feels towards members of outgroups. The scale I used was a development of a scale described by Dodd (1935) and Triandis and Triandis (1962). In it, the subject is asked to rate the four non-white groups of South Africa – Coloureds, Indians, urban Africans and rural Africans – along five dimensions ranging from 'I wish someone would kill them all' to 'I would marry a member of this group.'

14 I used many sources in these historical explorations, including works specific to South Africa as well as those pertaining to Africa as a whole:

Benson (1963), Bird (1968), Bunting (1969), de Kiewiet (1975), de Villiers (1964), Forman (1962), Henachsberg (1950), Hepple (1967), Izedinova (1977), Maclean, *et al.* (1866), Mansergh (1962), Marais (1961), Marquard (1969), Mbeki (1968), Mbiti (1970), Murphy (1972), Murray (1958), Rousseau (1960), Sachs (1965), Simons & Simons (1969), Troup (1972), Van der Merwe (1938), Van Jaarsveld (1961; 1975; 1977), Viatkina (1976), Walker (1957 and both volumes of Wilson and Thompson (1969).

15 Walker (1957) contains detailed descriptions (pp.98–102) of the criticisms made at the time by visitors to the colony. He cites de Mist, for example, who called them 'half-wild Europeans, rebellious and unreasonable in their behaviour'. They were suffering, he said 'from a complete corruption of their moral sense' (Walker, p.99). As Walker puts it, these were 'the fathers or grandfathers' of the men who took part in the Great Trek.

16 The phobic structure of this psychology is clear. Holland had bad memories for the trekkers, becoming colonists had removed the memory – when their status was threatened by the British, these memories were reactivated together with the institutionalized fear (the younger boers being taught to equate fear, loss of status and memories of Holland with the removal of the inferior status of their Africans). Trekking successfully buried the memories and allowed the boers to retain their symbols of security. Because reality was not faced and the real anxieties dealt with, the boers developed a fear of both the British and loss of their symbols of security. This is a phobia: the more the symbols of problems are attended to, instead of the actual problems, the more entrenched a phobia becomes.

17 By mid-1837, 5,000 trekkers (and more or less 5,000 servants) had crossed the Orange River. This figure had increased to 14,000 by 1845. Working from figures estimated by Houghton (1969), the percentage of Afrikaners in the Republics in the 1850s was 11% of the total for the Republics and the Cape Colony taken together. Thompson (1969) estimated that in 1865 the Republics had just over 50,000 whites while the white population for the Cape Colony was 181,582 at the same time (see also Maclean, 1866).

18 This was written into the constitution of the South African Republic (Thompson, 1969).

CHAPTER TWO

1 These actions are detailed in Bunting (1969) and included removal of Coloured voters from the common roll, removal of the right of Africans to be represented in white parliament, and the High Court of Parliament Act, which made parliament the highest court in the land – the Nationalist Party thus becoming in effect the final court sitting in judgement on its own laws. Other acts slowly and systematically strangled the legal right of whites and blacks to the expression of opposition. African Nationalist parties and communist parties were first banned; then multiracial parties such as the

Liberal Party; then existing parties were prevented from having multiracial membership, then from providing funds or assistance to political groups of other races. De Villiers (1969) is worth reading. He shows how one of the first acts of the Afrikaner Nationalists in 1948 was in fact to control its own Afrikaners so that those who had integrated with the English were identified and isolated and, if necessary, evicted.

2 Botha was South African Prime Minister from 1910 to 1919. Smuts, from 1919 to 1924. Hertzog ruled from 1924 to 1933, when he entered a coalition pact with Smuts until 1939. From 1939, Smuts ruled until 1948. Malan, Strydom, Verwoerd, Vorster and Botha, all hard-core Nationalists, followed.

3 From here on, when I speak of English, I mean South African English.

4 I have avoided giving more details about what turned out to be a revealing correspondence to protect the identity of the person he thought he was writing to. If he had known he was writing to me, he would never have admitted this.

5 The United Party, formed in 1934 (Smuts' party), advocated a Federal system of racial separation of power with whites in overall control. The Progressive Party, formed in 1959, advocated a qualified franchise; and the *Herstigte Nasionale* Party, formed in 1969, advocated extreme racial and Afrikaner-English separation. The study was reported and discussed in Lambley (1974a; 1976). Most samples, incidentally, in South African research are taken from young university students. They suffer, as my study shows, from being poor representatives of South African society.

6 The F. Scale cuts both ways. Those who score highly are authoritarian and can be said to be so because of an outward threat, real or imagined, but by the same token, low scorers can be said to be reacting to an authoritarian stimulus. Their rejection of authority may also arise out of fear. Given the complexity of the Progressive, non-authoritarian students scoring on the tests I gave them (discussed in the text), it was clear that the extreme scorers who turned out inevitably to be either Nationalist or Progressive, represented both sides of the authoritarian coin; the Nationalist students reacting to a social phobic symbol – the English – and the Progressive students to the underlying pressure of the Afrikaners' authoritarian behaviour.

7 I used the California Psychological Inventory for these studies (Gough, 1957) which has several measures of various types of socialization.

8 A few non-whites were permitted to attend white universities if their own universities lacked adequate facilities.

9 These interviews were greatly revealing and, I felt, accurate because adolescents are a great deal more frank about home life and debates than parents or younger children who tend to want to preserve an ideal image about home life.

10 The test I used was the Differential Personality Inventory developed by D. N. Jackson (Jackson and Carlson, 1969). Professor Jackson kindly gave me permission to use this test for research prior to its formal publication. The drug study is Lambley (1971a).

11 Political pluralism, as taught by this Professor of philosophy, was in

essence an attempt to justify by historical and philosophical argument, the ethic of *apartheid*. The same man, I believe, played a part in providing ideology for the government's Department of Information and in guiding their propaganda offensive in the late 1960s and 1970s.

CHAPTER THREE

1 And often was: nurses with clerical experience were often attached to the psychology unit to administer, score and interpret every kind of psychological test.

2 These are the initials for the Minnesota Multiphasic Personality Inventory, a well-known and widely used test developed in America in the 1940s and 1950s.

3 These, the so-called subjective tests, were not used officially at Valkenburg. They include the well-known Rorschach Ink Blot Test and Murray's Thematic Apperception Test. I studied them and did research on the Rorschach and schizophrenia at Valkenburg which was published in Lambley (1973a).

4 Excellent reviews exist in this area and marshal evidence to show quite clearly that great care has to be taken when certain types of drugs are in prolonged use. Crane, for example, has written extensively on the neurological side-effects involved, amongst which are Parkinsonism, akinesia, hypotension, drowsiness, jaundice, impotence and leukopenia. These, however, generally disappear when the patient is taken off the drug. Other more severe damage can be caused by overdosing. He cites the example of retinitis which can result in blindness (Crane, 1975). A good overview of this area was available in Cape Town while I was an intern in Klein and Davis (1969). Interestingly enough, I notice that the team sent by the American Psychiatric Association in 1978 (see Chapter One) also reported on this. They said that several of the *government* psychiatrists they interviewed 'had never heard of tardive dyskinesia' (p.14), one of the most serious side effects of neuroleptic drugs, and this was, they reported, 'despite the fact that their main responsibility was the core of chronic psychotic patients, most of whom were maintained on neuroleptics'. This was eight years after I had trained.

5 A psychiatric colleague of mine complained about this procedure and I believe that some modifications in the practice have since been introduced.

6 The reliability of some district surgeons has been amply demonstrated in Biko's case (Bernstein, 1978).

7 The significance of this will emerge later. The psychologist concerned was a respected member of the Afrikaans community – a former mayor of a *platteland* town, a former minister in one of the Afrikaans churches and, with the Superintendent, had been the state psychiatrist and psychological counsel in Cape Town for many years.

8 See: *The Report of the Commission of Inquiry into the Mental Disorders Act.*

Government Printer, Pretoria, 1972.

9 The South African Bureau of Racial Affairs, an academic institute set up by Afrikaners to counter the highly respected South African Institute of Race Relations – an anti-government body that has turned out a steady stream of critical papers for many years.

10 A Department of Health hospital closely associated with Stellenbosch University.

11 I published two papers detailing the kind of problems experienced in South Africa such as these. They are Lambley (1973c) and Lambley and Cooper (1975).

12 I have been told that the government provided the necessary funds for this and other similar propaganda ventures, another instance of the tight interrelationship existing between Afrikaans academic and government departments. I met and talked to Professor Van den Berg and was convinced that he himself was acting in all good faith and sincerity for what he believed was a good psychotherapeutic cause. I feel sure he was unaware of the use to which he was being put, as are many of the professionals who accept similar invitations.

CHAPTER FOUR

1 See for example: Duncan (1970); Hubbard, (1975); Randall, (1971a; 1971b) Van der Merwe, (1974); Whisson (1972).

2 Texts such as: Cilliers (1971; 1975), Manganyi (1973), Mechanic (1973) comment on the situation but present little in the way of evidence. Macrone (1975) found Africans to suffer from a 'boer phobia', but in analysing it he considered it to be exaggerated and that it functioned in an 'unrealistic fashion'. Lever's (1978) book on South African society describes social symptoms of distress like crime and poverty but without linking it specifically to *apartheid*. Most of the empirical studies conducted examine how comparable groups of whites and Coloureds fare on a range of psychological tests designed to measure an aspect of interest to the researcher. Davidson, for example, studied patterns of dominance and submissiveness in school children to see if the Coloured's inferior status resulted in a tendency to be submissive. Similarly, Mann investigated the Coloured person's sense of marginality in samples of schoolchildren in Natal to see if there was any evidence to support the popular idea that Coloureds had the kind of personality patterns associated with the position. Both studies failed to find any evidence of pathology or personality disturbance. Both are referred to in Mann (1957).

3 Orpen (1971). He used Rotter's 1-E Scale.

4 This is reported in Singer and Van der Spuy (1973). See also Edwards (1972) and Van der Spuy, *et al.* (1974).

5 Research results such as I have described above helped indirectly to further the government's overseas propaganda. Free researchers in free universities finding little wrong empirically carries a lot of weight in scienti-

fic communities. Books such as Rhoodie's *South African Dialogue* (1972) appeared at about the same time, in which government ministers engaged in 'frank and open' discussions about the country's problems with some of their opponents. All this helped to convince people that there was a growing *verligte* (enlightened) trend in Afrikaner thinking. Time, of course, showed these efforts for what they were: Fatima Meer, one of the contributors to Rhoodie's book, is not banned for conducting sociological research in Soweto to prove citizens' claims of police brutality.

6 Elusive because you need a government permit to get into a black location. The multiracial community allowed me to compare those in the same culture who experienced direct *apartheid* with those who did not.

7 Sam Lison worked with me on the first report prepared (Lambley and Lison, 1974) and made available to me at an early date the data from both his Honours projects and his Master's thesis (Lison, 1976). I bear the responsibility, however, for the interpretations of these studies presented here as well as for the indices presented.

8 See, for example: Gough, McKee and Yandell (1955) and, in particular, the discussions on institutionalised rebellion in Merton (1957).

9 This follows Dahlstrom, *et al.*'s (1972) review and description of this scale.

10 Two examples of overseas students were used to compare with our South African samples. These were those reported by Taft (1959) on American and Australian student samples. Greater use was made of the Australian sample because I felt it to be more culturally appropriate.

11 Halbower's study (1955) of people with this type of MMPI profile is relevant; he describes them as having chronic personality problems, being chronically tense, nervous, prone to worry. They also show marked feelings of inadequacy and inferiority.

12 See Goldstein and Rodnick (1975); Lambley (1973b; 1977a); Reis (1971); Seigel and West (1975). We are a long way from deciphering what causes schizophrenia but we do know the stresses are real, incredibly complex and subtle.

13 This was confirmed in a separate study in which I found Afrikaners, male and female, to be far less open and self-disclosing than English-speaking whites.

14 The procedure for calculating these indices is to be found in Dahlstrom, *et al.* (1972) and described in more detail in Welsh and Sullivan (1952).

15 I wrote a theory paper on *apartheid* based partly on these results in Lambley (1973c). The metatheoretical concepts I used there and throughout my work are expanded in Lambley (1970a, b and 1974b) and in my Doctoral dissertation, Lambley (1971b).

16 Psychological testing is a very subtle and complex process, not just a matter of test-scoring; you have to use different frameworks to identify the protocol style of the individual tested, ideas I developed in Lambley (1973d and 1974c).

17 Some experts make great use of symbolism in these cards based usually on Freudian concepts: if you see a spider, for example, it is usually taken to refer to you mother; if you see a tooth, then you have guilt about mastur-

bating. In my research, I found these symbols unreliable and inaccurate: if a person has dental problems, they tend to see teeth which is unfortunate for the masturbation hypothesis. What I found to be highly reliable and accurate was the form and level of functioning used by the person on the cards: if he showed a constricted or limited style of responding, the chances were this was how he behaved in real life.

18 One example: in the 1977 budget, increases for pensions were announced. Africans got R2 per month; Coloured, Indians and Asians got R4 per month; whites got R7.

19 There is a considerable literature on African and Coloured attitudes towards whites. A good review of the controversies involved is to be found in Lever (1978 Chapter 8). Not all researchers have found the Afrikaners favoured by non-whites as I did, but I should point out that the only studies that employed in-depth techniques such as mine did find this to be the case. See especially Brandel-Syrier (1971) and also Theron (1950).

20 I feel sure that this attitude of the police has a historical base. Afrikaners form the bulk of the force and, as I mentioned in Chapter One, in the boer communities of the nineteenth century officials were respected but apathetic. I think this is still the case.

21 There was one humorous instance of this. One of my white, Afrikaans patients used to act out his aggression towards a white neighbour, also Afrikaans, by phoning the police anonymously and reporting having seen '*Kaffir* women going into the place'. Police flying squad cars were there inevitably within moments, much to the glee of the patient. Once, though, returning home to find his home burgled and the intruder still in it, my patient phoned the police and had to wait two hours before anyone came.

22 Much of the information presented here about *Broederbond* activities was gathered later. See Chapter Seven for further details.

23 Where it could not buy out a company, it ensured that the company kept its prices high by creating the circumstances for losses to occur to the company. I am grateful to Dr Hans Retief and to Anton Maritz for much of this information.

24 African 'rights', for example, are looked after by the Department of Bantu Affairs.

25 One example of this kind of manipulation: the Dairy Board used to empty each month millions of gallons of excess milk into Cape Town harbour. The ostensible reason for this was that it would have been too expensive to transport it to African townships. The real reason was that it was part of government policy to keep milk costs high. Thousands of Africans work in Cape Town Docks – it would have been an easy task to let them have the milk, even at a small cost – or they could have transported it the short distance to Cape Town railway station through which hundreds of thousands of Africans and other non-whites pass every day. I was told that proposals for such a plan were submitted to the government but were turned down despite the fact that the party involved expected to make a *profit* from the enterprise.

26 Other evidence of the government's economic manipulations: in the 1977 budget, the government cut its subsidies on bread, maize and butter,

staples for the poorer people, by forty-five million rand. At a different level, in a report by Thomas and Marsay (1977) the belief that job opportunities for Coloureds in Cape Town had improved – much publicized by the government and offered as proof of progress – was assessed in a survey and found to be a myth. Of the 350 companies who were sent questionnaires, only eighty-seven replied. Those motivated to reply provided the basis for the findings. Since those who replied were obviously those who were already doing something to improve matters, no matter how small, it was clear from the survey that the real state of affairs – that is, in the employers of 91% of the Coloured labour-force – was even worse than the survey indicated. It is more than likely that the other companies did not reply because they were not motivated to help their Coloured people. If they were, they would have replied.

27 Such as holding multiracial parties, which in themselves are not illegal. The consumption of alcohol in an interracial communal context is, even in one's own home. The effect of this is the invasion of privacy in the home and of the act of hospitality. It is a strain – a multiracial gathering in one's private home is sufficient to attract the attention of a critical neighbour who may just make a complaint to the police who may just investigate the party – so hosts and guests never relax.

28 During the Cape Town riots in September – December 1976, the vanguard of the protesters, schoolchildren and adolescents, asked for the support of the African contract workers. But the latter refused to give up their spare time and went drinking instead of taking part in the protests. This created bad feeling between the labourers and the protesters which was immediately used by the police. Using their agents, they encouraged the labourers to attack the protesters and bloody fighting took place between the two factions. Once this occurred, the police moved in to help the contract labourers and to worsen the conflict. Riot police and conventional police furthered the process by arresting and intimidating protesters while leaving contract labourers unmolested.

CHAPTER FIVE

1 At government social work and welfare agencies, clients, the poor and the suffering, preferred seeing Afrikaans or English social workers because Coloured professionals were 'hard, unsympathetic and ruthless'. 'You can always weedle a welfare grant out of a white,' I was told, 'but never a Coloured social worker. They'd rather see you die.' I am indebted to Marie Theron, Johannes Vermaark and Hennie Terblanche, social workers at three separate agencies for this information.

When the government tried to replace white social workers in Coloured areas by Coloured social workers, there was uproar and protest from the communities involved, to the extent that the government had to slow down the pace of the changeover.

2 The Coloured or African child is born into a psychological framework in which to survive means to manipulate and to develop a culturally approved mask of indifference. To reject this development means to collapse, to become psychologically ill, to become abnormal in that culture and so to suffer. There are no other options. This is why, I believe, the younger black radicals have to fervently reject *everything* in the culture – it is the only way, in South Africa, to retain the sense of self, independent of the community.

3 These studies are reported in Frank (1971) and in Rabinowitz (1972).

4 CID and Special Branch are now closely integrated, and officers serve both sections at the same time and are often swapped around.

5 Television transmission began in January 1976. The English press was given nine months' grace to feel the pinch and to watch their circulation figures drop. Then, in September 1976, the *Citizen* was launched. Background moves were being made all the time, in 1975 and again in 1977, to buy into English printing houses. These were the kinds of operations that the Department of Information was involved in: co-ordinating and planning the various moves that ensured for the government a firm control over the English press. Note, incidentally the characteristic psychological ploys used by the police and the government to infiltrate the institutions involved. They were precisely those used on the Coloured community, described earlier and those used against the English universities.

CHAPTER SIX

1 This was not the end of my own personal intimidation. As a result of my actions at Valkenberg, my academic research, my refusal to comply with requests for information and my publications, I was ear-marked for 'special treatment'. This is too extensive to be dealt with here and will appear in my personal account of my life in South Africa, in preparation.

2 This, incidentally, was one of the hidden determinants of my experiences at the University of Cape Town described in Chapter Two. Banning outspoken lecturers combined with the pressures on the university, made it inevitable that the universities would attract and promote 'safe' options.

3 The data about the Border industry chicane was provided by two sources. One, a government economist and the other, a member of the Board of Directors of the company involved. I am grateful for the help given to me by several economists in South Africa, not only in this respect but in respect of informing me of Treasury policy and planning, tax evasions, budget deficit irregularities, pricing control boards, Land Bank operations, and the intricacies of Holding Company operations.

4 Shirley Jenner did an MMPI, Rorschach and clinical interview study on Karen Horney's Personality Theory. In return for my supervision, for doing some of the testing and agreeing to be her external examiner, she

used a sample made up of nearly all Cape Town's leading white radicals and gave me their protocols when her study was completed. Her report is in Jenner (1974). Shirley died in mysterious circumstances shortly before I left South Africa.

5 Anton Van den Bergh kindly supplied me with details about these techniques.

6 The Bureau of State Security.

7 In South Africa, the police have the power to detain witnesses indefinitely, ostensibly to protect them; in reality as a means of making people talk and holding them incommunicado. Threat of this form of arrest is often used to make uninvolved and innocent people talk.

8 Described in detail in Lambley (1977b), the paper I was working on at the time of my flight.

9 One example of how operations are interlinked: the Rent Act of 1966 froze rents in all flats put up in and before that year. These are administered by the Rent Board which had offices in each region. The owners of these flats have to submit lists of tenants to the board so that at any one time, the chairman of the board knows exactly who is in which flats. Now, students often rent these properties because they are cheap. When the police take names of politically involved students, these are, in time, passed to the local Rent Board chairman. Now, the Rent Board is continually at war with the property owners some of whom are taken to court for cheating the act and increasing rents or similar malpractices. In private arrangements between these landlords and board chairmen, select students or other radicals are evicted in return for the Rent Board turning a blind eye to the owner's profit-making activities.

CHAPTER SEVEN

1 I examined a sample of school textbooks, comics and photostory magazines (which were very popular amongst young and old before the advent of television) in 1969 and again in 1976. School textbooks varied little in the interim years presenting a strictly Afrikaans-orientated interpretation of the history of South Africa and presenting *only* the South African authorities' point of view and policies after 1948 (see also Auerbach, 1965). Material used in 'youth preparedness' lectures for schoolchildren was even more avidly Nationalistic. Comics and photostories, however, changed radically between 1969 and 1976. In the latter years, after the Angolan 'adventure' of the South African forces and long before the government officially admitted to its part in Angola, militaristic themes dominated in over 55% of the literature surveyed (as compared with less than 10% in 1969) and violence, both visually and in terms of words used, increased from 30% in 1969 to over 85% in 1976. The comics and photostories consistently portrayed South African agents, spies and policemen in action against foreign invaders, Africans, communists and white traitors. Most of

the material I studied was published by one of two companies, both, I believe, controlled by the *Broederbond*.

2 I frequently had to clear research material, textbooks and certain journals with this board before I could continue with some of my work – particularly that on the history of South Africa and in conducting psychotherapy with sexually disturbed patients. I had to apply for permits to obtain, among other things, Alex Comfort's *Joy of Sex* and to have my subscription to the *Journal of Sex Research* filled.

3 It also decides which races will see and read which films and books. *The Godfather*, for example, was for viewing by whites only. Some films can be seen by whites and Coloureds but not Africans.

4 The parliament of South Africa is the highest court in the land – which means in effect, the National Party Caucus.

5 I was told that *any* police investigation in South Africa that appears to involve *Bond* activities is referred to a secret section within the police, set-up to detail how much the investigations may reveal.

6 I am grateful to Jill Steenkamp for this information. With her help I was able to collect data from nine mothers who had their babies adopted and so establish the procedure involved.

7 Derogatory terms for Africans and Coloureds respectively.

8 I was unable to get hold of one of these manuals. I am quoting from someone else who did and as it was told to me.

9 It is, incidentally, a criminal offence to deter or dissuade anyone in South Africa from performing his national service.

CHAPTER EIGHT

1 I am grateful to Sadie Forman for discussions on this point about Bram Fischer, his personality and his upbringing.

2 John Vorster got into Parliament in 1953. Prior to that, he had been in the Afrikaner Party, not in the Nationalist Party; his wartime activities with the *Ossewabrandwag* had made him risky in the eyes of Malan and Strydom and he was not trusted by them. Only when the two parties united did he get in – through the back door, as it were.

3 An extreme pro-Nazi right-wing paramilitary Afrikaner organization that operated during World War Two.

4 This was a statement made to me by a businessman long before Van den Bergh's fall from grace and when he was still the most feared and powerful man in South Africa.

5 The evidence from the IQ testing indicated a temporal impairment – shown by only two low scores out of ten (of $z=85$) – rather than a major impairment of functioning. Truly hebephrenic schizophrenics show the reverse: impairment on all but one or two tests. Tsafendas' scores showed him to be withdrawn and cut off – interpreted in court as schizophrenia – but not demented in anything like the degree claimed. Anyone, in fact any

normal-neurotic person in the same frightful and shocking situation, would show the same kind of fall-off in performance. If you took Tsafendas' IQ test results (ten sub-tests) and asked a clinician to evaluate them blind – that is, without knowing who he was – they would say, and I quote: 'Highly intelligent, creative adult male with some personality problems.' I did, in fact, take Tsafendas' results and gave them to other clinicians to rate blind. No one said he was schizophrenic or even severely disturbed. They noted that in some instances, his sub-test results showed an extremely high level of intellectual functioning.

6 One example that I remember clearly: Tsafendas saw a leg on one of the Ink Blot cards but was not sure if it was a rat's leg or a rabbit's. This very example was used in court to substantiate his schizophrenic diagnosis: '. . . such jumbled and nonsensical reactions are typical of schizophrenia which typically include bizarre or unusual detail . . .' This statement comes out of a text book and the statement is true but the example is not. It is not unusual to get this kind of response in intelligent adults; what the examiner was confusing in this instance was the confabulatory response category into which he thought Tsafendas' 'Leg' response fell, which it did not. This kind of loose and often inaccurate reflection marked the psychological analysis presented in court.

7 Cooper had several misgivings about the proceedings. He thought perhaps the authorities were covering up their own lax security procedures and having Tsafendas declared insane helped them avoid being responsible in any way for the assassination.

8 One might be tempted to dismiss these views easily because they originated from patients and lower levels of staff. There is now fairly conclusive evidence in my opinion, however, from studies done in America, that these are the very people who most often and consistently can tell whether or not a patient is shamming (Rosenham, 1973).

9 One of my patients, an Afrikaans businessman who lived in a select Afrikaans suburb and some of whose neighbours were parliamentarians, said the following to me at the time of Watergate: 'One day, the world is going to find out about *our* Watergate and believe me, it is going to make President Nixon look like a good fairy.'

The people who spoke to me about the feelings of the 'average' *Broeder* towards Vorster's role in Verwoerd's death seemed to accept that there was a connivance between Vorster and Van den Bergh and other people. Their attitude to this in turn was nonchalant *as if* they were used to this kind of thing.

10 Working from figures provided in Bunting (1969) and de Villiers (1969), the *Broederbond*'s membership grew from 2,672 in 1944 to 6,768 in 1964. If one estimates that its membership increased under Vorster's rule to between 10,000 and 15,000, then there were roughly two or three *Broeders* for every hundred adult male Afrikaners, based on the 1970 population census figures. Of this number, over 3000 were believed to be hard-core Verwoerdians.

11 South Africans are used to election violence but most of it had been directed against opposition, English-orientated parties – this campaign

was the first since 1948 against an Afrikaans opposition and it was marked by the high degree of organization involved and the systematic destruction of the HNP's campaign in most areas.

12 Van den Bergh helped Vorster into power by releasing in rumour form blackmailing data he had obtained on Ben Schoemann – Vorster's main rival for the premiership. A businessman told me that one of the functions of BOSS has been to set up a series of massage parlours and prostitution chains in several major cities – particularly Pretoria and Cape Town, the seats of power. These are financed and run by the Bureau of State Security and have sophisticated electronic listening devices and filming equipment. The main function of the enterprise is to trap top Afrikaans officials.

13 The fact that Steve Biko died in Port Elizabeth came as no surprise to me. Vorster has special relationships, personal and official, with police and security officers in the Eastern Cape, established there before, during and after the war. Port Elizabeth has long been known as the most brutal and ruthless division in the security police; because of Vorster's patronage, its officers, on countless occasions, have been protected from being reprimanded by regional police chiefs.

14 I have no way of confirming these statements. I can only repeat them and remind the reader that I have only reported evidence that many people confirmed independently.

CHAPTER NINE

1 Permanent force officers had long resented Van den Bergh's intrusion into army matters. This was so pervasive that even non-commissioned officers expressed this opinion to me. I was informed by a highly reliable army source that BOSS' intelligence services were far more adept at internal, white espionage than at foreign data collection. According to this officer, the invasion of Angola was only undertaken after Van den Bergh's service had reassured the army High Command that they faced little substantial opposition. When things turned out to be very different and, incidentally, the army lost raw troops in numbers that caused distress, the army began to take steps to insure that it never again had to rely on BOSS.

When Soweto blew up, it was Van den Bergh and BOSS again that came in for criticism. His inadequate intelligence briefings that he presented to the Cabinet ensured that many ministers made complete fools of themselves in the eyes of the Afrikaner community by making grossly rash predictions that they inevitably had to take back the next day.

Both these events caused many Afrikaners within Vorster's circle and in the military to question his hold on power and his ability to manage Van den Bergh. They were frightened, it is clear, by the unrealistic atmosphere at the top that had buckled in the face of real threat.

Bibliography

Abdi, Y. O., 'The problems and prospects of psychology in Africa', *International Journal of Psychology*, 1975, 10, pp. 227–234.

Adorno, T. W., Frenkel-Brunswik, E., Levinson, D., & Sanford, R. N., *The Authoritarian Personality*, New York, Harper, 1950.

Allport, G. W., *The Nature of Prejudice*, New York, Doubleday, 1954.

Archibald, D., 'The Afrikaners as an emergent minority', *British Journal of Sociology*, 1969, 20, pp. 416–426.

Auerbach, F. E., *The Power of Prejudice in South African Education*, Cape Town, Balkena, 1965.

Barth, A. T., & Noel, D. L., 'Conceptual frameworks for the analysis of race relations', *Social Forces*, 1972, 30, pp. 333–348.

Benson, A., *The African Patriots*, London, Faber, 1963.

Bernstein, H., *No. 46 – Steve Biko*, London, International Defence and Aid, 1978.

Bird, J. (Ed.), *The Annals of Natal. Volumes I and II*, Pietermaritzburg, 1888.

Brandel-Syrier, M., *Reeftown Elite*, London, Routledge and Kegan Paul, 1971.

Bunting, B., *The Rise of the South African Reich*, Harmondsworth, Penguin, 1969.

Cilliers, S. P., *The Coloureds of South Africa*, Cape Town, Bauier,

1963.

Cilliers, S. P., *Appeal to Reason*, Stellenbosch University publishers, 1971.

Cilliers, S. P., 'The social, political and economic implications of industrial progress with particular reference to the position of the Coloured population', *Social Dynamics*, 1975, I, pp. 45–52.

Cilliers, S. P., & Joubert, D. D., *Sosiologie: n' systematiese inleiding*, Stellenbosch, Kosmos, 1966.

Close, M. E., Kinloch, G. C., & Schlemmer, L., 'The Afrikaners as an emergent minority; an alternate view', *British Journal of Sociology*, 1971, 22, pp. 200–205.

Colman, A. M., 'The measurement of attitudes towards Africans. A unidimensional scale with high discriminating power', *Psychologia Africana*, 1971, 14, pp. 32–37.

Colman, A. M., & Lambley, P., 'Authoritarianism and race attitudes in South Africa', *Journal of Social Psychology*, 1970, 82, pp. 161–164.

Crane, G. E., 'Clinical psychopharmacology in its 20th year', in R. Cancro (Ed.), *Annual review of the schizophrenic syndrome*, New York, Brunner Mazel, 1975.

Cryns, A., 'African intelligence: A critical survey of cross cultural intelligence research in Africa south of the Sahara', *Journal of Social Psychology*, 1962, 57, pp. 283–301.

Dahlstrom, W. G., Welsh, G. S., & Dahlstrom, L. E., *An MMPI handbook. Volume I*, Minneapolis, University of Minnesota Press, 1972.

Danziger, K., 'Ideology and Utopia in South Africa', *British Journal of Sociology*, 1962, 13, pp. 59–75.

De Kiewiet, C., *A history of South Africa*, Oxford, Oxford University Press, 1975.

De Villiers, R., 'Afrikaner nationalism', in M. Wilson and L. Thompson (Eds.), *The Oxford History of South Africa, Volume II*, Oxford, Oxford University Press, 1969.

Dodd, S. C., 'A social distance test in the near-East', *American Journal of Sociology*, 1935, 41, pp. 194–204.

Duncan, S., 'The plight of the urban African', *South African Institute of Race Relations*, Topical Talks No. 23. 1970.

Edwards, D. J. A., 'EPI profiles of black and white South Africans', *Rhodes University*, unpublished study, 1972.

Evans, J. L., *Children in Africa; a review of psychological research*, New York, Teachers College Press, 1970.

Forman, L.; 'The birth of African nationalism', *Africa South*, 1961 5, pp. 48–55.

Frank, M., 'Transvestism and ego identity', *University of Cape Town*, unpublished Course 3 project, 1971.

Goldstein, M. J., & Rodnick, E. H., 'The family's contribution to the etiology of schizophrenia; current status', *Schizophrenia Bulletin*, 1975, pp. 14–63.

Gough, H. G., *California Psychological Inventory Manual*, Palo Alto, Consulting Psychologists Press, 1957.

Gough, H. G., McKee, M. G., & Yandell, R. J., 'Adjective check list analyses of a number of selected psychometric and assessment variables', *US Army. Officer Education research Laboratory*, technical memorandum, OERL – TM – 55 – 10, 1955.

Halbower, C. C., 'A comparison of actuarial versus clinical prediction to classes discriminated by MMPI', *Dissertation Abstracts*, 1955, 15, p. 1115.

Henachsberg, E. S., *The Group Areas Act; an explanation*, Durban, Butterworth, 1950.

Hepple, A., *Verwoerd*, Harmondsworth, Penguin, 1967.

Hines, J. S., 'A theory of racial conflict', *Social Forces*, 1971, 30, pp. 55–60.

Houghton, D. H., 'Economic development 1865–1965', in M. Wilson & L. Thompson (Eds.), *The Oxford History of South Africa, Volume II*, Oxford, Oxford University Press, 1969.

Hubbard, M., *African poverty in Cape Town 1960–1970*, Johannesburg, Institute of Race Relations, 1975.

Izedinova, S., *A Few Months With the Boers*, Johannesburg, Perskor, 1977.

Jackson, D. N., & Carlson, K. A., 'Convergent and discriminant validation of the Differential Personality Inventory', *University of Western Ontario, Department of Psychology, Research Bulletin*, Oct. 1969, No. 129.

Jenner, S., 'Karen Horney's theories of neurosis: An empirical clinical study', *University of Cape Town*, M.Sc. Thesis, 1974.

Katzen, M. F., 'White settlers and the origin of a new society', 1653–1778', in M. Wilson & L. Thompson (Eds.), *The Oxford History of South Africa, Volume I*, Oxford, Oxford University Press, 1969.

Klein, D. F., & Davis, J. M., *Diagnosis and Drug Treatment of Psychiatric Disorders*, Baltimore, Williams and Wilkins, 1969.

Kuper, L., 'Political change in plural societies', *International Social Science Journal*, 1971, 23, pp. 594–607.

Lambley, P., 'The use of a forced-choice F-Scale in the prediction of prejudice and social distance attitudes of a sample of South African students', *University of Cape Town*, unpublished course 3 project, 1968.

Lambley, P., 'Authoritarian trends in contemporary psychology; The dominance of the paradigm', *Psychological Reports*, 1970 (a), 27, pp. 575–582.

Lambley, P., 'Psychology and epistemology: Operationism revisited', *Psychological Record*, 1970 (b), 20, pp. 229–234.

Lambley, P., 'Student drug users: Some personality characteristics', *University of Cape Town*, unpublished working paper, 1971 (a).

Lambley, P., 'A theory of existential psychology: The role of values in psychology and psychotherapy', *University of Cape Town*, Doctoral dissertation, 1971 (b).

Lambley, P., 'Authoritarianism and prejudice in South African student samples', *Journal of Social Psychology*, 1973 (a), 91, pp. 341–342.

Lambley, P., 'Behaviour modification and the treatment of psychosis', *Psychological Record*, 1973 (b), 23, pp. 93–97.

Lambley, P., 'Psychology and socio-political reality: *Apartheid* psychology and its links with trends in humanistic psychology and behaviour theory', *International Journal of Psychology*, 1973 (c), 8, pp. 73–79.

Lambley, P., 'Rorschach scores and schizophrenia: An evaluation of Weiner's signs in clinical practice', *Journal of Personality Assessment*, 1973 (d), 37, pp. 420–423.

Lambley, P., 'Racial attitudes and the maintenance of segregation:

A study of the voting patterns of white, English-speaking South Africans', *British Journal of Sociology*, 1974 (a), 25, pp. 494–499.

Lambley, P., 'A theory of existential psychology', *Humanitas*, 1974 (b), 2, pp. 419–424.

Lambley, P., 'The dangers of therapy without assessment', *Journal of Personality Assessment*, 1974 (c), 38, pp. 263–265.

Lambley, P., 'Voting behaviour and the maintenance of segregation: A reply to Lever', *British Journal of Sociology*, 1976.

Lambley, P., 'Preliminary statement of a theory of schizophrenic functioning', *Psychological Research Associates Working Papers*, 1977 (a), 4, pp. 38–80.

Lambley, P., 'Psychological terrorism in South African radical communities', *Psychological Research Associates Working Papers*, 1977 (b), 4, pp. 110–159.

Lambley, P., & Cooper, P., 'Psychotherapy and race: Interracial therapy under *apartheid*', *American Journal of Psychotherapy*, 1975, 29, pp. 179–184.

Lambley, P., & Gilbert, L. H., 'Forced-choice and counterbalanced versions of the F-Scale', *Psychological Reports*, 1970, 27, pp. 574–550.

Lambley, P., & Lison, S., 'The psycho-social effects of *apartheid*: An MMPI study of English-speaking and Coloured South African students', *University of Cape Town*, unpublished paper, 1974.

Lever, H., *South African Society*, Johannesburg, Jonathan Ball, 1978.

Lison, S., 'An MMPI based study of the personality characteristics of three groups of South African students', *University of Cape Town*, MSc. thesis, 1976.

Loubser, J. J., 'Calvinism, equality and inclusion: The case of Afrikaner Calvinism', in S. N. Eisenstadt (Ed.), *The Protestant Ethic and Modernization*, New York, Basic Books, 1968.

Macrone, I. D., *Race attitudes in South Africa*, Johannesburg, Witwatersrand University Press, 1965.

Macrone, I. D., 'Reaction to discrimination in a colour-caste society', in S. J. Morse & C. Orpen (Eds.), *Contemporary South Africa: Social Psychological Perspectives*, Cape Town, Juta, 1975.

Maclean, J., *et al.*, *Compendium of Kaffir Laws and Customs*, Cape Town, 1866.

Manganyi, N. C., *Being-black-in-the-world*, Johannesburg, Spro-cas-Ravan, 1973.

Mann, J., 'The problems of the marginal personality: A psychological study of a Coloured group', *University of Natal*, Doctoral dissertation, 1957.

Mansergh, N., *South Africa. 1906–1961*, New York, Praeger, 1962.

Marais, J. S., *The Fall of Kruger's Republic*, London, Clarendon Press, 1961.

Marquard, L., *The People and Policies of South Africa*, Oxford, Oxford University Press, 1969.

Mbeki, G., *South Africa: The Peasants' Revolt*, Harmondsworth, Penguin, 1968.

Mbiti, J. S., *African Religions and Philosophies*, New York, Anchor Books, 1970.

Mechanic, D., '*Apartheid* medicine', *Society*, 1973, 10, pp. 36–44.

Merton, R. K., *Social Theory and Social Structure*, New York, The Free Press, 1957.

Metrowich, F. R., *Africa and Communism: A Study of Success, Setbacks and Stooge States*, Pretoria, Voortrekkers, 1967.

Morse, S. J., & Orpen, C. (Eds.), *Contemporary South Africa: Social Psychological Perspectives*, Cape Town, Juta, 1975.

Murphy, E. J., *History of African Civilization*, New York, Thomas Crowell, 1972.

Murray, A. H., *The Political Philosophy of J. A. de Mist*, Pretoria, Haum, 1958.

Orpen, C., 'Authoritarianism in an authoritarian culture', *University of Cape Town*, Doctoral dissertation, 1970.

Orpen, C., 'Internal-external control and perceived discrimination in a South African minority group', *Sociology and Social Research*, 1971, 56, pp. 445–448.

Orpen, C., 'Sociocultural and personality factors in prejudice: The case of white South Africa', *South African Journal of Psychology*, 1973, 3, pp. 91–96.

Park, R., *Race and Culture*, New York, The Free Press, 1950.

Parsons, T., *Societies: evolutionary and comparative perspectives*, Englewood Cliffs, Prentice Hall, 1966.

Pettigrew, T. F., 'Regional differences in anti-Negro prejudice', *Journal of Abnormal and Social Psychology*, 1959, 59, pp. 28–36.

Pettigrew, T. F., 'Social difference attitudes of South African students', *Social Forces*, 1960, 38, pp. 246–253.

Pinderhughes, C., Spurlock, J., Weinberg, J., & Stone, A., 'Report of the committee to visit South Africa', *American Psychiatric Association*, 15 May 1979.

Pokroy, W., 'Authoritarianism in an authoritarian culture', *University of Cape Town*, unpublished course 3 project, 1971.

Rabinowitz, S., 'A multidimensional personality study of male transvestite homosexuals and male homosexuals', *University of Cape Town*, MA thesis, 1972.

Randall, P., *Some Implications of Inequality*, Johannesburg, Sprocas, 1971 (a).

Randall, P. (Ed.), *South African Minorities*, Johannesburg, Sprocas, 1971 (b).

Reiss, D., 'Varieties of consensual experience: III. Contrasts between families of normals, delinquents and schizophrenics', *Journal of Nervous and Mental Disease*, 1971, 152, pp. 73–95.

Rex, J., 'The plural society: The South African case', *Race*, 1971, 12, pp. 405.

Rhoodie, N., *South African Dialogue*, New York, McGraw Hill, 1972.

Robbertse, P. M., 'Rasseverskille en die sielkunde', *South African Psychologist*, 1967, Monograph No. 72.

Rogers, C. R., *Client-centered Therapy*, Boston, Houghton Mifflin, 1951.

Rogers, C. R., 'Persons or science?', *American Psychologist*, 1955, 10, pp. 267–278.

Rogers, C. R., 'Some issues concerning the control of human behaviour', *Science*, 1956, 124, pp. 1057–1066.

Rogers, C. R., 'A therapist's view of the Good life', *Humanist*, 1957, 17, pp. 291–300.

Rogers, C. R., *On Becoming a Person*, Boston, Houghton Mifflin, 1961.

Rosenhan, D. L., 'On being sane in insane places', *Science*, 1973, 179, pp. 250–258.

Rousseau, F. P., *Handbook of the Group Areas Act*, Cape Town, Juta, 1960.

Sachs, E. S., *The Anatomy of Apartheid*, London, Collets, 1965.

Scheepers Strydom, C. J., *Black and White Africans*, Cape Town, Tafelberg, 1967.

Siegel, R. K., & West, L. J., *Hallucinations*, New York, Wiley, 1975.

Simons, H. J., & Simons, R. E., *Class and Colour in South Africa, 1850–1950*, Harmondsworth, Penguin, 1969.

Singer, G., & Van der Spuy, H. I. J., 'Personality patterns of white and coloured South Africans', paper presented at the South African Psychological Association conference, Pietermaritzburg, 1973.

Smith, M. G., *The Plural Society in the British West Indies*, Berkeley, University of California Press, 1969.

Taft, R., 'A cross-cultural comparison of the MMPI', *Journal of Consulting Psychology*, 1957, 21, pp. 161–164.

Theron, E., 'Die Kleurling en die houding van die Blanke', *Journal of Racial Affairs*, 1950, I, pp. 21–28.

Thomas, W., & Marsay, A., 'Coloured job opportunities and advancement', *University of the Western Cape*, survey conducted by the Institute for Social Development, 1977.

Thompson, L., 'Co-operation and conflict: The highveld', in M. Wilson & L. Thompson (Eds.), *The Oxford History of South Africa, Volume I*, Oxford, Oxford University Press, 1969.

Tiryakian, E. A., 'Sociological realism: Partition of South Africa', *Social Forces*, 1967, 46, p. 211.

Triandis, H. C., & Triandis, L. M., 'A cross-cultural study of social distance', *Psychological Monographs*, 1962, 76, No. 540.

Troup, F., *South Africa*, London, Methuen, 1972.

Van den Berghe, P. L., 'Race attitudes in Durban, South Africa', *Journal of Social Psychology*, 1962, 57, pp. 55–72.

Van den Berghe, P. L., *Race and Ethnicity*, New York, Basic Books, 1970.

Van den Berghe, P. L., '"Ethnicity"; the African experience', *International Journal of Social Science*, 1971, 23, pp. 507–518.

Van den Berghe, P. L., 'Integration and conflict in multiracial societies', *Social Dynamics*, 1975, I, p. 3.

Van der Merwe, H. K., 'Some sociological aspects of nutrition and development in South Africa', *South African Medical Journal*, August 1974, 48.

Van der Merwe, P. J., *Die trekboer in die geskiedenis van die Kaap-kolonie, 1657–1842*, Cape Town, 1938.

Van der Spuy, H. I. J., 'The psychology of South Africa', *New Society*, 1974, 30, pp. 671–673.

Van der Spuy, H. I. J., Barkusky, Z., Davar, E., Frampton, G., Lison, S., Shamley, D., & Singer, G., 'Racial discrimination and personality: The neurotic South Africans', paper presented at the 18th International Conference of Applied Psychology, Montreal, 1974.

Van der Walt, J. A., Maritz, F. A., & Strauss, J., *Rassesosiologie*, Pretoria, Academica, 1967.

Van Jaarsveld, F. A., *The Awakening of Afrikaner Nationalism*, Johannesburg, Perskor, 1961.

Van Jaarsveld, F. A., *From Van Riebeeck to Vorster, 1652–1974*, Johannesburg, Perskor, 1975.

Van Jaarsveld, F. A., 'Suid-Afrika, 1984: Afrikaner waarheen?', *University of Cape Town*, summer school, February 1977.

Van Rooy, A. J., 'Sosiale en sielkundige factore wat bydra tot vorming van die persoonlikheid van die Kleurling', *South African Psychologist*, 1971, 1, pp. 11–17.

Viatkina, R. R., *The Foundation of the Union of South Africa*, Moscow, 1976.

Viljoen, A. G., & Grobler, E., 'A comparison between the moral codes of American, Korean and a group of Afrikaans-speaking South African students', *Journal of Social Psychology*, 1972, 86, pp. 147–149.

Walker, E. A., *A History of Southern Africa*, London, Longmans, 1957.

Welsh, D., 'The growth of towns', in M. Wilson & L. Thompson (Eds.), *The Oxford History of South Africa, Volume II*, Oxford, Oxford University Press, 1969.

Welsh, G. S., & Dahlstrom, W. G. (Eds.), *Basic Readings on the MMPI in Psychology and Medicine*, Minneapolis, University of Minnesota Press, 1956.

Welsh, G. S., & Sullivan, P. L., 'Booklet-card, card-booklet item conversion tables for the MMPI', *Psychological Abstracts*, 1952, 26, p. 652.

Whisson, M. G. (Ed.), *Coloured Citizenship in South Africa*, Cape Town, The Abe Bailey Institute, 1972.

Wilson, M., 'The hunters and the herders', in M. Wilson & L. Thompson (Eds.), *The Oxford History of South Africa, Volume I*, Oxford, Oxford University Press, 1969.

Wilson, M., & Thompson, L. (Eds.), *The Oxford History of South Africa*, two volumes, Oxford, Oxford University Press, 1969.

Zubaida, S. (Ed.), *Race and Racialism*, London, Tavistock, 1970.

Index